Faith To Raise The Dead

Written by Michael King

Abundant Life Series: Book 1

This book and other titles by Michael King can be found at TheKingsofEden.com
Available from Amazon.com, Createspace.com, and other retail outlets where applicable.

ISBN-13: 978-1946252012 (The Kings of Eden Press)
ISBN-10: 1946252018
Printed in the USA

Table of Contents

Part 1 - The Theology of Resurrection

Part 2 - Practical Resurrection

Dedication

I dedicate this book to Sage, Sophia, and Scarlett. You three are always ready to help me pray to raise the dead, and your love for Jesus grows in leaps and bounds even as you do. I look forward to the day each one of you has your first resurrection, but until then I will be content to watch you grow in the love and power of the Spirit.

Acknowledgments

Thank you to Tyler Johnson for being a forerunner, friend, and letting me bounce ideas off you at all hours of the day or night. You have been and continue to be a great encouragement to me as we pursue this abundant, immortal, resurrection life of Jesus Christ. I love you buddy.

A special thanks to Wanda Gladney and Jeannie Fortuna for speaking to me and sharing your stories—I know those experiences were costly to you, and they have helped shape my perspective on this subject. I honor you both for being pioneers in this area, and for standing steadfastly on the word of God to receive the fullness and promises of life God has designed for your families.

Thanks to Lisa Savage for helping compile the Resurrection verses in the Appendix—your work is appreciated and helpful to many.

To the members of the *Raise The Dead Initiative*, thank you for your ongoing pursuit of resurrection life and for partnering in intercession with God and one another. Even when we don't see an answer to our prayers, we are pushing together against a death-culture to see the life of Christ manifest in miracles.

Thanks to Sunshine L Brown King, my wife, editor, and best friend. You are *often* a captive audience as I sort out my thoughts, and you have had to experience far more than your fair share of my learning process—I appreciate your many contributions to this book. Thank you also for your tireless love and support; and for choosing to walk alongside me every day.

Foreword

I am excited for you: You are about to embark on an adventure into a new place with God that you likely have not yet traversed. *Faith to Raise the Dead* is a roadmap into new revelation, dimensions in God, and a renewing of your first love.

What struck me as I read this wonderful book was the tone of invitation that Michael takes. Many times books that deal with the supernatural and making the impossible possible actually cause the reader to feel less spiritual than is needed to attain the great miracles of old. This book is not like that. Rather, it is a humble invitation into the journey that Michael personally walked out in discovering the tangible, practical, mysterious, goodness of God. As you read you will feel your spirit engage truth and the courage of faith will rise in your heart.

Michael is a forerunner. This means that he speaks simply, candidly, and without fear, mainly because he doesn't know how far gone he is compared to the masses. It is innocent: Forerunners are simply the first to obey. Michael has rightly allowed his "normal" to be dictated by faith in what the Bible claims to be true. That is no crime, but sadly this sets him apart from the beliefs of the masses, and what he says could be interpreted as crazy. The truth is, forerunners are seen as crazy until what they have been saying for decades actually manifests in fullness on the earth. From that point on, they are hailed as heroes, leaders, and prophets, ahead of their time.

Instead of disregarding or passively ignoring what is foreign, it would be wise to receive what God has for us with an open heart and mind. If it is Biblical, it is fair game, regardless how impossible something seems to be in the natural. For those of us who are already on board with going after all that God has for the Church, prepare for guidance and practical wisdom. I especially appreciated the second half of the book, not because the first wasn't just as good, but because very few people are offering legitimate counsel on resurrection topics like gaining access, when to stop praying, and how to love a family who just lost a loved one while still standing in faith. These topics are where the rubber meets the road after a person has internalized the reality of God's goodness and love.

I was honored to read this book—it encouraged me deeply. I am thankful to God that others are unashamedly carrying the banner of life and life abundant for the world is in desperate need of it now more than ever. Follow Michael in this journey, on a road less traveled, that leads to a Kingdom shining with light from another world. Like Robert Frost said in his poem *The Road Not Taken*,

> *"I shall be telling this with a sigh*
>
> *Somewhere ages and ages hence:*
>
> *Two roads diverged in a wood, and I—*
>
> *I took the one less traveled by,*
>
> *And that has made all the difference."*

Tyler Johnson
Founder and Director, Dead Raising Team
Author of *How to Raise the Dead* and *The Dead Are Raised*
www.OneGlance.org
www.DeadRaisingTeam.com

Preface

I have believed in current-day resurrection for a long time, but in the past I didn't have an avenue to pursue it, nor did I see the extent of the need in the Body of Christ, but that changed in 2010. My journey to actively pursue resurrection began at a Spiritual Hunger Conference that year hosted by the International Association of Healing Rooms. I was starting nursing school the next week, and my wife and I drove six hours from Portland, Oregon to Spokane, Washington for their annual event. It was there I was introduced to Tyler Johnson, the founder of the Dead Raising Team (DRT) and at the time of writing this, he and his wife Christine have ministered faithfully for over ten years, releasing the message of God's goodness and His desire for abundant life. I forget how many sessions Tyler spoke at, but for me, one was all it took. Partway through the conference we were introduced by a mutual friend, and he handed me a single CD teaching of his called *The Theology of Dead Raising*. I listened to it on the drive home—twice—and from then forward, I was hooked.

My wife didn't really understand why I was so into raising the dead, but she was very supportive nonetheless and has continued to be since then, even when I bring home fresh roadkill to pray over it. Since then, we have had to deal with issues such as "where do I store the dead animal body when I'm not praying for it?" We came to an agreement on a 3-day maximum for all roadkill I find and bring home. Yes, these are the things my wife has to deal with in my pursuit of resurrection. Nevertheless, in October of 2011 I founded the social media group *Raise the Dead Initiative (RDI)* as I became a part of two serious attempts to resurrect some acquaintances' loved ones. That group, which has evolved into its own facet of our ministry, has grown to nearly 2,000 members in the past five years, and has been an ongoing training ground for myself and many others as we have learned to deal with the good, the bad, and the ugly in regards to death and resurrection.

It is my ardent hope that this book will speed you along the path of raising the dead, and if you have come across this text as a result of having recently lost a loved one, I extend my deepest sympathy, and an encouragement that God is only ever good in spite of this dark hour you are in. May the grace of the Lord Jesus Christ, the love of the Father, and the fellowship of the Holy Spirit be with you.

Multiple and abundant blessings,

Michael C. King

Part 1:

The Theology of Resurrection

Chapter 1

Back to Basics

When talking about raising the dead, one of the first things that comes to mind is an image of praying over a body. In actual practice it is daunting when standing there only to realize "I'm supposed to make him/her alive again? That's impossible!" Yes, technically it is, but God is in the business of doing the impossible, and when we start to think like God does, what was once unattainable starts to look extremely probable. This is why the resurrection process begins with one thing: Changing our thinking.

For centuries church members in all denominations have been taught many things about God that simply are not true, and in order to optimize success with raising the dead we need to revamp our understanding of God, take another look at what the Bible actually says about Him, and re-evaluate our long-held beliefs and what these things change for us. Then we will look at what we have actually been commanded to do. This means that we must go "back to basics" before heading on to the deeper stuff—which in reality isn't deep at all. The apostle Paul put it this way:

> In fact, though by this time you ought to be teachers, you need someone to teach you the elementary truths of God's word all over again. You need milk, not solid food! Anyone who lives on milk, being still an infant, is not acquainted with the teaching about righteousness. But solid food is for the mature, who by constant use have trained themselves to distinguish good from evil. Therefore let us move beyond the elementary teachings about Christ and be taken forward to maturity, not laying again the foundation of repentance from acts that lead to death, and of faith in God, instruction about cleansing rites, the laying on of hands, the *resurrection of the dead* [*emphasis mine*], and eternal judgment (Hebrews 5:12-6:2).

Resurrection is meant to be an elementary teaching of the faith, but more often than not it is shoved in a back corner somewhere, and I'm not entirely sure why. I have good friends who have had family members die and when I have politely offered to help pray for resurrection, they were resistant—to this day the deceased are still no longer with us. What I find so strange is that they are Charismatic and believe in resurrection, which usually means they would be open to it more than others of different denominations. It saddens me, actually, that what Jesus meant to be a basic part of the life of the believer has become this super-spiritual thing that special people do instead of what it is meant to be—part of a normal day in the life of a follower of Christ.

To truly understand God's will for resurrection, we need to grasp a few things first: God's original plan, His nature, and the purpose of healing. God's original plan was simple: Live forever. He didn't ever have to actually come out and say it because it was just that way. We know this is true however because of what transpired in the Garden in Eden. If you need a refresher on the story reread Genesis Chapters 2 & 3.

In chapter 2, verses 16-17, "The Lord God commanded the man, 'You are free to eat from any tree in the garden; but you must not eat from the Tree of Knowledge of Good and Evil, for when you eat from it you will certainly die.'" Eating of the tree of the knowledge of good and evil caused death. Romans 5:12 says, "Therefore, just as sin entered the world through one man, and death through sin, and in this way death came to all people, because all sinned . . ." Once Adam and Eve ate from the forbidden tree, they lost their innate immortality and became mortal. Having unleashed death upon themselves and the rest of creation, Adam and Eve were powerless to fix it, so God intervened. The first thing He did was prevent the pair from eating from the Tree of Life again. Genesis 3: 22 states, "And the Lord God said, 'The man has now become like one of us, knowing good and evil. He must not be allowed to reach out his hand and take also from the tree of life and eat, and live forever.'" While this seems harsh, there is more to it than appears at first glance. We have been taught that because they didn't die immediately that what occurred was spiritual death, which did happen to a certain extent, but it is by no means the whole story and it is a doctrine that has thrown us off-track ever since. From the instant Adam and Eve ate the forbidden fruit their bodies began to decay. The life of God in that new world was so fresh that in spite of an imminent death sentence it took their bodies nearly a thousand years to wear out! How do we know God wasn't preventing them from living forever? We have to remember that Adam and Eve had free access to the Tree of Life prior to eating from the Tree of

Knowledge of Good and Evil. They had *already* been immortal up to that time. God warned them that if they ate of the one tree that they would die—not because they would instantly drop dead, but because they lost their immunity to death and became subject to it. What God was doing was preventing their bodies from becoming immortal *in their fallen state.*

I once heard Kirby Delanerolle, cofounder of WOW Ministries in Sri Lanka, share a stunning revelation regarding this matter, explaining what God did in Genesis 3 to protect His children's access to the Tree of Life. Genesis 3:24 says, "After he drove the man out, he placed on the east side of the Garden of Eden cherubim and a flaming sword flashing back and forth to guard the way to the tree of life." God in His infinite kindness sent an angel with a flaming sword to guard the *way* to the Tree of Life. On the one hand it might seem like God was preventing Adam and Eve from taking the fruit, and in that moment He legitimately was in order to protect the couple, but the angel's job was not only to guard the tree, but the way to the tree. In other words, God was concerned about our access to life so He made sure that there is always an open road back—we will visit this again in the next chapter. That "guarded way" was brought to completion in Jesus Christ through His death and resurrection on the cross. The fact remains that God's will has always been for mankind to live an immortal and abundant life.

What does this mean for us? First, it puts the Garden events in a brand new light. God was acting as a kind and protective Father when He set up boundaries for His kids, not because He was angry with them but for their well-being. This could be compared to a fire in a fireplace. It heats the house in winter so we don't freeze, but we still have to keep our children from playing with it because we don't want them getting burned. Likewise, God knew that His kids were about to get hurt badly if He didn't act and prevent them from consuming the fruit of the Tree of Life in their fallen state. His solution was to stop the immediate danger and set an angelic guardian in place to temporarily restrict access while also protecting entry for the future.

If we accept that God's original plan was for man to never die, it stands to reason that God isn't a big fan of death. And really, He isn't—death is God's enemy, in total opposition to His life-giving nature. In spite of this, the Church has taught us that God kills people. Well, we don't like to put it in such harsh and uncultured language, preferring the more delicate version of "God takes people home" but we can't honestly have God "taking people home" without Him killing them. Either God kills people to get them to heaven or death is an enemy and God doesn't kill, but we can't have it both ways. We will look at this a bit more in a future chapter, but let me throw out a verse for you to chew on until later. First Corinthians 12:25-26 says, "For he [Jesus] must reign until he has put all his enemies under his feet. The last enemy to be destroyed is death." Death is an enemy—God's enemy, and therefore ours as well.

If God values life immensely and He never meant for mankind to die, it only stands to reason that He would make a provision for resurrection. In fact, it's hard for God *not* to value life because it's His very nature. John 1:1-4 says, "In the beginning was the Word, and the Word was with God, and the Word was God. He was with God in the beginning. Through him all things were made; without him nothing was made that has been made. In him was life, and that life was the light of all mankind." Jesus and God are one and the same so this passage shows that God's nature—the very essence of His being, is made of life. It is impossible for God to want anything *other* than life for us because to do so would be against His nature. Jesus expressed yet again in John 10:10 how much he values life

19

saying, "The thief comes only to steal and kill and destroy; I have come that they may have life, and have it to the full." Full, abundant life is what Jesus is after for all of us, and he stopped at nothing short of *His* death to wrest the power of death from the enemy, thereby giving us the authority to command the dead to rise again.

To recap, resurrection from the dead is a basic doctrine that is predicated on the facts that:

- God never intended for us to die
- God desires life for us above all else
- Jesus destroyed the power of death

In the next chapter we are going to look at the goodness of God—and what bearing that has on resurrection.

Chapter 2

The Goodness of God

When we want to understand God's perspective on death and His desire for us to live in abundant life, we must begin by understanding His nature. When Moses asked God to reveal His glory, his innermost nature, God said the following: "And the Lord said, 'I will cause all my goodness to pass in front of you, and I will proclaim my name, The Lord, in your presence. I will have mercy on whom I will have mercy, and I will have compassion on whom I will have compassion'" (Exodus 33:19). God wanted to reveal His nature to Moses, so He simplified the explanation of who He is to the very core essence of His being. God's goodness *is* the simplification of His nature. He is good, and he shows mercy and compassion. I think it is important to point out here that Moses was living under the Old Covenant with all its rules and regulations—yet when he asked God to show him His glory, God didn't mention a single thing about being a righteous judge, about vindication against evil, about sin, wickedness, destroying the immoral, or anything else—God only spoke of His goodness.

The reason this is important is because the Church has been incredibly off-base when it comes to our focus. As a whole, we have been excessively sin-focused and have narrowed in on the Tree of the Knowledge of Good and Evil—always asking ourselves the internal question "is it good or is it evil?" I'll tell you a little secret: whether it's good or evil, we're still eating from the *wrong tree*. God prioritizes goodness, mercy, and compassion, all of which rise from the Tree of Life—even in the Old Testament! He wasn't overly concerned about sin because God knows that when we get a deeper revelation of how immensely and utterly good He is, we too will emulate that nature. Not only that, but Jesus came to destroy the power of sin and to set us free from its bondage—so God isn't threatened by sin and He isn't afraid we will be destroyed by it either! We need to shift our focus onto goodness, righteousness, mercy, love, the other fruit of the spirit, and all manner of things that bring life.

God's goodness is all-encompassing—and understanding His goodness changes how we view, well, everything. This shift in perspective, viewing life from a place of being conscious of His goodness at work in and for us, will significantly change the choices we make. Think about it—if we believe God is good, we will expect Him to act in ways that align with His goodness. I personally grew up learning that our Heavenly Father was this fearful authority figure who was waiting for me to step out of line—and when I did, He was going to give me Heaven's version of a spanking. Jesus, on the other hand, was kind—He was nice, loving, and He was my friend. While it would be nice to say that my experience was isolated; unfortunately, it is common.

As I grew older and got to know the Father better, both through my own experiences and better, more accurate teaching, I came to understand a new perspective—that Jesus and the Father are the same. It's true—and the Bible actually says so. John 10:30 says, "I and the Father are one." It's so simple—Jesus is exactly like the Father in every way. Hebrews 1:3a states it another way, "The Son is the radiance of God's glory and *the exact representation of his being* (*emphasis mine*), sustaining all things by his powerful word." God doesn't have split personalities, one of whom is angry and judgmental all the time and the other whom is kind. No, the Father, the Son, and the Holy Spirit are all 100% alike in their nature because they are literally the same being! As I began to understand this, it started to shift how I thought about God—and how I understood His will. What this meant for me was that I couldn't think of God as a taskmaster and Jesus as my kindly friend. If Jesus is kind then so is the Father, and if God is a harsh disciplinarian then Jesus must be too—except that Jesus has never represented Himself that way, even in scripture, so it simply cannot be true of the Father.

If we know that Jesus and the Father are one, we can look at the life of Jesus and recognize that if Jesus acted a certain way, the Father will too. Think about it—if God isn't angry and is instead the kindest person we have ever met, then He is going to act in ways that align with that goodness. What is that going to look like? Healing for every disease, every time. Resurrection for every death. A solution for every problem, whether it be job loss, finances, disease, relationship issues, and more. There is literally nothing that God does not want to fix because He hates the things that cause us pain. He hates the things that destroy our lives. He hates death, disease, and every other problem, so God actively works to display His power on our behalf to improve our quality of life.

It's really that simple. I used to believe that our life mission was to win the lost above all else, and while that is important, this salvation we preach has to actually look like something here on earth, not just in some far-off heavenly reality after we die. What exactly *is* this Good News we are preaching anyway? That God is just barely kind enough that He will keep us from a burning torment of His making, but only if we shape up our ways and struggle our whole lives to prove to Him we really want it? There are a number of things wrong with that version of the narrative, but in short, no—God is far more interested in giving us good gifts, in being kind to us, in demonstrating His love to us, than He is in watching us trying to grovel in His general direction to prove we deserve His love. God is so good He is not hindered by our fallen state—because His nature doesn't change. Malachi 3:6 even states it point blank saying, "I the Lord do not change." What else about that do we need to know?

God Does Not Cause Calamity

Let us look at this logically. If God and Jesus are the same, and God doesn't change, then regardless of what we read in the Bible, we have to understand that God is good first and foremost, as revealed to Moses, and that God does things like Jesus did. Our old perspective of God as an angry heavenly dictator waiting to smite us has to get tossed out—immediately and permanently.

We see this sort of theological error played out to the extreme in the life of Job. This man, for reasons I cannot possibly fathom, is held up by many modern-day Christians as the poster-child for understanding God's nature, and Job is most often quoted when people believe God has done bad things to them. They usually have used the book of Job to develop a theology that says God has a master plan and purpose for causing calamity, and that we shouldn't blame Him when He either afflicts us or doesn't stop Satan from afflicting us. They use this same book to develop a deranged view of God's sovereignty and thus explain bad things as "God having a plan." I'm fairly certain that Jesus had something much better in mind when He said in Luke 19:10, "The Son of Man has come to seek and save that which was lost." Jesus never once used calamity to teach people a lesson. He didn't use it to help build their character. No, when Jesus saw misery he would fix it, as was prophesied in Isaiah 61—he bound up the brokenhearted and traded out negatives for positives. If someone was weeping, he would bring joy; if despair and depression, he would gladden their heart. Isaiah 42:3 spoke of Jesus in this manner, "A bruised reed he will not break, and a smoldering wick he will not snuff out. In faithfulness he will bring forth justice . . ." He doesn't kick us when we are down; instead, He is faithful to bring justice to right that which is wrong.

God doesn't cause or allow bad things to happen to us so we can learn and grow because He isn't an abusive Heavenly Father—and that's what He would be if He did! There is not a single instance in the life of Jesus where we can see Him allowing or leaving alone sickness and infirmity to teach someone, nor do we see a single instance where He suggests that God causes disease. The *only* possible reference one can find where this could be the case is in John 9:1-7, where it says:

> As he passed by, he saw a man blind from birth. And his disciples asked him, "Rabbi, who sinned, this man or his parents, that he was born blind?" Jesus answered, "It was not that this man sinned, or his parents, but that the works of God might be displayed in him. We must work the works of Him who sent me while it is day; night is coming, when no one can work. As long as I am in the world, I am the light of the world." Having said these things, he spit on the ground

and made mud with the saliva. Then he anointed the man's eyes with the mud and said to him, "Go, wash in the pool of Siloam" (which means Sent). So he went and washed and came back seeing (English Standard Version, ESV).

In the above passage, it seems at first glance that Jesus says God caused this man to be born blind so that God might do a miracle, yet that is not what happened at all. I once heard Bill Johnson, senior pastor of Bethel Church in Redding, CA explain what he believes that passage is saying, and I have to agree with him. What Bill shared is that if we remember the ancient Hebrew language doesn't have punctuation, we can essentially move commas and periods around as we desire based on how we perceive it should be translated—because translation is more like an art than a science. Oftentimes a translator has to make his best guess because languages have different syntax, sentence structure, and articles, and words have very different meanings. Hebrew and Greek both have words that are very pregnant with meaning, whereas most English words are fairly specific and only mean one or two things, which can be a nightmare for Bible translators. With this in mind, if we alter the punctuation, which is perfectly legitimate to do in this instance, it gives a very different message. The passage in John 9 would say, "Jesus answered, 'It was not that this man sinned, or his parents. [Period added here] But that the works of God might be displayed in him, [comma placed here] we must work the works of him who sent me while it is day; night is coming, when no one can work.'"

Wow—isn't that an amazing difference? With just a few punctuation changes, no longer is God causing disease so Jesus can heal a man and somehow give God more glory by fixing a problem He caused to begin with, but instead Jesus is doing God's work when someone is afflicted inexplicably. And it's not all that inexplicable either, as explained earlier—sickness is Satan's domain. Acts 10:38 says, ". . . how God anointed Jesus of Nazareth with the Holy Spirit and power, and how he went around doing good and healing all who were under the power of the devil, because God was with him." This verse points out quite clearly that when people need healing, it is because they are under Satan's power in some way. That man wasn't born blind because of his or his parents' sin—he was blind because of demonic oppression, and Jesus in His kindness, mercy, and love healed him.

I cannot recount the number of times I have heard statements from people saying things like, "God must think I am really strong to be giving me the burdens He is placing on me." That notion comes from a poor understanding of 1 Corinthians 10:13, where the common thought is that God is placing a weighty and negative burden on people—but only just as much as they can handle because He is testing them. I cringe inside every time I hear someone refer to that verse and use it to explain how God is afflicting them because they are completely misquoting the verse, not to mention grossly misjudging God's nature. The truth is that 1 Corinthians 10:13 has nothing to do with being given burdens by God that we can bear—it's about dealing with temptation. It says, "No temptation has overtaken you except what is common to mankind. And God is faithful; he will not let you be tempted beyond what you can bear. But when you are tempted, he will also provide a way out so that you can endure it" (1 Corinthians 10:13). Nowhere at all does it say anything about God giving us problems, trials, or burdens. It simply states that God will protect us from being tempted into sin beyond our ability to resist and will help us to do so. It has nothing to do with the absurd notion of God laying burdens on us to test us. There is a saying that goes, "Everything happens for a reason. Sometimes that reason is that you are stupid and make bad decisions." While that's not true of every situation, the saying rightly illustrates that bad things do happen for reasons other than God causing them.

As mentioned previously, it is really easy to blame God for problems, saying that "God allowed it to happen," and that is a common view, albeit an inaccurate one. God has given mankind free will, and as such we have the right to make decisions, even if they are evil ones. Why do school shootings and suicide bombings, rape, theft, murder and abortion, bank robberies, bullying, pedophilia, and all sorts of base behaviors occur? They have nothing to do with some sort of higher divine plan that God has set up to test us, and they most certainly do not say anything about God's goodness being flawed, or Him allowing those things as a form of judgement. So what do they mean? If we believe we have free will, then that also means we have free will to bring problems down on our own heads, and the demonic realms are more than happy to assist us in that endeavor without needing a theology that says God is an abusive punisher.

The Issue of Sovereignty

One of the things people often fail to understand is how God's sovereignty works, and this has a major impact on how we view responsibility for calamity and whether or not we can believe that God is truly and only good. One of the major benefits we receive as followers of Jesus is that we get to see life as it exists with something no one in the Old Testament or even those in Jesus' day had: a revelation of Jesus and His finished work on the cross. We see a much clearer picture than Moses, David, the Prophets, or anyone else did, and the story it tells is far different than what they experienced. The Hebrew belief of sovereignty, as it is with most other cultures, is a bit fatalistic, in that whatever happens must be God's will—because God is in charge, right? Wrong! We must understand the difference between the fatalistic Hebrew-version of sovereignty and *actual* sovereignty, because this has a major bearing on who is responsible when things go wrong in our lives.

Sovereignty has to do with who is in charge. The fatalistic view says that *because* God is in charge, everything goes His way. News flash—almost every major religion explains bad things as being "the will of the gods" or as Islam suggests, that "Allah wills it." This fatalistic view is congruent with the overall belief system of Judaism—and most certainly with historical Judaism if not that of the present day. According to the SCJ, an online resource network for cultural Judaism, in Jewish thinking, every spiritual being is an emissary of God—whether an angel or a demon. There is no "other opposing force" in that religion because Satan (known as HaSatan) is understood to be God's employee. The line of thought is that Satan has no soul, is thus incapable of free will, and is sent by God to test and challenge us, making our free will choice to choose Him more meaningful (S.C.J FAQ). I see nothing in the Bible to suggest that Satan lacks free will as he clearly used it when he rebelled against heaven. The idea that God would purposefully make things harder for us to somehow prove that we "really want Him" is demonstrative of something an abuser would do, not our good, kind, loving Heavenly Father. Jesus cleared this up in John 10:10 when he explained that He and Satan are in direct opposition to one another and do not work on the same team.

This issue can be seen at various points throughout the Bible, especially in the lives of David and Job. One of these glaring inconsistencies can be seen when comparing verses that discuss the reason why David conducted a census of Israel. 2 Samuel 24:1 says, "Again the anger of the Lord was kindled against Israel, and he incited David against them, saying, 'Go, number Israel and Judah.'" Interestingly, 1 Chronicles 21:1 speaks of this same event, yet it says,

"Then Satan stood against Israel and incited David to number Israel." There are three main explanations for this disconnect between the verses:

The first view says that Satan works for God. As has already been explained, this is the Hebraic view which is completely inaccurate and has been otherwise disproven by Jesus. The second view says that God uses Satan to accomplish His will—almost like a contract employee. Satan doesn't work for Him, per se, but God somehow tricks Satan into doing the dirty work He doesn't want to sully His Divine Hands with. This is also clearly untrue. God is the "Father of the heavenly lights, who does not change like shifting shadows" (James 1:17). He isn't deceitful or false (Isaiah 23:9; 1 Peter 2:22). Does God take bad things and make good out of them? Yes. Does He covertly get Satan to do bad things *in order to* turn them into good things? No. If there is no darkness in God, no deceit, no falsehood, then he doesn't have a secret contract set up with Satan to afflict people to "get the job done." This option is simply impossible and is entirely unscriptural. The third and final explanation, which is incidentally the most logical and sensible, is that clearly both verses cannot be true. Saying something like this about scriptures tends to get people's hackles up, but continue reading with an open mind to see why I say this. Under the Hebraic perspective, because they viewed Satan as working for God, if Satan incited David to number Israel then theoretically God did too because Satan did it at God's command. Although this is categorically false, the ancient writers did not know this and so wrote it from the limited view of God they had at the time. They believed God was involved in the matter, so one of them wrote it that way, whereas the other stated the facts—that Satan was responsible. I believe we can forgive the author of 1 Samuel for this shortcoming because it wasn't his fault—he lacked the revelation of Jesus Christ, and as a result, wrote out of what he understood about God at that time.

Just for a moment, let us think about what it would actually mean if God did incite David to take a census. For those unfamiliar with the text, David had previously been instructed by God to *not* count his people. Some people actually believe that God set David up, pushing him to number the people, then punishing the man after the fact for doing it. Think about it—who tells someone not to do something, then suggests they do it, only to punish them when they go ahead with the plan? I'll tell you—torturers trained in psychological warfare and abusers. This is a case of "actions speak louder than words" and if God is inconsistent between His actions and deeds, then David really isn't to blame. If God did come along and subtly push him to do it, we could argue that David was actually following God's will when he complied. This entire thread of reasoning is convoluted, but that's because this idea is so illogical to begin with. Fortunately, God is delivering us from these nonsensical beliefs we have long been taught in the Church. Satan is anti-God and these passages, when understood in the right context, demonstrate this yet again. God did not push David to disobey; he gave in to Satan's tempting as 1 Chronicles 21:1 shows us clearly.

Job, the man whom the book of Job is written after, is another prime example of this breakdown between the Hebraic view of God and the Christ-centered perspective. In Job 1 the text shows us Satan having a conversation with God, with Satan asking God to let him test the man. In the text, God agrees and pulls back His divine protection to allow Satan to afflict Job. There are a myriad of problems with this passage, and many of them have led people into strange beliefs about God using calamity. Again, remember here that the historical Hebraic perspective of this passage was one where Satan was working *for* God when he afflicted the man, but because in

31

reality they are not teammates, then God wasn't "in on it" with Satan, regardless of what you read from this Old Testament book written by someone with a culturally limited view of God's nature.

In Job 1 where Satan and God have this discussion, I must first point out that the writer wasn't exactly standing in the Heavens at the time. What he wrote in that chapter is basically pure conjecture and is quite probably a literary device and not meant to be read literally. I think we have to take that heavenly conversation with a grain of salt to begin with, but there is more. I suggest that the God seen in Job 1 is very much unlike the God as revealed through Jesus, and this again comes back to the Hebraic perspective. The writer would have believed that Satan's task was to afflict Job and test him *for* God. Since that's not true, we really have to question the theological usefulness of that chapter to begin with. Furthermore, there are additional inconsistencies, which largely have to do with how Satan is able to afflict people in the first place.

Job 1:1 says, "There was a man in the land of Uz whose name was Job; and that man was blameless, upright, fearing God and turning away from evil." The Hebrew word *tam* is the word for blameless and could also be correctly translated as *upright, completely innocent, pure* or *perfect*. We already know there is no one perfect other than Jesus, so Job couldn't actually be sin-free and rather was a very moral man. *Very moral* still means the man sinned from time to time, so we have to understand that from a spiritual perspective, Job wasn't free and clear of Satan's afflictions to begin with. What do I mean by this? There are two ways Satan and the forces of darkness are able to harm us: through entry in our lives via our unrighteousness, or through breaking spiritual laws and attacking us in spite of heaven's prohibitions. Job was a very righteous man, but not perfect—thus, his imperfections would be potential cause for demonic entry into his life. Furthermore, Job had a good bit more fear than might appear at first glance, and fear opens doors to the demonic. Consider Job 1:5, "When the days of feasting had completed their cycle, Job would send and consecrate them [his children], rising up early in the morning and offering burnt offerings according to the number of them all; for Job said, 'Perhaps my sons have sinned and cursed God in their hearts.' Thus Job did continually." In Job 3:25 he declares, "What I feared has come upon me; what I dreaded has happened to me." Job sowed fear of bad things happening to his family every single day through his beliefs and actions, and as a result reaped those very things he was afraid of. I suggest that Job, through fear, was responsible in part for the opening needed to afflict him, and when the enemy gets an inch, he takes a mile—which is the other way he does it, by simply breaking spiritual laws and afflicting regardless of circumstances.

One of the things I have heard people say as a result of this verse is that Satan has to ask God for permission to harass people. I'll be honest, there are so many verses in the Bible that demonstrate this to be untrue that I simply don't have room to list them all. Rather, I will expound on the *one* other verse people use to proof-text this notion, Luke 22:31, where Jesus says, "Simon, Simon, Satan has asked to sift all of you as wheat." Interestingly enough, the word *asked* in that passage could just as easily (and just as accurately) be translated at *demanded* or *desired*. It seems much more reasonable and a better translation to say that Satan *desired* to do so but was unable to succeed because as the next verse, Luke 22:32 says, Jesus prayed that even though he knew Peter would fail, Jesus had a plan to redeem him and bring Peter back. Think about it—if the will of God was to have Satan attack Peter, then it would make no sense for Jesus to pray for him as that would put Jesus in opposition to the Father's will of affliction. However, because God has no will of affliction, Jesus rightly demonstrated the Father's heart by praying for Peter's deliverance. Luke 22:31 does not prove anything in regards to Satan's need to get permission from God to harm people. If anything, it proves the opposite—that Satan is a lawbreaker and actively rebels against God's will as revealed in Jesus Christ, and Jesus stepped up to the plate to put a stop to it.

When we travel toward the end of the book of Job, after thirty-four chapters where he and his friends complain and argue with one another as they wax poetic, there was another piece Job missed in this whole God-affliction-picture when he claimed, "The Lord gives and the Lord takes away, blessed be the name of the Lord." Job didn't understand that God wasn't responsible for the taking-away he experienced—that was the work of Satan. Anything that God *does* take away is only going to be those things that hinder His love from being displayed. People attempt to brush off understanding why God causes calamity with pithy sayings such as "God works in mysterious ways." He really doesn't. God increasingly reveals Himself and His ways to us. While there is mystery, we continually unravel those mysteries. Where the Hebrews believed that God caused bad things, we now have the revelation of Jesus, so we have a different standard to go by that conclusively says God doesn't cause misfortune and calamity at all. We have to bring this whole Job-fiasco back into context with Jesus at the forefront because He and the Father are completely alike. If Jesus was doing his thing in Job's day, He would have resurrected his sons and daughters and He would have restored Job's fortune—or he would have prayed and prevented Satan from stealing and killing in the first place. I should mention here that in spite of Satan's destruction, God in His goodness still restored all of Job's wealth and gave him new family to help bring joy in place of those he lost because *that* is what God is like. We can no longer afford to prioritize the inferior revelation of Job over the superior revelation of Jesus Christ.

The True Meaning of Sovereignty

We have looked at the lives of both David and Job to see how this fatalistic Hebraic view of God's sovereignty negatively colors how we understand God's nature. We have been able to see how this archaic mindset has pushed us to believe things about God that are false due to a lack of understanding about the authors' beliefs when writing the Old Testament, and how it has influenced our understanding of what it means for God to be sovereign. A much more accurate and *useful* view of sovereignty recognizes the difference between absolute dictatorial control and simply being the one in charge. God is sovereign. It's positional, meaning it denotes the status He holds as the One Who Is Above All Things. It doesn't necessarily mean He always gets His way. Yes, in spite of being the Supreme Ruler of the Universe, God doesn't always get His way. Need an example? Adam and Eve. God was very clear that His wishes were for them to not eat the fruit of the Tree of Knowledge of Good and Evil, yet they ate the fruit anyway. Thus, it is clear within just the first few chapters of the Bible that God doesn't always get His way. Need some more examples? Moses hitting the rock instead of speaking to it as instructed (Numbers 20:8-12). The Israelites refusing to take the Promised Land as directed (Numbers 32:10-13). Sampson letting Delilah cut his hair against instructions (Judges 16:17-20). Israel insisting on a king when God wanted them to have judges and prophets instead (1 Samuel 8:6-9; 19-22). The Bible is full of such examples—need I go on? I'm sure you can think of some times in your own life when you didn't obey God—and thus God didn't get His way. With that in mind, how does this whole sovereignty thing actually work?

Let us look at a current-day example to explain this concept: The President of the United States is generally "in charge" of the U.S.A.

(and yes, while that position isn't a dictatorship, just work with the example). Yet, somehow, we still have thieves who rob and steal. Is the President somehow no longer Commander-in-Chief because there are lawbreakers? Of course not. It just means that he (or she) isn't getting his way when people break the law. It also means that the President will send out the police to enforce the law and bring the lawbreakers to justice, make them pay restitution and restore that which was stolen or damaged. God is the same way. Just because Satan steals, kills and destroys (John 10:10) doesn't negate God's power. It doesn't negate His sovereignty, but it *does* mean God is not getting His way. Honestly, what kind of Cosmic Idiot would God have to be to say, "I'm going to create a being that I design and instruct to commit evil so that I can, as Jesus, go around fixing that evil that he causes—acts that I told him to commit in the first place?" It's entirely illogical, and for good reason—it's nonsense. Satan is a lawbreaker. He didn't really care that he was not supposed to cause Job's calamity—he did it anyway. He doesn't really care that he isn't supposed to afflict us—he does it anyway. That's why it is *our* job to enforce God's will in the earth.

Oh—there's one more thing. When we get upset as to why bad things happen in the earth, it's not because God doesn't care or isn't truly good—it's because He delegated authority of earth to us humans, and He is expecting *us* to fix things. Psalm 115:16 says, "The highest heavens belong to the Lord, but the earth he has given to mankind." This means that it is our job to enforce His will and we shouldn't complain that God is abandoning or afflicting us when things go wrong—we need to pray and fix them. However, God hasn't left us alone. The Holy Spirit indwells us to be a counselor, guide, and helper (John 14) and He sends us angels to help out as well (Hebrews 1:7).

I often hear that even if God didn't tell Satan to do something directly it is still indirectly His fault because "He permitted it to happen." I suppose we could ultimately blame everything on God for the sole reason that He created us to begin with, and if we never existed we would never have bad things happen to us, but even that argument is a red herring. This line of reasoning completely ignores the intricate interplay between the various spiritual laws set forth. While the claim could be made that because God set the laws of creation up making it so we have free will that He is still "allowing" bad things to happen, I believe that to be a gross oversimplification of the matter.

God set up spiritual laws in the cosmos at the beginning of creation, once—laws that He does not break. He isn't making ongoing choices of who deserves intervention and whom He should "allow" Satan to afflict. In creation He decided that all created beings can make their own choices, including angels (else how could Satan have rebelled and fallen?), called the Law of Free Will, which incidentally was required in order to give us the capacity to love. This is possibly the most pivotal and deciding factor behind why people think God ignores some problems. He isn't ignoring them—we collectively choose evil in spite of His attempts to get us to choose otherwise.

Sometimes bad things happen because various laws are in conflict with one another. God input the Law of Sowing and Reaping that says whatever we put out, we get back in like kind (Galatians 6:7). The problem is that we can reap what we *did not sow* when we become a victim of someone else's free will to do evil—but often they are sowing and reaping victimization because they, too, were a victim once. While some would argue God's sovereignty means He can do anything He wants, for reasons I only partially understand that's just not how He set things up. Amos 3:7 even says,

"Surely the Sovereign Lord does nothing without revealing his plan to his servants the prophets."

God created the Law of Involvement that basically says God's created beings must be involved in His interaction in the world. The Law of Involvement is why prayer is important—because if God could do whatever He wanted whenever He wanted, we wouldn't need to pray and ask Him to do things. It is extremely counterintuitive, and quite confusing, to try to figure out what God can and can't do because anything God doesn't do is as a result of self-limitation at the beginning of creation. On the one hand there are verses that say God can do literally anything, but there are others that suggest strongly He has limited His power to that which includes us. One verse in favor of the God-can-do-anything view is Matthew 19:26 which says, "Jesus looked at them and said, 'With man this is impossible, but with God all things are possible.'" On the other hand a verse that points to the need for our involvement is Ephesians 3:20 which says, "Now to Him who is able to do exceedingly abundantly above all that we ask or think, according to the power that works in us . . ." This passage says that God can do more than we can ask or think—but it is conditional—*according to the power already working within us*. This is why prayer is so incredibly vital—because prayer is a sort of spiritual transaction with God that brings His involvement into our circumstances. When we pray God releases heavenly power and angelic forces to answer our prayers and solve our problems. These spiritual laws do not in any way denigrate or undermine God's sovereignty—He is still the one in charge, but as with the previous example of the US President, who is subject to the laws of the United States in spite of being "in charge", God is subject to the rules He has made as well.

God's Goodness Revealed

Now that we have a clearer picture of how sovereignty works, having looked at scriptural examples in the lives of Job and David, I want us to look further into how a different view of scripture supports the revelation of the goodness of God. There are many different scriptures that can be read in a new light with this revelation that God is good, and Genesis 3 is a perfect example. When God kicked Adam and Eve out of the Garden of Eden, He didn't simply make them leave—he made a number of pronouncements which always used to sound extremely harsh to me. In Genesis 3:15-16 it says, "'And I will put enmity between you and the woman, and between your offspring and hers; he will crush your head, and you will strike his heel.' To the woman he said, 'I will make your pains in childbearing very severe; with painful labor you will give birth to children. Your desire will be for your husband, and he will rule over you.'" This scenario has never sat well with me, even as a child, so more recently I did a little digging. After looking those verses up and researching further, it seems to me that the translators made some assumptive errors when translating the text. What God pronounced to them weren't actually curses, but an explanation of changes that would take place—changes as a direct result of their choices, a version of sowing and reaping with a really quick turnaround. Try reading it another way: *There will be enmity between you and the woman and between your offspring and hers; he will crush your head and you will strike his heel. Turning to the woman he said, "Your pain in childbearing will become severe, and with painful labor you will give birth to children* (Genesis 3:15-16). The subtle but significant change is the difference between whether God is saying He will afflict them versus that they have brought affliction on themselves due to their choices; I suggest the latter is the more accurate version.

On first read it seems like God cursed Adam and Eve to have a really hard life, saying "I will cause these things to happen" when in reality what happened was their sin released decay into their environment which began the process of death and decay in their bodies, and God simply stated "these changes will take place." While that might seem like splitting hairs to some, it makes a big difference when we play things out. If we serve a God who is willing to curse us with pain and problems when we make mistakes, we are in big, and I mean *big* trouble. The opposite side of that is if I make a bad decision and reap the consequences of my stupidity, I don't turn around and blame God for cursing me—I recognize I was a dolt and need to make better choices the next time around. Likewise, since God didn't curse man and woman and simply informed them of the natural results of their behaviors—enmity between the serpent and them and increased pain in childbearing, it can be rightly understood that He was warning them for their benefit of the changes that were ahead. And while giving His children advanced warning in and of itself is quite kind of God, there's more, but I want to point something else out first.

In that same chapter in Genesis, God went searching for Adam and Eve while the two went hiding. God already knew what was going on, but didn't just cause the earth to split and bump them out of the Garden or send a wind to carry them away. He sought them out and spoke to them because He loved them. He didn't just abandon them; He warned them of the pending results of their actions. God didn't turn His back on them—He even declared prophetically in His warning to them that even though the serpent would bite at their heels, there would come a day they would crush the serpents head—which we have seen the fulfillment of this prophecy by Jesus Christ. God never abandoned them, and even when He was explaining how they would reap what they had sown,

God decreed a way out for Adam and Eve and the rest of humanity to come. We have been taught that God is a taskmaster, but this alone demonstrates something far more true—that God is and has always been first and foremost the God of Love.

That alone would have been enough for God to demonstrate His kindness and love, but He did not stop there. At the end of that chapter the Bible says the following: "And the Lord God said, 'The man has now become like one of us, knowing good and evil. He must not be allowed to reach out his hand and take also from the tree of life and eat, and live forever.' So the Lord God banished him from the Garden of Eden to work the ground from which he had been taken. After he drove the man out, he placed on the east side of the Garden of Eden cherubim and a flaming sword flashing back and forth to guard the way to the tree of life" (Genesis 3:22-24). This section of text shows us something I find rather profound. It looks at first glance like God says, in essence, that "because man sinned, then I don't want him to live forever—his fate and punishment is death." It seems like in order to prevent Adam and Eve from healing themselves with the fruit of the Tree of Life, God kicked them out of the garden and then placed an angel with a massive flaming sword as a guard to keep them out. But that's only a cursory reading of the text without any understanding of God's heart in the matter.

I covered this a bit previously, but we will go into further depth here. Read from a perspective of God's goodness, it says something *entirely* different. God knew that if Adam and Eve ate of the Tree of Life while in their fallen, sinful state, they would still gain immortality, but that version of immortality would come with the price of being *forever bound in sin.* God already had a plan arranged by which He would redeem all of mankind, but it would only work if they hadn't forever seared sin into their bodies by eating of the Tree of Life before Jesus redeemed them. Thus, He made them leave as a safety precaution to protect them—setting an angel and a flaming sword to guard the way to the Tree. This act of God's is actually a significant prophetic picture of what He was going to do to redeem mankind. Note that the scripture doesn't say that God sent an angel *with* a sword, but that God sent an angel *and* a sword. This again seems like splitting hairs but it matters simply because an angel with a sword would give the picture of someone who is getting ready to attack anyone who comes to the path—but what if that wasn't the angel's goal at all? The angel was a guard of two things—one, to keep Adam and Eve away from the tree temporarily, and two, to guard *The Way*. Yes, I believe that this angelic guard's job was to open up the path to redemption. Jesus Christ stated in John 14:6 that, "I am *the way . . . (emphasis mine)*"—and Genesis 3:24 says that the angel guards that way. The sword represents the word of God, and the flames signify purification—that God would send His Word—Jesus (John 1:1), to purify and remove all sin and allow us access to the Tree of Life once again. While God couldn't allow access at that moment, He was still protecting the way for the future—so that *all* could find their path home. Pretty cool, right? What used to look like God was angry and getting ready to kill now shows us that He was actually planning redemption from the very beginning! Revelation 22:1-3 confirms this concept, saying:

> Then the angel showed me the river of the water of life, as clear as crystal, flowing from the throne of God and of the Lamb down the middle of the great street of the city. On each side of the river stood the tree of life, bearing twelve crops of fruit, yielding its fruit every month. And the leaves of the tree are for the healing of the nations. No longer will there be any curse. The throne of God and of the Lamb will be in the city, and his servants will serve him.

Pre-redemption the Tree of Life simply wasn't safe for Adam and Eve any longer, but after the cross we see the Tree of Life has multiplied into a species of tree that is readily and openly available for everyone, yielding fruit year-round and with the leaves used to heal the people of every nation. There is no longer mention of anything guarding, removing access, or in any way preventing people from partaking of this gift from God.

So now the big question: what does this have to do with resurrection? Everything. Think about how absolutely, stunningly kind God is to allow us to raise the dead. Death is a horrible, terrible thing—and while there are streams of thought that talk about it as a transition and "passing through" to another wonderful phase of life, let's be honest—death is horrible. There is often physical pain, not to mention regret, grief, and loss. Death rips families and friends apart. It creates conflict, fear, and much heartache for everyone involved. There is literally nothing good about death! There's a reason God told Adam and Eve not to eat of the Tree of the Knowledge of Good and Evil—so they wouldn't die. Death isn't just a phase or a step or a bump or whatever other ridiculous descriptor people like to use to minimize its significance. It is an abomination against God's plan for us because God has plans for hope and a future and for long life and blessings (Jeremiah 29:11), not death—it's not in *His* plan for our lives. Do you have any idea how much heartache and pain death brings into the world? Of course you do—every single person on this planet has been touched in a negative way by the death of another. And while one could make the argument that some people die well and pass on a legacy, how much better a legacy could they pass on if they continued to live? Death is evil and God has given us a solution for the problem in Jesus Christ.

43

Do you know what God told me one time He was teaching me about raising the dead? He said, "Anyone who wants to learn how to raise the dead must first be convinced of my goodness." How can faith for resurrection be built on anything less? If we don't believe God is good, and that He rewards us, then how can we expect to receive anything from Him? That is being double-minded, and as James 1:6-7 says, "But when you ask, you must believe and not doubt, because the one who doubts is like a wave of the sea, blown and tossed by the wind. That person should not expect to receive anything from the Lord." We all have doubts, but God wants to bring us to a place where we never doubt His goodness. You see, it's not that God doesn't want to give us good things when we doubt, but that doubt is putting our faith in what God *won't* do—and what we believe and ask for, we can have. This is why we so often don't receive what we think we are requesting because our doubt is essentially a prayer asking God to *not* give us what we ask. As we become convinced in the deepest parts of our souls that God is kind, good, and loving, and that "Every good and perfect gift is from above, coming down from the Father of the heavenly lights, who does not change like shifting shadows" (James 1:17) then I believe we will see a vast increase in our answered prayers, both in general and in regards to resurrection. It's time for a Goodness Revolution!

In the next chapter we are going to look at how our view of God's goodness influences our understanding of death, and how that perspective changes what we believe and how we live.

Chapter 3

The God of Life Does Not Kill

In the last chapter we looked at how God's nature is entirely and completely good and how we have learned a misrepresentation of it, partly through inaccurate scripture translation. In this chapter we are going to look at even more misunderstood Bible passages that give us a faulty understanding of who God is and what He is like. This will help us to apply our new perspective to the topic of death and paint a clear new picture—that the God of Life does not kill.

One of the most difficult things I have run into with others as I have walked out my journey to live in resurrection power was the idea that God might not want to resurrect an individual. After all, how did I know if God took the dead person home or wanted him to stay dead? I once had a conversation with my father-in-law where I recounted a failed resurrection attempt. His response? "The Lord knows His timing and calls some to be with Him sooner than we might think."

My response? "I don't think God kills people." You see, in light of the last chapter's discussion, I have a hard time believing that God kills, especially when the person in question in that scenario was a twenty-five year old woman who died suddenly of a brain aneurysm and left a grieving fiancée, family, friends, and a whole bunch of unlived-life behind. Really?? We think that "God's timing" involves killing a young woman through one of the many medical conditions Jesus died in order to protect us from?

The quick reply to my response was, "Well, the Lord doesn't kill people, He just takes them home." I'm afraid that in my quickness to respond, I left behind the religious mindset that would have made his idea have any substance at all. Can someone please explain to me how we can claim someone died of a brain aneurysm which presumably was the Lord "taking her home," yet in the same breath one can also say He didn't kill her? It's impossible to explain because it is simply not true. We have for far too long given ourselves over in religious circles to cognitive dissonance in our beliefs. We use confusing and convoluted thought-processes in order to explain tragedies that elude easy explanation. Worse still, we attribute those tragedies to the God of Light and Love as though somehow He is perpetrating these literal crimes against humanity. Instead of acknowledging what the Bible clearly states in John 10:10—namely that there is a thief loose in the world who kills and destroys and who is nothing at all like God, we make up well-meaning and pious-sounding arguments that sound persuasive enough that many people fall for them. Those who don't are usually those wise enough to just play along and keep their mouths shut or can see past that charade and thus want nothing to do with the Church to begin with. I used to believe the same as my father-in-law, but I eventually discovered that over time the Church developed convoluted theology to explain tragedy. The problem is that this line of reasoning is so obtuse that it can't stand up to even simple scriptural scrutiny. It just plain doesn't work. I think it would be far more authentic if we started questioning random acts of darkness and labeling them as such instead of attributing them to God for lack of better understanding of the details. Incidentally, if we were to do so, the rest of the world might want what we have because glaring theological flaws would be gone.

To illustrate this issue with God killing, let us take a trip back to ancient Egypt and visit what happened with Moses and the plagues—you know, the one where God supposedly killed everyone's firstborn? Let's start off by considering the events in light of God's immense intelligence. If God kills people, then God is also exceedingly stupid, and by stupid I mean unintelligent, dimwitted, daft, dense, slow, retarded, cognitively delayed, and dumb. But God doesn't kill, so clearly He isn't stupid either.

How can I say this? Easy. Back in Exodus, the Bible says the Lord went and killed the firstborn in all of Egypt. Yet while in previous chapters He was able to protect everyone in Goshen from the plagues, according to the common Church narrative somehow in Chapter 12 God lost track of where Goshen was located such that He had to have everyone smear blood all over their doors (Exodus 12:12-13) to keep Him from forgetting not to kill the Hebrews, even though Matthew 10:30 and Luke 12:7 say He knows how many hairs are on each of our heads. Maybe God had amnesia? Maybe God was really constipated or was having a temper tantrum? I don't know, but what I do know is that the "God killed all the firstborn" narrative actually doesn't even add up with God's nature, much less His intelligence level. Yes, let's consider how smart God is. In a split moment and with a single utterance He formed all of the intricate interactions between atoms, subatomic particles, the atomic forces of gravity, strong force, weak force, and electromagnetism, and much more. He designed and created orbits for planets, stars, solar systems, and galaxies. He formed intricate weather patterns, water currents, and patterns of movement for tectonic plates. Yet somehow, in the midst of this supreme galactic-level intellect, supposedly God can't tell the difference between the people he wants to kill and the ones to keep alive without someone else posting red markers on the doors. And while I understand the prophetic significance of the blood on the doors as a signpost pointing to Jesus, it doesn't change the fact that Jesus protects us *from evil*, not from our Heavenly Father.

What is *much* more likely than God being forgetful is that through sin—by Pharaoh's hardness of heart and through the slavery and oppression of the Jewish people, the enemy gained legal access to cut off the firstborn of *all* of those in Egypt from the land. This would have *included* the Hebrew slaves who lived in Goshen because they were owned by the Egyptians, thus falling under the same curse and enemy attack. The *only* way they were able to be saved was that God spoke to Moses and provided protection for those in Goshen to avoid the enemy attack, thereby sparing their lives. The Bible shows us that the blood sacrifices of animals were able to cover over sin and essentially delay it for a time, which in this case prevented the Angel of Death from killing in those households who had performed the sacrifice. In reality, anyone who put blood on their doorposts, including Egyptian households, were saved because God is in the business of abundant life and a blood sacrifice would have covered over the sin of the Egyptians just as easily as it did for the Hebrews. However, because presumably no one told the Egyptians about this divine "skip me" card (since it was also the Hebrew get-out-of-slavery-free card), their firstborn all died.

If you read through Exodus 12, you will see that in verse 23 it says that, "When the LORD goes through the land to strike down the

Egyptians, he will see the blood on the top and sides of the doorframe and will pass over that doorway, and he will not permit the destroyer to enter your houses and strike you down." If we read this at face value, it seems abundantly clear that God killed people. However, when we dig further the passage reveals more. Remembering that the Hebrews believed Satan was an agent of God and reading it again, it is clear that the "Lord" didn't actually go through the land. Look—the word for "The Lord" in that passage is *Jehovah*, but the word for "destroyer" is *shachath*. It says Jehovah is going and killing people, but he won't let the shachath to enter their houses and strike them down. Well, which is it—is the Lord killing people, or is the destroyer striking them down? Because it certainly isn't both. If God is standing at the door of each house that has lamb's blood on the doorjamb and is preventing a destroyer from entering, that is clear imagery of a guardian and protector, not of the top-level spiritual assassin He is opposing. In Isaiah 54:16b it says, "I create the destroyer so he might devastate" and it uses the word *shachath* again. Keep in mind that the writer of Isaiah was still living under the Hebrew perspective that the destroyer works for God instead of against him, which simply means that the writer *thought* God gave destroying spirits their jobs when He in fact did not. In fact, 1 Kings 22:22 and 2 Chronicles 18:21 show a spirit choosing its own function. God wouldn't ever tell a destroyer opposed to His will to destroy—that spirit would have decided all on its own.

Taking a further look at the passage in Exodus, it doesn't even make sense on a cursory read. God is going through the land to strike down the Egyptians, but when he sees the blood on the doorpost he won't let a third party, the destroyer, enter the house to kill. But I thought the passage said God was the one doing the killing? The scripture verse really doesn't make any sense all on its own without additional insight. However, since in John 10:10 Jesus divorces the notion that God can be the destroyer, citing that destruction is the work of the thief, the choice to blame God for the enemy's handiwork is no longer available to us.

If a believer walks up to another believer, at least in the USA, and says, "God is good, all the time," the most likely response will be "All the time, God is good." I'm not sure where this call-response saying began, but it is a common belief that God is good, and the Bible supports this fact with countless verses that restate the same thing from different angles: "His mercy endures forever" (Psalm 136:1); "In Him there is no darkness at all" (1 John 1:5); "God is love" (1 John 4:8). While we generally believe God is good, we almost never follow that line of thinking consistently throughout the entire Bible, nor do we apply it to present-day life. We cannot in one breath extol the goodness of God and in the next breath blame Him for killing people and causing massive earthly destruction, or other such acts that are usually attributed to the Wrath of God. The Bible is clearer than some might believe about God's goodness, and it is all contained in Jesus.

As I mentioned in the previous chapter, Jesus is the exact copy, image, likeness, and representation of God (Hebrews 1:3). In other words, when Jesus said, "I and the Father are one," He meant it. They are 100% alike. Interestingly enough, the single time Jesus ever engaged in "wrath" against anyone was when they were hindering access to the Father's love and forgiveness, and that only happened once, in John 2. While Jesus did freak out on some people who were preventing others from accessing God, he also never killed anyone. I once heard a teaching on the John 2:15 passage that turning over tables and using a whip to drive cattle out was how the merchants in the temple court closed down at the end of the day. The text states that he whipped cattle, not people, and I don't think He was angry at the sheep—he was just herding them like everyone else in their day did. The ultimate point here is that Jesus wasn't getting ready to off anyone, so neither is the Father. He isn't sitting at the edge of the universe with lightning bolts in his hand waiting to smite evildoers. Instead, He is exactly like Jesus, who had dinner with prostitutes, extortionists, *and* hypocritical Jews (the "Christians" of his day), and he loved all without reservation. So what does this mean in regards to death and life? God didn't just go around randomly thrashing everyone who stepped over the line. Why? He loves them—and because it's not what Jesus is like, we know it's not what the Father is like either. This really messes with some people because the first thing they do is run to the Old Testament and start referencing all of the verses where it says God killed someone, or start spouting quotes from a confusing and largely symbolic book at the end of the Bible that no one clearly understands to begin with. I don't think most of us honestly expect to have a beast with horns rising out of the sea anytime soon to rule over the nations, nor some other beast rising out of some subterranean crack in the earth to represent the sea-beast to the nations, but this is what a literal reading of Revelation 13 would give us. Even some of the finest scholars argue for a symbolic interpretation of that book, and either way there is no clear consensus on the subject.

Jesus not only did *not* kill but laid his life down *in place* of others; the Father is just the same, which means by simple logic, Father God is not a killer. The funny thing about it is that the New Testament actually agrees with what I am saying in multiples of places, but this truth has been incredibly hard for many followers of Jesus to hear! 2 Peter 3:9 even says flat out that, "God is not willing that any should perish (die)..." So is the Bible all a lie then? By no means, but parts of it certainly are greatly misunderstood, and as I have said before, I suggest those parts are poorly translated—or at least interpreted with an inferior understanding of God's nature. What would happen if someone were to translate the Bible from beginning to end with a firm understanding of God's goodness? I thank God that He is bringing us from glory to glory and is revealing new and deeper revelations about His nature. Twenty years ago the idea of God being good to the point that He doesn't kill would have been considered heresy; twenty years from now we will find it taught as foundational truth. What changes is not the scriptures themselves, but our understanding of how they are meant to be interpreted. It is unarguable that God used Martin Luther to change the Church's beliefs about salvation by grace, but the Bible remained the same. It is verifiable fact that God used Asuza Street and other similar events to reignite the understanding of the gifts of the spirit in the Body of Christ, but nothing about the Bible changed. Likewise, God is using men and women today to not just bring new revelation, but to restore revelation Jesus taught long ago that has since been lost—all with the same book people have been using for thousands of years. I believe this understanding that God does not kill is just one of the many beliefs God is restoring to the Church, His precious Bride.

I will be the first to tell you that there are lots of passages in scripture, specifically in the Old Testament, that I don't yet understand and currently have no explanation for. I cannot explain the verses that say that God killed hundreds of thousands of people because it's not in His nature to do so. What I *can* grasp with impunity is that Jesus and God are one, and that Jesus revealed himself to be the one who *gives* life, not the one who takes it away. While some people think that my inability to "explain away" what they believe the text clearly states is heretical, I'm fine with that. As mentioned before, the Hebrew mindset that says all death comes from God is behind those beliefs—and I've already explained that view is inaccurate. Thus, while I can't always say what *did* happen, I know what didn't—God did not and does not kill.

I recognize all of this is a bit strong for some, so let me explain it another way. As I have already shown that God is a good God, please explain to me how a God who is good and kind and loving would go around killing people? We call that a split personality—one personality of which would be either a psychopath or sociopath. Truthfully, if that is the God we serve, we literally would be better off not going to heaven—because in that case heaven would be ruled by a psychotic divinity who changes His mind at a whim—and with an omnipotent ruler with that level of crazy at the helm, who knows when you are going to get the short end of the stick! The world already understands this notion and in some cases this is the reason individuals rebel against the idea of such a God—the very God that we Christians often present to them. No wonder some people reject the truth—because they know in their hearts that version of God really isn't true! The actual truth is that God doesn't change, isn't sociopathic, and heaven is a wonderful place—and that is all because God is good. With that, we can confirm with certainty that God not only does not kill, but that He actively opposes death.

As I said before, we have for too long relied on Job's limited and inaccurate view of God as one who gives *and* takes away instead of trusting in the perfect revelation of God found in Jesus Christ. It's time we moved on from the rancid milk of God-kills thinking and try chewing on the meat of the Word that speaks of this God who raises the dead, heals the sick, gives hope to the hopeless, and brings light in the darkness. Instead of living a powerless gospel that saves no one at all and instead relies on death to get us to heaven, I'm believing in the Jesus who promised abundant life. Colossians 2:9 says, "For in Christ all the fullness of the deity lives in bodily form, and you have been given fullness in Christ, who is the head over every power and authority."

Why is this whole "God doesn't kill" thing so important to dead-raising? It's about faith—and while it might seem to some like impractical theology, it's quite practical when you get down to the details. Faith looks like something—and when it comes to raising the dead, it looks like praying God will bring someone back to life. If you have a belief that says God kills some people and "wants them home" with Him, it instantly erodes faith—it's not even subtle. There is no room for resurrection if you are constantly questioning whether God wants to bring him or her back to begin with. The enemy will incessantly whisper in your ear that God wants that one dead, that praying to bring him back is against God's will., that the person won't resurrect because he sinned and earned death, that Jesus needs him more in heaven, that his work is being done from "the other side," and that death isn't actually that bad—it's just a simple transition from one phase of life to the next. All of these are nice-sounding *lies*. It's simple: Satan and the rest of the demonic realms want people dead, and they have for a very long time. Resurrection is a significant threat to them, and they will do anything they can to stop it. The *very first thing* they will attack is your faith, and the belief that God kills is one of the top faith-assassins out there.

It goes beyond that though. We all want to do what we see God doing, and if we don't understand God's nature as purely good, it becomes hard to join Him in His work. When we understand clearly what God is like, it becomes easier to know how to pray in any and every situation. We renew our minds to deeply understand that, "Every good and perfect gift is from above, coming down from the Father of the heavenly lights, who does not change like shifting shadows" (James 1:17). We stop seeing disease as something God is giving us to teach us something. We stop seeing theft, relational strife, and other problems as God testing us. We understand that in the same way that God gives good gifts and doesn't change, He isn't a shady figure making mafia-style deals with the devil in a back room somewhere in heaven.

In the next chapter we are going to look at what healing and decay actually are, some of the ways we contribute to death, and will look at a few more verses with a different perspective, seeing how God has given us power over life and death.

Chapter 4

The Power of Life

All this talk about life and death makes minimal sense if we don't understand what is actually going on in the body when we talk about these things. What actually *is* life? What is death? They are pretty self-explanatory at first glance, but when we take a deeper look at life and death there are two ways to consider the matter. On the one hand, and especially when thinking of things spiritually, life and death aren't actually opposites. Life is a state of being and death is simply the absence of that state. On the other hand, especially regarding physical health, life and death can be viewed as opposites. Healing is a manifestation of life, and the more life energy at work in someone's body, the healthier he will become. The corollary is that disease and decay are manifestations of death, and when someone gets sick, unless that person is healed, he will die. Purportedly, John G. Lake, founder of the original Healing Rooms (after the method of John Alexander Dowie), stated that sickness was simply "incipient death." According to Dictionary.com, the definition of the word *incipient* is "beginning to exist or appear; the initial stage of." In other words, sickness and disease are simply the initial stages of death beginning to appear in the body. Why does this matter? Because death is the work of the enemy. If sickness is basically embryonic death, then healing is likewise the equivalent of embryonic life. When more life energy is at work in the body, a person will heal, but when more death-energy is at work, he will get sick, grow old, and eventually die. We can only have healing—and likewise resurrection, if the life at work in a body is greater than the death at work. We will look in the latter portion of this book at how to practically engage that life to resurrect someone, but first we need to understand how we contribute to both life and death on a daily basis—with our words.

We have to remember that our words have power. The Bible says in Genesis 1:27 that we are made in God's image, which means more than just looking like Him—our redeemed and/or unfallen nature mirrors His nature— including His abilities as a Creator. God has made us in His likeness, and we are co-creators of our world. In Deuteronomy 30:19, God spoke to the people of Israel and explained it this way, "This day I call the heavens and the earth as witnesses against you that I have set before you life and death, blessings and curses. Now choose life, so that you and your children may live." We get a choice to live or die, be healthy or be sick, and it has a lot to do with the words we speak, the thoughts we think, and the ideas we believe. Proverbs 18:21 says, "The tongue has the power of life and death, and those who love it will eat its fruit." We can literally pick which power is at work in our lives based on the things we say— because regardless of which we choose, we will eat its fruit.

The Bible and modern science agree on the fact that we help create our reality. The Observer Effect is a term used in quantum science based off an experiment originally performed by Thomas Young in the 1800s, but has since been improved upon. I don't recall where I first read it, and the following explanation grossly oversimplifies numerous studies over decades for brevity of explanation, but the experiment is as follows: According to author Keith Mayes' website, *Theories With Problems*, scientists wanted to know how electrons would behave under certain conditions where the inanimate object had to make a "choice." If a single electron was shot toward a thin sheet of metal with two open slots next to each other, which one would it go through? Ultimately they found a number of unique and surprising results, but of particular note was that how the electron behaved changed based on the expectation and observation of the researchers! If they expected it to go through one slot, it did. If they didn't have an expectation, it could be a particle going through a single slot or an energy wave passing through both of them, and if different people expected different things, it would appear as both a particle and a wave at the same time (Mayes). Their so-called outside observation was in fact entering into an undefined relationship with this electron, influencing the results.

For those who aren't science-geeky like me, another example can explain this concept—the thought experiment physicist Erwin Schrodinger created about his cat. The way his idea goes is that if Schrodinger put his cat in a box, is the cat alive or dead? While we can make an educated guess about the state of the cat, it's not actually possible to know with 100% certainty whether the cat is dead or alive until we actually open the box and check. When we don't look in the box, the cat can be thought of as existing in two theoretical states at the same time: dead and alive. When we observe the cat, it is clearly noted to be one of the two. While not a perfect example, our observation pulls the cat out of two *potential* states into one *actual* state. Likewise, the Observer Effect states essentially that our interaction with reality, even if that interaction is passive as an outside observer, changes the very fabric of creation down at the subatomic level to the point of forcing matter to choose one state or another. But then, the Bible has known this for millennia, saying things like, "For as he thinks within himself, so he is" (Proverbs 23:7a). It is strange in some ways to think that our beliefs directly alter our reality, but it's true.

Science has also been able to prove that we can actually "sow" our beliefs and emotions. Scientists at the HearthMath Institute have been able to measure various spectra of energy waves being emitted from the brain and heart—even to the point of being a few feet or even a few yards out from the body (McCraty). Some people call it an aura, magnetic field, or energy field, but our body is complex and on a moment-by-moment basis, we literally send out our thoughts and emotions into the universe. Galatians 6:7 says, "Do not be deceived, God is not mocked; for whatever a man sows, this he will also reap." It makes a mockery of God and the way He has designed creation to think that we can sow without reaping. In other words, when we say things, or even just think or feel, we emit the energy signature of those emotions, thoughts, and words to the world around us, and according to what we sow out, we are going to get it back. It's just like when God said, "Let there be light" in Genesis 1:3 and it was so. God spoke the entirety of creation into being—and what is sound, if not a frequency or wavelength of energy that happens to match the spectra of frequencies our ears can detect. Likewise, light is another frequency of energy that our eyes are able to detect—although there are far more wavelengths of light than we can perceive. It would be more accurate to say that God released energy and then light manifested in response, but regardless of the specific details, He has given us that same ability to a lesser degree.

Whether we speak out loud or think in our minds, we emit signals that change our world. It is not that surprising, then, that Philippians 4:8-9 admonishes us to pay attention to the things we think: "Finally, brothers and sisters, whatever is true, whatever is noble, whatever is right, whatever is pure, whatever is lovely, whatever is admirable—if anything is excellent or praiseworthy—think about such things. Whatever you have learned or received or heard from me, or seen in me—put it into practice. And the God of peace will be with you." When we align our thoughts with good things, we find God brings us peace and harmony. The corollary of that is when we align our thoughts with darkness and perversion, the enemy brings us chaos and despair. Angels and demons are able to see that spiritual light or darkness and are attracted to it accordingly, so we can literally choose which spirits we are surrounded by based on our thoughts.

Jesus spoke on this topic in Matthew 5:27-28 when He said, "You have heard that it was said, 'You shall not commit adultery.' But I tell you that anyone who looks at a woman lustfully has already committed adultery with her in his heart." If our beliefs put out energy to co-create the thing we think, then when we lust we are already sowing into adultery, and even if we haven't actually done the deed yet, we have already performed it in our hearts. If we sow it out long enough over time, we will eventually end up committing adultery because we have created that reality for ourselves.

There is far more information on the Observer Effect and quantum reality than I cover here, but if you are interested in reading more, you can start with Masaru Emoto's *Messages in Water* series—books which show through pictures the effects of our thoughts, words, and emotions on water, the single molecule that makes up the majority of the human body. Suffice it to say that he, too, found that our words can produce life or death depending on what we speak.

Peter, Jesus' disciple, ran into this very phenomenon when he dealt with a couple named Ananias and Sapphira. This couple is most-well-known for what people presume is being killed by God for lying. I suggest a different narrative—that Peter killed them—read on and I will explain. In Acts 5:1-11 it says:

> Now a man named Ananias, together with his wife Sapphira, also sold a piece of property. With his wife's full knowledge he kept back part of the money for himself, but brought the rest and put it at the apostles' feet. Then Peter said, "Ananias, how is it that Satan has so filled your heart that you have lied to the Holy Spirit and have kept for yourself some of the money you received for the land? Didn't it belong to you before it was sold? And after it was sold, wasn't the money at your disposal? What made you think of doing such a thing? You have not lied just to human beings but to God."
>
> When Ananias heard this, he fell down and died. And great fear seized all who heard what had happened. Then some young men came forward, wrapped up his body, and carried him out and buried him.
>
> About three hours later his wife came in, not knowing what had happened. Peter asked her, "Tell me, is this the price you and Ananias got for the land?"
>
> "Yes," she said, "that is the price."
>
> Peter said to her, "How could you conspire to test the Spirit of the Lord? Listen! The feet of the men who buried your husband are at the door, and they will carry you out also."
>
> At that moment she fell down at his feet and died. Then the young men came in and, finding her dead, carried her out

and buried her beside her husband. Great fear seized the whole church and all who heard about these events.

The term "great fear" in the last verse of that quote doesn't mean "reverence and awe." It is the Greek word "phobos" which literally means fear, dread, or terror (Strong). There's nothing godly or holy about being afraid that God is going to smite you for lying. We covered this in Chapter 3 already—God doesn't kill, so we start with that premise and we look at context. Based on the actual meaning of the word "fear" as used in that passage, everyone in the church wasn't in awe of God but was scared they were going to be the next to die if they messed up even a little bit.

Put this in a bit more perspective. Did the Holy Spirit state somewhere in the text that Peter was to kill them? Did Holy Spirit say that God wanted to kill them? No and no. Did Peter curse them with his words and decree their death? It's hard to say whether he cursed Ananias, but he was definitely judging him pretty harshly and pretty clearly pronounced to Sapphira that she was going to die. Even if Ananias died because the enemy came in through his lying and killed him, Peter definitely was the one who killed Sapphira, and who is to say that his judgment of Ananias wasn't the foothold the enemy needed to cause his death?

Looking a bit deeper, whose money was it anyway? It wasn't Peter's for sure. Ananias wasn't right to lie, but he didn't have to share any of his money to begin with—and he certainly didn't deserve to die for it. Not only that, but where did this "lay it at the apostles' feet" thing start? There certainly is no scriptural precedent for it. What is my point here? Peter seemed to get a bit of a power trip out of the situation, and his solution was to pass judgment. Jesus told the disciples back in John 20:23, "If you forgive anyone's sins, their sins are forgiven; if you do not forgive them, they are not forgiven."

Peter held Ananias in judgment, not forgiving his sin, and in the very moment that Peter spoke judgment against him, he died. I believe that Peter killed him, because when the glory of God is present, everything is accelerated. I explain this concept of acceleration and share an example of this in a story about a phone call later in this chapter. Nevertheless, in that glory atmosphere, the pronouncement of judgment Peter made rapidly bore fruit—and as the payment for sin is death (Romans 6:23), when Peter held Ananias' sin against him, Ananias received the payment in full right at that time.

We have to take a serious step back and look at Peter's actions and the power of death he wielded with his tongue. What would it mean for our lives if every time we messed up, we had to fear being killed? Lying is certainly not the worst crime one can imagine; did they really deserve to die for it? This death-cursing for sin is literally the exact opposite of the gospel of Jesus Christ who died on our behalf, for us, as us, and took all our sin upon himself. Romans 8:1-2 says, "Therefore there is now no condemnation for those who are in Christ Jesus. For the law of the Spirit of life in Christ Jesus has set you free from the law of sin and of death." The Bible is clear that we are no longer bound to death under sin, but as seen with Ananias and Sapphira, that doesn't mean we can't still kill people with our thoughts and words. In fact, Jesus spoke in Matthew 5:21-22 about this, pointing out that those who are angry with one another are already condemned to judgment as if they had murdered—because that is the root of what is in their heart. What we understand in the present day is that if someone thinks a thought, he has already sent out that murder-energy, so on some level he has sown into co-creating the murder even if it hasn't manifested physically yet. In this case, Peter spoke out that Sapphira was going to die—and it happened almost instantaneously.

One of the things that can happen when we get deeper into the glory realms of God is that our words become more powerful and the time it takes to see things manifest from the time we speak it shortens considerably. I was once in a time of prayer with my wife and some friends and an issue came up where we needed to speak to someone and she wasn't answering her phone. I could feel the active presence of God all around us, and I pointed to the cell phone, spoke the woman's name and commanded her to call. Literally, within fifteen seconds, the phone rang because she was calling. God wants us to understand that when He says He has made us in His image, and that the power of life and death are in our words, He means it.

I was talking to a friend once who pointed out that Peter's language problem didn't stop with Ananias and Sapphira—he also cursed Simon the Sorcerer (also known as Simon Magus) in Acts 8.

> When Simon saw that the Spirit was given at the laying on of the apostles' hands, he offered them money and said, "Give me also this ability so that everyone on whom I lay my hands may receive the Holy Spirit."
>
> Peter answered: "May your money perish with you, because you thought you could buy the gift of God with money! You have no part or share in this ministry, because your heart is not right before God. Repent of this wickedness and pray to the Lord in the hope that he may forgive you for having such a thought in your heart. For I see that you are full of bitterness and captive to sin."
>
> Then Simon answered, "Pray to the Lord for me so that nothing you have said may happen to me."
>
> After they had further proclaimed the word of the Lord and testified about Jesus, Peter and John returned to Jerusalem, preaching the gospel in many Samaritan villages (Acts 8:18-25).

This sorcerer saw in the spirit that the Holy Spirit was being transferred when the apostles laid their hands on people and prayed. As a nonbeliever (who was basically wanting to convert), he really had no idea of the ways of the Kingdom and didn't know that you can't buy spiritual power—because in his world, he could! People paid Simon for his services, and if he needed sorcerous ingredients or magical services from someone else, he would purchase it as well. The sorcerer lived in a power-for-pay culture, so the fact that he was willing to shell out bucks for the Holy Spirit is actually pretty telling— it meant he was sincere about wanting to be able to impart such a wondrous gift!

Peter's response to this was exceedingly harsh and without love. His answer was essentially "You are going to die. You will never minister the Spirit to others, and you can only hope that God will forgive you because it is apparent that you are sinful." What?!? Since when has that *ever* been the response to someone having interest in the gospel? It is clear he was a sinner—haven't we all been in that position at one time? That's the key message of the gospel—that while we were sinners, Jesus forgave all of our sin because He is merciful and good. Peter in no uncertain terms refused him salvation—even when Simon repented, on the spot, in what was a very mature response, saying, "Pray to the Lord for me so that nothing you have said may happen to me" (Acts 8:24).

Let's face it—Simon was a sorcerer and a pagan leader of his day and knew about the power of the tongue. He heard Peter and he must have been thinking, "You literally just cursed me—and I know because I've done this to people before too. You're just tons more powerful than I am, so I am in *big* trouble." The text would have stated as much if Peter had prayed for Simon, but the last sentence in that passage didn't mention a thing about it, so Peter probably ignored him and walked off, presumably with the same prideful attitude it seems he had when he killed Ananias and Sapphira. Interestingly, since Peter cursed and rejected Simon, it is not too surprising to find that there are multiple references in old texts to Simon Magus, an important figure in Gnosticism, as being a Babylonian priest who started a hybrid religion that was a cross between Judaism and Babylonian paganism. History is pretty clear about this, to the point that he eventually elevated himself to god-status and had a statue of himself erected in Rome (Martin 9). How would things have gone differently if Peter had decided not to outright refuse Simon to take part in the gospel and also curse him to death?

Jesus was clear with the disciples on how we are supposed to speak, and as His followers our goal is the same. He was pretty adamant in Luke 9 about this as well:

> And as they went, they entered a village of the Samaritans, to prepare for Him. But they did not receive Him, because His face was set for the journey to Jerusalem. And when His disciples James and John saw this, they said, 'Lord, do You want us to command fire to come down from heaven and consume them, just as Elijah did?'
>
> But He turned and rebuked them, and said, 'You do not know what manner of spirit you are of. For the Son of Man did not come to destroy men's lives but to save them.' And they went to another village. (Luke 9:52b-56, *NASB*)

If we read the text above it gives us a certain perspective, but I imagine the conversation between them could have gone a little something like this:

James and John said, "Let's call fire down and burn them all!"

Jesus in turn was like, "Whoa guys, let's back that up. You *really* don't get it, do you? The mission is not to kill everyone who upsets us. We're not Elisha who gets angry at kids and then sends bears after them. I mean, who doesn't need a good mauling, right? Or like Elijah—'Hey there, your platoon was sent to take me to the king? Fireball from heaven! How do you like them apples?!?' Guys, I came to help people and fix things, not destroy everyone."

The disciples, Peter included, were starting to come into their authority—which was exactly what Jesus had been trying to teach them; the problem was how they were going about it.

This misuse of the tongue and carnal judgment isn't limited to the Bible—men and women of God throughout history have done this very same thing. Saint Vincent Ferrer, a Dominican Priest and missionary from the late 1300s once had a mute woman come up to him. She began to sign to him asking for some bread and for the ability to speak. While she was signing, her tongue became loosed and she began to speak, continuing her request. St. Vincent promised her bread, but *took back her speech* because he said she wasn't going to make good use of it (Hebert 167). Think about how horrible of a thing that was. The woman came to him asking for help because she was unable to solve the problem herself. There is a good likelihood she had been mute from birth—and yet when God saw fit to heal her, this man thought it was appropriate to revoke Heaven's gift. I don't see a single place where this sort of behavior is evident in the life of Jesus, but rather Acts 10:38 says, ". . . God anointed Jesus of Nazareth with the Holy Spirit and power, and . . . he went around doing good and healing all who were under the power of the devil, because God was with him." The life of someone who is filled with the Spirit should look like it did for Jesus—healing those who the devil had oppressed, not re-oppressing them after they receive their healing. And while St. Vincent is known for prolific miracles and for setting many people free from darkness, sickness, and infirmity, I can say without a doubt that he missed it on this one. I think if the saint were here today he would agree with me. We have to learn to use our words and the power that God has given us responsibly because the choices we make directly impact others' lives.

St. Vincent wasn't the only one to do this sort of death-speaking over people. St. Philip Neri, who lived in the 1500s, raised the dead and healed many. However, there is one less-flattering story where he spoke death over a woman and she died. St. Philip had been visiting a woman in Rome repeatedly over the course of a month because she had been ill. One day she was in considerable agony and after he left, he felt like he should go see her again, so he turned around. Those present apparently thought she was going to die the next day, but seeing her agony he prayed for her, then spoke up and commanded her soul to leave her body. She died that very moment.

His reason for prayerfully killing her was that she would have "run the risk of giving way to certain temptations" (Hebert 125). While I recognize I am second-guessing the man roughly 500 years after the fact, it seems quite strange to me that this man who was well-acquainted with divine healing only had death to hand out in this situation. I believe he heard God when he felt he was supposed to go visit her again, but I suggest God intended another outcome. If the Lord revealed that she was going to give way to some kind of temptation, whatever that would have been, the obvious solution would have been to continue to intercede for her total healing and that she bear up under temptation, not ensure she died swiftly. It is not only entirely contrary to the nature of God, but it literally does not make any sense why he would have chosen to pray her into the grave instead of persevering to pray her well once more. This only further proves my point that oftentimes *we* are the ones who decide whether life or death reigns in a situation based on the choices we make and the words we speak and pray.

Remember that situation where I commanded someone to call and within fifteen seconds she was calling us? Imagine if that was me praying over a body and within fifteen seconds of commanding life, he sat up? The power in our words is immense, so is imperative we understand this ability God has given us. We have the capacity to *speak life* where there is death and turn a situation completely on its head. When someone dies, it is our job to command life into the situation and to undo what the enemy has done. As we grasp this power of speech we will develop a reputation as those who raise the dead. And while it may get inconvenient, that reputation for speaking life will be what wakes us at 3 am with a person crying on the other side of the phone begging for us to pray over a body. The power of life is in our tongues—so let us steward it well!

I realize I have spent a considerable amount of time in this chapter reviewing Peter and other saints' poor use of words, but I believe it is important. If we don't understand that our words have power and we are irresponsible with them, we could kill someone with our speech just as easily as Peter and the other saints did. It's really not that far-fetched. Peter was a man with flaws just like you and me. He was about as human as human can get. He was zealous, but also had a temper. He bumbled around but meant well—and often God would use him to do some really cool stuff. If Peter the bumbling clown was one of Jesus' top disciples, we really don't have any reason to believe we are so much better than him that we will never make similar mistakes—but there are some mistakes we cannot afford to repeat; cursing people to death is one of them. If we value life then we need to not just stop death-cursing, but go one step further and use our words to command life. In closing, we have to remember the goal. We can choose to cultivate an inner culture of life based on what we think and say, or we can cultivate a culture of death. Only one of those two will effectively raise the dead, so we must choose wisely and get in the habit of doing so each day.

Chapter 5

Power and Authority for Resurrection

It is easy to say that we have power and authority to raise the dead, but how do we know? How do power and authority even work, and how can we use them effectively? This chapter will attempt to answer these questions and more. First, we will look at the difference between power and authority and how they function. Next, we will look at the power and authority God has given us, which qualifies us as servants of God who have the permission, right, and even duty to raise the dead. Finally we will look at how to wield them to accomplish things here on earth—all of which applies directly to resurrection.

Power and authority can be a bit confusing because they are both related yet function in different ways; at the same time, they overlap. Someone can operate in both at the same time, and I suggest that increasing in one has the potential to help one increase in the other, but that is also not a guarantee.

Power is fairly straightforward and is basically as it sounds—ability, strength, virtue, capacity. All of these are words to describe this force or energy. It can be used to cast out demons by force or regenerate damaged tissue, even creating missing body parts. Power can be used to cause people to experience spiritual encounters. Jesus often used it to heal people, especially when in crowds and large groups. Luke 5:17 states, "One day Jesus was teaching, and Pharisees and teachers of the Law were sitting there. They had come from every village of Galilee and from Judea and Jerusalem. And the power of the Lord was with Jesus to heal the sick." Again Luke 6:19 says, "…and the people all tried to touch him, because power was coming from him and healing them all." We have since learned what Jesus knew, that using spiritual virtue directly is one method to fix earthly injury, sickness, and disease. Taking it one step further, this same energy that can heal bodies can also raise the dead. If those missing body parts can find themselves regenerated through God's power, then this same force of life that originates from God can be used to reinsert the soul and spirit back into that same body and resurrection will occur.

Most church-goers, or at least those who are familiar with the charismata, or spiritual gifts, are familiar healing others with power. This is because the altar call—where after preaching the speaker will call those in need of prayer to the front of the room, is common. In most church services, the stage has been set for displays of power through worship and preaching, and the Bible has given a precedent that the Lord will confirm the words spoken with signs and miracles to follow alongside them (Mark 16:20). During the altar call, other parishioners who have been designated to pray will do so with those responding. These ministers often tap into what is referred to as a "corporate anointing" which is a way of describing that they have engaged a larger flow of healing power than they might normally access on their own without that energy-atmosphere in place. When that power is present it is a good time to do anything—especially raising the dead.

The downside to this particular method is that people rarely die in the middle of a church service. It would be nice if they could simply wait to have their life-threatening heart attacks until Sunday morning during the ministry time, but sadly it rarely works that way. As such, there will be times when the "power present to heal" isn't all that present for healing or resurrection. This doesn't halt our efforts as even Jesus felt virtue flow out from him at times when there was no corporate atmosphere (Luke 8:43-48), but when it isn't readily available, we must have other ways to get the job done. We could try creating a corporate atmosphere, but this tends to be inconvenient and often impractical. In such circumstances, raising the dead through authority fits the bill quite nicely.

Authority is a little harder to explain, but by definition it is delegated power—the right to give orders and enforce obedience (Dictionary.com). While simply being delegated power makes it sound pretty similar to power, authority is different in its function. Power is raw energy whereas authority is based on a governmental system. For example, a police sergeant has authority given to him by the ruling power, which means he has the right to call the shots in a particular region to the extent that his authority covers. However, what happens if that sergeant is a small, slender man and gets into a fistfight with a beefy 250-pound muscular criminal? In a fight the cop is over*powered*—but he could still win. How so? It is possible that the criminal will recognize the policeman's authority and surrender without coming to physical blows. Even if the lawbreaker does not surrender, the sergeant may force him to give up, not through the use of his own personal strength, but by sending the many police under his command. In other words, while a single cop may not be strong enough to fix the problem through power, by using his authority the twenty policemen under him are more than sufficient to arrest the criminal, no matter how much the man resists.

I give another example of this in my book *The Gamer's Guide to the Kingdom of God*, where I explain power and authority using the Disney movie *Aladdin*.

> Early on in the movie, Aladdin the orphan is walking through the marketplace with Princess Jasmine who is disguised as a commoner. The city guards apprehend Aladdin and are about to arrest him. Three guards are present, all bigger than she, but that doesn't matter. She simply takes off her disguise and orders them as the Princess to let him go. In that situation Jasmine would have been easily overpowered by the guards, but they are required to listen to her. In an interesting twist, the guards tell her that her authority is no good in that situation for one reason alone—someone with greater authority than she gave the command to apprehend Aladdin. (King, *Gamer's Guide* 245)

Both Jasmine and the guards respond to authority that is greater than their own, and ultimately the one with the highest level wins, regardless of how righteous or unjust they are. The Kingdom is no different. As we engage and increase in authority, even demons are required to respond to us whether they want to or not. Believers who are not accessing a wave of power conveniently put at their disposal can still use authority to heal the sick, raise the dead, and cast out demons. Authority can even be used to command the natural elements, as is shown in Matthew 8:23-27:

Then he got into the boat and his disciples followed him. Suddenly a furious storm came up on the lake, so that the waves swept over the boat. But Jesus was sleeping. The disciples went and woke him, saying, "Lord, save us! We're going to drown!"

He replied, "You of little faith, why are you so afraid?" Then he got up and rebuked the winds and the waves, and it was completely calm.

The men were amazed and asked, "What kind of man is this? Even the winds and the waves obey him!"

A similar story is found in Luke 8:24-25, but both passages clearly demonstrate that whether it was the atoms of the air making up the storm itself or spirits causing the storm who obeyed him, at Jesus' command it all stopped. Everything in all of creation outside of God himself will respond to the right level of authority when put in use.

Now that we know what power and authority are and have a general idea of what they can do, how do we know that we have the same power and authority that Jesus had? Also, how do we know that we can use it to raise the dead and manifest the Kingdom of God here on earth?

The New Testament is full of many stories, but the most pivotal one upon which the rest of the Bible hinges is the death, resurrection, and ascension of Jesus of Nazareth. The Bible tells us that after he died, Jesus spent time in hell, engaging those who had died long before (1 Peter 3:18-20; Ephesian 4:9). The details are unclear, but at some point during the three physical days of Jesus' death, he also wrested the keys of death and hell away from Satan. Revelation 1:10 states, "I am the Living One; I was dead, and now look, I am alive for ever and ever! And I hold the keys of death and Hades." When Jesus took those keys, he triumphed over death from a legal perspective. Where sin had been able to infiltrate and take dominion over the earth through Adam's sin, Jesus permanently cancelled all legal rights that death and destruction held over us, then he rose from the dead and delegated authority to us, his followers, to reverse death, loss, and destruction wherever it may be found. The results of this legal transaction were first evidenced in Matthew 27:50-53 where it says:

> "When Jesus had cried out again in a loud voice, he gave up his spirit. At that moment the curtain of the temple was torn in two from top to bottom. The earth shook, the rocks split and the tombs broke open. The bodies of many holy people who had died were raised to life. They came out of the tombs after Jesus' resurrection and went into the holy city and appeared to many people."

People who had been dead, possibly even for years, came back to life. If Jesus' death caused the dead to rise, how much more will his spirit living in us do much more?

In Matthew 28:18-20 Jesus spoke to his disciples and said, "All authority in heaven and on earth has been given to me. Therefore go and make disciples of all nations, baptizing them in the name of the Father and of the Son and of the Holy Spirit, and teaching them to obey everything I have commanded you. And surely I am with you always, to the very end of the age." In telling them to go, and by consequence the rest of us who are His disciples as well, Jesus has delegated His authority to us to minister the gospel (the good news of life), with an instruction to obey everything He commanded. One of my favorite verses is Matthew 10:7-8, "As you go, proclaim this message: 'The kingdom of heaven has come near.' Heal the sick, *raise the dead (emphasis mine)*, cleanse those who have leprosy, drive out demons. Freely you have received; freely give." Jesus gave the command to raise the dead and has since passed that authority on to us. What this means is that, as I said at the beginning of this chapter, we have the right, privilege, and *duty* to raise the dead. A friend of mine puts it this way: Raising the dead isn't a suggestion—it's a command!

We don't always think about this fact, but Jesus actually spent close to forty days with his disciples after his resurrection, presumably teaching them about the things that had changed now that he had conquered death and returned. On the final day he was with them, he told his disciples about power that was going to come from Heaven enabling them to perform His will in the earth:

> On one occasion, while he was eating with them, he gave them this command: "Do not leave Jerusalem, but wait for the gift my Father promised, which you have heard me speak about. For John baptized with water, but in a few days you will be baptized with the Holy Spirit."
>
> Then they gathered around him and asked him, "Lord, are you at this time going to restore the kingdom to Israel?"
>
> He said to them: "It is not for you to know the times or dates the Father has set by his own authority. But you will receive power when the Holy Spirit comes on you; and you will be my witnesses in Jerusalem, and in all Judea and Samaria, and to the ends of the earth" (Acts 1:4-8).

This baptism of power took place only ten days later on the day of Pentecost. In Acts 2:39 Peter explained that, "The promise is for you and your children and for all who are far off—for all whom the Lord our God will call." Since we, too, have been called by God to be heirs of His Kingdom, then we also must receive the Baptism of the

Holy Spirit and be given that same power. There are many good books one can read to learn more about this topic, but a good place to start is Derek Prince's book *Baptism in the Holy Spirit*. When we receive the Baptism of the Holy Spirit we receive a new measure of power above and beyond that which we receive at salvation to do such things as raise the dead, heal the sick, and generally destroy works of darkness. While I will not say Baptism in the Spirit is a requirement to raise the dead, if we are serious about this, it is something we will be unwilling to do without.

Since God has delegated both power and authority to us to raise the dead, there are some additional considerations. While it is fruitless and otherwise impossible to try to measure our power or authority to see if it is "enough" to raise the dead, we would do well to understand that power and authority do come in levels. We must always act under the assumption that God has equipped us with everything we need for that task in that moment, but I believe it is helpful to understand what these levels look like, and where we see them in scripture.

Second Corinthians 3:18 says, "And we, who with unveiled faces all reflect the Lord's glory, are being transformed into his likeness with ever-increasing glory, which comes from the Lord, who is the Spirit." There are other translations which express it a bit differently. The KJV and NASB say "from glory to glory" and the ESV and NET say "from one degree of glory to another." If we expand the translation of the passage based on the original Greek, it says that as we behold the Lord we "undergo metamorphosis into God's likeness, separating ourselves entirely from one level of exalted splendor and departing into another level of exalted splendor" (Strong). In simple terms, we can advance in levels of power and glory. Experience and even simple observation show us that as believers our spiritual journey works exactly like this—with progression in levels of glory. The Bible talks about how as beginners, we crave pure spiritual milk—the easy stuff, but as we grow into maturity, we need deeper spiritual sustenance—the solid food of spiritual growth (Hebrews 5:12-14; 1 Corinthians 3:2). Water Baptism and Baptism of the Holy Spirit are two easy ways to begin our process of leveling up, but overall, it is a gradual journey as we engage our relationship with God more deeply. The good news is that Holy Spirit is given to us as a guide to help us on our way (John 14:26). I discuss this phenomenon in more detail in my book *The Gamer's Guide to the Kingdom of God*.

The Body of Christ is coming into a greater revelation on the authority of the believer. We now understand that we can command the elements to respond to us such as Jesus did when he spoke to the storm (Mark 4:35-41), we have been given the right of influence over sickness and disease, and by authority we are able to cast out demons. Yet, simply having authority is not enough—we must learn how to use it wisely. To do this, it is crucial we gain a greater understanding of God's purpose in giving us authority and what He expects us to do with it.

Authority comes in levels as well, but where with power we are able to gradually increase in the amount of raw heavenly energy we can work with, all authority has already been given to us as per Jesus's proclamation in Matthew 28:18-20. The difference we see in our lives between the "all authority" Jesus declared was His and ours through Him and what we walk in now has to do with the difference between being children and *mature* children of God.

The Bible speaks about authority in a number of places, but it begins with our position. The reason we have the right to wield God's authority is our Sonship (Romans 8:16)—not just as ones who have been adopted in, but legitimate children, made so by Jesus Christ. When Paul spoke to the Romans about adoption, he knew they understood the permanent and irreversibly binding rights and authority a child received when he or she was adopted, but when he wrote to the Jews he was not speaking about adopted children, but rather that we are born from above and are new creations with God's DNA within us. Jesus spoke the same to Nicodemus, saying he must be re-born from above (John 3:5-8). As legitimate children, we have all of the rights and responsibilities of God's heirs; we are heirs alongside Jesus (Romans 8:17; Galatians 4:7).

To understand what this means influences both how we use authority and how we live in general, so we need to grasp what the Bible says about sonship with God. Galatians 4:1-2 explains it like this, "What I am saying is that as long as an heir is underage, he is no different from a slave although he owns the whole estate. The heir is subject to guardians and trustees until the time set by his father." In other words as God's children, we have to have others watch over us—and not just other believers, but Holy Spirit and even the angels to help us grow into maturity. In the same way that we wouldn't let a three year old have full reign of the house, likewise God doesn't necessarily give us everything without some limitations early on. This isn't to keep us from things, but to safeguard us until we mature.

This idea holds true when studied out in the scriptures. The New Testament uses a few different words that usually translate as "child"—the words *nepios, teknon,* and *huios.* A *nepios* son is basically an infant or young child and needs constant supervision. A *teknon* child is like those mentioned in Galatians 4:1-2 above—one who still needs an authority figure to watch over him and help him with daily affairs, but who is no longer a baby. A *huios* son (or daughter) has become a mature member of his household and is able to wield the full authority he possesses as an heir.

To understand our authority and role as believers we need to know the difference between *nepios, teknon,* and *huios* sons. Not all the verses in the Bible that refer to sonship and being children of God can be read the same way. 1 Corinthians 13:11 says, "When I was a child, I talked like a child, I thought like a child, I reasoned like a child. When I became a man, I put the ways of childhood behind me." The word child here refers to a *nepios* son—one who is literally a baby and is extremely childish in his ways. Romans 8:16-17 says that we are *teknon* sons of God, who are older but still need assistance. The verses state, "The Spirit himself testifies with our spirit that we are God's children. Now if we are children, then we are heirs—heirs of God and co-heirs with Christ if indeed we share in his sufferings in order that we may also share in his glory." The point I believe Paul was making here was that as immature sons and daughters of God that we are still heirs—not having yet inherited the fullness, but that Holy Spirit resides within us and marks us with God's seal, designating us as His children for all time and allowing us the legal right to inherit the fullness He has planned for us. This is as differentiated from a *huios* son, which Paul mentions only two verses prior. Romans 8:14 says, "For those who are led by the Spirit of God are the children of God." The word children here is better translated as mature children or mature sons/daughters of God. Even Jesus, when it states that he is God's only begotten son (John 1:18, 3:16, 3:18; 1 John 4:9), is referred to as a *huios* son.

Those *huios* sons and daughters, led by God's Spirit, are brought into maturity and are able to wield their authority as heirs of God's estate, and His estate extends beyond the earth into the entire cosmos, even the heavens. As such, we as believers need to learn to operate in our God-given authority to help manage that which we have been given. It is for this reason that Romans 8:19-22 speaks of *huios* sons, saying:

> For the creation waits in eager expectation for the children of God to be revealed. For the creation was subjected to frustration, not by its own choice, but by the will of the one who subjected it, in hope that the creation itself will be liberated from its bondage to decay and brought into the freedom and glory of the children of God. We know that the whole creation has been groaning as in the pains of childbirth right up to the present time.

Creation is on the edge of its seat waiting for the Body of Christ to step up and take our place as mature sons and daughters of God who are actively stepping into our inheritance and role to govern not just the nations, but the cosmos.

While all the Greek words provide one level of understanding, I believe there is a key principle here that is important to understand—one that gets lost amidst the meanings of the various words if we don't focus on taking it a step further. Matthew 25:14-30 tells of the parable of the talents, but more than that it speaks to the result of those who have purposed to go through the learning process versus those who have avoided learning how to use what they have been given. Verse 29 says, "For whoever has will be given more, and they will have an abundance. Whoever does not have, even what they have will be taken from them." The significance here has to do with what it means to act and live as a *huios* son versus a *teknon* son.

Those of us who operate in the prophetic can get so focused on hearing what God is saying that we only do what we see the Father doing (John 5:19) and miss the fact that God's desire isn't just to teach us to hear Him. While that is a good goal, He wants to develop us a few steps further. If we are eight years old and ask our earthly father to help us count the money for a purchase we want to make, that is normal. If we do the same at age twenty-five, that is abnormal.

By age twenty-five we should have learned not just how to count small bills, but also how to manage and balance a budget, do our taxes, and possibly even how to invest and/or run a business. Much more is expected of an adult child (*huios*) than would be expected of the eight year old child (*teknon*).

Now that we have a better grasp of what power and authority are, how they operate, and how we can increase in both, we need to understand how to *wield* them. While what I discuss here is going to explain how to wield authority and power in a general sense, I will also attempt to clarify what that means more specifically when it comes to raising the dead.

Something I have a hard time understanding is this attitude in the church that says we must always ask God's permission before we do things. There is a measure to which this is wise and a measure to which it is foolish. God expects us to learn and grow, and as we do this, we should be learning about how God runs His Kingdom and the rights and responsibilities we possess. While a new believer will probably have a lot of questions about what he or she is "allowed" to do, a mature believer shouldn't still be wondering about these sorts of things as often. Questions like "Does God want to heal that person?" shouldn't even come up in a mature believer's mind— because he or she should be so well acquainted with God's nature and will that he already knows the answer is "yes" and the next question is simply "how shall we make it happen?" A mature believer should be able to start to minister healing and get mid-course guidance from Holy Spirit instead of waiting for a unique word from God in that moment for permission to start praying.

Where people get hung up on this subject is what I mentioned before in John 5:19 when Jesus stated that he only does what he sees the Father doing and that he can do nothing on his own. Some people are so concerned that they will step outside of the will of God that they have to get a word of knowledge just to know which bag of apples to buy at the grocery store. That is the exact opposite of the *huios* maturity God wants to bring us and verges on *nepios* immaturity—the work of babies and toddlers. What some people don't seem to understand is the difference between a now-word based on God saying something specific in a moment and grasping the general will of the Father.

As I have emphasized earlier in this book, it should go without saying that God is good, and He doesn't hide his personality or ways from us. He isn't deceitful, pretending to be one way but actually behaving another way—He is straightforward in expressing His nature (James 1:17). If we don't see Jesus acting a certain way, then the Father isn't that way either (Hebrews 1:3) because they are one and the same (John 10:30). As such, we can understand who God is, what He is like, and recognize that because God doesn't change (James 1:17; Hebrews 13:8) we can know what His will is in many situations without needing to ask. Furthermore, we have authority as sons in those situations where *we* are to determine what needs to be done, then carry it out.

To give a real-life example, I am a nurse and I work on a hospital unit. I work three scheduled twelve hour shifts each week for roughly 156 shifts per year. I should not have to ask God at the beginning of each of those 156 shifts if I have permission to pray for or with my patients that night. I work to serve broken people. Each and every one of them is someone Jesus died to heal, save, and deliver. As I have heard Minister Todd White say once when preaching, "Show me the one Jesus didn't die for and that's the one I won't pray for." That quote says it all. When I understand my authority as a son of the Most High King, I don't need to get special permission or a prophetic word from God each and every day. "God, it is shift number 47 for the year. Do I have permission to heal the sick tonight?" It sounds ridiculous when posed this way, yet how many people actually live like this? How many people fail to understand the authority we have been given as sons and daughters of God? Jesus was very clear in John 10:10 about his work and Satan's: "The thief comes only to steal and kill and destroy; I have come that they may have life, and have it to the full." Jesus is in direct opposition to any work of the enemy, and we have the same right and responsibility to destroy works of darkness and release abundant life into the world around us. This is an important concept to understand as we look at raising the dead, and we will explore this issue of permission further as we try to walk in resurrection power.

To do this well, however, we need to combine the general will of God with His specific will in a particular moment. While this may sound contrary to what I have been explaining above about why we don't need to ask God for permission to perform His will, there is more to it than that. In prior paragraphs I have been emphasizing the need to learn and know God's general will due to *immaturity* in the Body of Christ, but there is a balance that needs to be reached in each and every situation.

The general will of God could be understood as allowing us to operate on protocols. My friend Praying Medic has explained this well in the past, and I am using an example he has shared with me here—one I have seen and put into action as well. In the medical field, protocols are orders that are pre-signed by the doctor that allow nurses, paramedics, and other staff to operate outside of the bounds of their scope of practice in certain pre-defined situations. Because these orders are agreed-upon in advance, as long as I, the nurse, remain within the bounds of that protocol, I am covered in situations that require me to do more than my nursing scope normally permits. The only time this does not work is if I step outside of the additional rights permitted me by that document. God has given us protocol in

Jesus Christ saying things like, "As you go, proclaim this message: 'The kingdom of heaven has come near.' Heal the sick, raise the dead, cleanse those who have leprosy, drive out demons. Freely you have received; freely give (Matthew 10:7-8). We don't need to ask permission to do the things we have been commanded to do—God gave us a protocol.

On the other hand, as mentioned before, we also need to do what we see the Father doing, and we need to listen to what God is saying to us (Revelation 2:7, 11, 17, 29; and 3:6, 13, 22). When we don't know what to do, are unfamiliar with the situation, or just need general wisdom and counsel, we are prudent to ask God and listen to His guidance. In reality, even in situations where we start by operating from within the protocol, we need to stay open to hearing the Spirit's voice leading and guiding us as we walk it out.

Inner healing and deliverance are perfect examples of this. Jesus has given us authority over unclean spirits to cast them out (Matthew 10:1), but in the moment, we also need revelation. What is the entry point or stronghold that has made it so the demon has been able to remain? What emotional issues are hindering the deliverance, and what mindsets and feelings need to be corrected and healed so the person can live in freedom? These come by revelation, and while some basic protocol can be used to get the process started, eventually we will have to hear from God in that moment for that person if we want to be effective.

In my own family, I tend to operate first out of protocol, whereas my wife is geared more toward being Spirit-led in the moment. That doesn't mean that I am not Spirit-led, but that I am less reticent to step out in situations where a clear word from God has not come through. The reason for my way of doing things is that in any situation where death, loss, or destruction are present, as a son of God, I understand I have permission to intervene and don't need a special instruction from Him. On the other hand, my wife tends toward intervening only if she feels God urging her to do so. Which of us is correct? Neither, or both. We must know God's will both generally and individually. I tend to start with protocol when I either want to or am instructed to, changing course as needed based on Holy Spirit's guidance in that moment. My wife tends to move forward only if she feels specifically nudged or directed to do so. Neither of us are wrong, but both of us have settled into a comfortable rhythm in the way we each operate in cooperation with Holy Spirit. With that said, either method or a combination of the two is fine provided we understand we have that underlying authority to begin with.

When it comes to raising the dead, making use of this authority is important. In fact, did you know that Jesus used authority to heal the sick? There was one encounter in particular that Jesus had with a Roman centurion that surprised Jesus, but it was because the centurion was able to correlate what he understood about the military with how Jesus exercised heavenly authority. In the New Testament Luke writes:

> He was not far from the house when the centurion sent friends to say to him: "Lord, don't trouble yourself, for I do not deserve to have you come under my roof. That is why I did not even consider myself worthy to come to you. But say the word, and my servant will be healed. For I myself am a man under authority, with soldiers under me. I tell this one, 'Go,' and he goes; and that one, 'Come,' and he comes. I say to my servant, 'Do this,' and he does it."
>
> When Jesus heard this, he was amazed at him, and turning to the crowd following him, he said, "I tell you, I have not found such great faith even in Israel." Then the men who

had been sent returned to the house and found the servant well (Luke 7:6-10).

While at times Jesus would heal with sheer quantity of power, that's not how he did it in this situation—he knew that God had placed legions of angels under his command and that he was able to command healing to the desired location because the angels would bring the healing wherever he instructed. When we pray, we ought to pray with authority, expecting results from the things we command. Instead of praying "request" prayers for the dead to be raised, we should command the life back in their bodies!

I have prayed for many people for healing, and while I first began to pray with an expectation of using power, which usually involved touching them as long as possible to let the power continue to flow, as I began to understand my authority I started to change how I prayed when in public. Once I was walking down the street and saw a woman walking with a cane. Curious as to why she had the cane, I asked the Lord and received a word of knowledge that her knee was affected. I approached her and struck up a short conversation, asking why she had the cane. Often when I talk to random strangers I find simple questions of curiosity like this can be disarming and friendly, as well as good conversation starters, which allows me to pursue further and offer healing. It turned out she had arthritis in her left knee which made it difficult for her to walk. I prayed with her three times, each time her knee getting less painful until the last time she was able to stomp her leg on the ground pain free. When I prayed, I wasn't looking for a wave of power to show up and I never touched her. I spoke a command, and as I did so the cells in her body, the arthritis, and the angels responded to my command and carried out my decree. That is an easy example of how authority is used in prayer, and whether healing the sick or raising the dead, the method doesn't change—because the same life of Jesus that can heal sicknesses is the same one that will bring life to the dead.

When raising the dead with power, it may or may not happen in such a way that it is apparent that power is present at that time. While not a guarantee, someone could sense that the atmosphere feels electrically charged or "alive" in some way. There may be physical sensations that accompany this such as trembling of your hands or legs, or a tingly feeling on the skin. I have had times where a sensation of power descended upon me from above, blanketing my head as if someone was pouring oil on it, and on my hand as if I had put gloves on, both my head and hands feeling supercharged with energy. In situations such as that, the best plan is to lay hands on the deceased if at all possible; if they are located elsewhere at that time, physically touch an object that can be placed with them later, much as Paul did in Acts 19:11-12 when it states, "God did extraordinary miracles through Paul, so that even handkerchiefs and aprons that had touched him were taken to the sick, and their illnesses were cured and the evil spirits left them." The same life of Christ that can cure illnesses and cast out demons is the same powerful life that can raise the dead. On the other hand, someone could feel nothing—but that doesn't change whether power is being released or not. Sensations are a potential indicator, but not a requirement. Often people feel nothing but get healed anyway. As long as we are getting results, it doesn't matter which way it happens.

In this chapter we have looked at power and authority in significant depth, gaining a better understanding of what they are, how they function, and how we can use them to raise the dead. We have also looked at what the Bible says about our right to wield power and authority. In the next chapter we are going to look at faith—both what it is and how we use it.

Chapter 6

Faith to Raise the Dead

Faith is a word that is used readily in most Christian circles, but I think it is uncommon that people understand what faith actually is, what it does, and how to use it, not to mention that many teachings on the subject are sorely lacking. Typically people preach out of Hebrews 11:1 about "now faith is" and talk about "NOW-faith." They might go through the gospels and talk about great faith (Matthew 8:10), small faith (Matthew 6:30), or the mustard seed of faith (Luke 17:6), or they will talk about how "faith is evidence of things hoped for and the substance of things not seen" in Hebrews 11:6, and how if you have just a little you can cast a mountain into the sea (Matthew 17:20). While all of this is true, and is both foundational and important, we tend to stay at the basics—where faith is substance and evidence, can be big or small, and apparently you don't need much to play a game of toss with mountains. Nevertheless, there aren't half as many people getting the kind of results that the Bible suggests we should be getting when we operate in it. Part of this is because we lack good teaching not just on what faith is, but on how to put it to work.

To be fair, part of the reason faith is so difficult to teach well is that it is hard to describe. It is the thing that "gets stuff done" but because we can't measure it, we cannot easily quantify results and test what works and doesn't. I suggest that faith is best understood as an intangible and immeasurable force or energy—the spiritual power that accomplishes things and changes reality. Paul said, "Now to him who is able to do immeasurably more than all we ask or imagine, according to His power that is at work within us . . ." (Ephesians 3:20). What I believe Paul alluded to here is that the force of faith we emit influences what happens around us. While God is able to do more than we can ask or think, there is something about the power of faith *at work within us* that makes a significant difference.

Whenever we do anything in prayer, we make use of this spiritual force. Think of it as a transaction or purchase where when we spend our faith-currency, and if we spend enough of it, we are able to "buy" the results we seek. If we don't have enough faith to spend in one go, we may have to use our faith on a layaway program, which is why some things take prayer over time, and sometimes even fasting to accomplish. Keep in mind that this talk about spending faith as a currency only works and/or makes sense if faith is quantifiable. While we cannot quantify it in the physical realm at this time, I cannot prove that the angels have that same limitation—I suspect that angels actually can and do measure our faith when it comes time to put things into action. Here's why: Revelation 5:8 speaks of the prayers of the saints as being collected in golden bowls. In Revelation 8, those prayers are referred to as incense, and that incense made up of prayers is combined with the fire of God then thrown back down onto the earth. In that passage, the end result of the prayers and fire being thrown back to the earth were colossal, earth-shattering changes. If we pull this together with the fact that the Bible mentions multiple times that God acted when "times had reached their fullness," I believe we can get a working model of what happens when we pray.

Consider that prayer is measured in faith-units, and the golden bowls are like a bank. Each time we pray, we deposit faith-units into our bowl-banks. Then imagine that each prayer request has a certain unit-requirement to reach before it can be answered—its own personal bowl bank. When we loose great faith, it doesn't take much to fill the bowl whereas if we release only a little faith, it is going to take a while for the bank to reach capacity and get answers. On some level, our prayers—how much and often we pray and how faith-filled we are as we do so—determines how soon and how often we get answers. On the other hand, we live under grace, and while there is a transactional partnership between us and heaven, Jesus is also our Chief Intercessor who sits at the right hand of God. As such, and even as shown in Revelation 8, our prayers get mixed with fire from the altar—which means Jesus helps us out as well. We also have to remember that we are in a spiritual battle and sometimes the enemy hijacks our results even when the bowl has been filled and the answer sent, forcing us to start over again without even being aware of it— yet another reason to pray things through to completion.

Why is this whole faith-unit and prayer-bank thing important? While a single prayer might not seem significant, I believe the above verses from Revelation demonstrate the principle I am describing— that there are mathematical, measurable quantities of power needed to bring change onto the earth, and they are usually released through prayer. Like with the golden bowls, when the necessary amount of time had passed, the so-called "fullness of time," God moved. When we pray, we have the disadvantage of not knowing when these spiritual bowls have become full, but when they do, the answers we seek are sent to us. When we want to break through into something new, we may need to pray until that bowl is filled, and only then will we get our answer. The same goes for healing, raising the dead, or anything else. When we pray we want to get results, and if we don't understand that faith plays a significant role in our prayers being answered, we won't make it a priority. When we understand the importance of faith, we will do things to guard and protect that faith as well as to enhance it. So how can we activate, enhance, and increase our faith to raise the dead? Read on.

The first thing we can do is settle the primary issues in our minds once and for all. What are these issues? Look back at the previous chapters. Is God inherently good? Does God kill? Does He want this person to live? Do we have power and authority to raise the dead? If we cannot answer these questions at the drop of a hat with surety, then somewhere deep down we haven't really settled the matter in our hearts. We need to understand how important these subjects are, and it is impossible to overstate. Our beliefs about who God is, what His will is, and what we are permitted or able to do can make the difference between whether we are wishy-washy and ineffective or can stand in faith for resurrection. Ephesians 6:16 speaks of a shield of faith, which is a much-needed part of our spiritual armor when we try to bring the dead back to life. When we have the above foundational truths as our basis, the shield of faith keeps the enemy from attacking our minds with arrows of crippling doubt that cut off access to empowered prayer. Sure, we might be able to keep praying, but when that doubt sets in and truly takes root, the power is gone and we are left largely with empty words. I don't say this to scare anyone, but to drive the point home that faith is immensely important to resurrection and we have to use it both as a weapon and a shield.

One important thing to note is that our thoughts while we are praying influence the level of faith we release. When our minds are focused in doubt, we are unable to access the faith within us to the same degree as when we are focused on God's great ability to work on our behalf. A great way to help expand and encourage ourselves, both immediately and long-term, is "By building yourselves up in your most holy faith and praying in the Holy Spirit (Jude 20). The gift of tongues is just one of the tools we have at our disposal to help strengthen faith making it readily available to us when we pray. Because faith is an intangible substance, it can be difficult to know if we are operating in it or not. I truly wish there was a device, much like in the classic *Dragonball* and *Dragonball Z* cartoons of my childhood, which measured power levels so we could know objectively when we have hit the mark. Lacking this, we have to use the tools we have at our disposal. Over time I have learned to sense when I am operating in high levels of faith based on what it feels like. The best I can describe is that it is like a sense of confidence. When I experience this feeling or inner sensation, it is an indicator that I am accessing faith at the level I seek. I can usually feel the emotion rising up within me when this occurs. If one lacks this sensation that does not guarantee he lacks faith—rather this is my experience and one indicator that might be helpful to some.

When in front of a dead body, I have hit this time and again in my own thoughts—this issue that God doesn't want to raise the person. It's a mental struggle at times in spite of what I already know. When we set out to raise the dead, the enemy hits us as hard as he can in an attempt to undermine our faith. We *have* to be grounded in what we know to be true so we can walk it out. One of the things that helps encourage my faith is to listen to, read about, and ponder/meditate on immortality. I think of places Jesus said things like, "The one who believes in me will live, even though they die; and whoever lives by believing in me will never die . . ." (John 11:25b-26). Verses like this boost my faith, reminding me that God is always and ever about life.

God shared something with me once when I was asking Him to help me be more effective in healing ministry. He said to me, "You can get an increase in one of two ways: Either heal a bunch of people and eventually work your way up into a breakthrough, or you can get a better revelation." He didn't disclose what that would look like at the time, but it was clear to me that a deeper, higher, better revelation is the more effective way to go, for the reasons discussed here—it bolsters our beliefs and provides a better launching pad to release the force of faith in prayer. While that particular view will not speak to everyone, the underlying principle remains—as we get a higher understanding of what God is doing, it will undergird our faith better than a lower-level version. All truth is from God, but some truths are deeper, more substantial, and more life-giving than others.

In the coming chapter we are going to look at resurrection stories in the Bible, various resurrections that have been recorded in history, and we will also look at some testimonies of resurrections that have happened in the current day. My hope is that your faith will be encouraged and stirred to new heights as you encounter the many things the Lord has done both in the past and present, and that these testimonies will help expand your faith as you seek to raise the dead in the future.

Chapter 7

Resurrections Past and Present

In the last chapter, and the chapters prior, we looked at a variety of beliefs and ideas that can help us to have a foundation for our faith that God raises the dead. In spite of all the "right" beliefs, there is something about experiences and stories that stir our faith in a completely different way. With this in mind, this chapter is designed with the goal of stirring faith through stories. Featured here are a combination of stories in the Bible, throughout history, and even in the present-day, all with the goal of building up our faith and stirring a hunger in our hearts to see God do the same through us. While only a few of the scriptural testimonies of resurrections are featured here, the complete set of resurrection stories found in the Bible are located in Appendix I.

Biblical Resurrection

2 Kings 13:20-21

"Elisha died and was buried. Now Moabite raiders used to enter the country every spring. Once while some Israelites were burying a man, suddenly they saw a band of raiders; so they threw the man's body into Elisha's tomb. When the body touched Elisha's bones, the man came to life and stood up on his feet."

Luke 7:11-15

"Soon afterward, Jesus went to a town called Nain, and his disciples and a large crowd went along with him. As he approached the town gate, a dead person was being carried out—the only son of his mother, and she was a widow. And a large crowd from the town was with her. When the Lord saw her, his heart went out to her and he said, 'Don't cry.'

Then he went up and touched the bier they were carrying him on, and the bearers stood still. He said, 'Young man, I say to you, get up!' The dead man sat up and began to talk, and Jesus gave him back to his mother."

Acts 9:36-41

"In Joppa there was a disciple named Tabitha (in Greek her name was Dorcas); she was always doing good and helping the poor. About that time she became sick and died, and her body was washed and placed in an upstairs room. Lydda was near Joppa, so when the disciples heard that Peter was in Lydda, they sent two men to him and urged him, 'Please come at once!'

Peter went with them, and when he arrived he was taken upstairs to the room. All the widows stood around him, crying and showing him the robes and other clothing that Dorcas had made while she was still with them.

Peter sent them all out of the room; then he got down on his knees and prayed. Turning toward the dead woman, he said, 'Tabitha, get up.' She opened her eyes, and seeing Peter she sat up. He took her by the hand and helped her to her feet. Then he called for the believers, especially the widows, and presented her to them alive."

Resurrection Throughout History

Jesus has been raising the dead throughout history, but if one didn't make a study of Catholic Church writings, it would be very easy for such stories to go unheard. While hundreds of these stories exist, I have picked out a few that I believe capture the essence of God's resurrection power. I aimed specifically for stories that are either touching in a special way or go far beyond the bounds of what we normally consider possible in order to stretch our faith. I will say that given just how many unique, precious, and sometimes mind-blowing miracles various saints performed, it was difficult to pare down the many resurrection stories to the few I have shared here. These stories come from Anthony Hebert's work, *Saints Who Raised The Dead*—a compendium of over 400 resurrection stories that have been documented throughout Church history.

Margaret of Castello

While this story isn't specifically about raising the dead, it does involve someone who is dead releasing the life-giving power of God.

I thought it was both "out there" and unique enough to be worth sharing here.

Margaret of Castello was born a deformed cripple and spent much of her early life ignored and abused by her parents. She spent some of her earlier life learning from the castle chaplain, and these lessons stuck. Her parents abandoned her when she was twenty after failing to be healed by the church. She spent her time limping around helping and serving others, and eventually joined the Third Order of Penzance of St. Dominic. At the time she didn't know more than a dozen Psalms, but the night she joined she received a divine infusion of knowledge and without learning them she knew all 150 overnight. Margaret performed a number of miracles during her lifetime, including levitation and raising the dead, but the story that struck me most was one that happened, ironically, just after her death.

Margaret died at age 33, and the crowd present demanded that the prior of the church bury her inside the church vault as a saint even though she had yet to go through the Catholic beatification process (Note: in Europe at that time, the Catholic Church was the only denomination in existence). At her funeral, a set of parents brought their crippled, mute, hunchbacked daughter right up to the coffin with a loud demand: "Margaret, you are a friend of God and you too are a cripple. You know how much you suffered in this life—have mercy on our daughter and pray to the Lord that He would heal her. Suddenly, Margaret's left arm raised itself up from the funeral bier, reached over, and touched the deformed little girl, who was instantly healed. This once-mute girl began to cry out and shout that Margaret had healed her. The family celebrated and the whole church went wild. The prior had no further objections to her burial and her body was placed inside the church (Hebert 77-79). I love this miracle because not only does it demonstrate the grace and mercy of our Lord, it shows that literally nothing is impossible with

God. While it is strange enough that Margaret remained dead during the healing and did not come back to life, it is equally remarkable that the parents' plea for help did not go unheard, even though the woman they sought in order to receive help from the Lord had already died. If dead people like her can heal, much as Elisha's bones did with another man in the Bible (2 Kings 13:20-21), how much more can we who are living release the resurrection life of Christ to those around us?

Anthony of Padua

Saint Anthony of Padua was born on August 15, 1195. His family members were prominent citizens as his grandfather was governor, but Anthony eventually became a monk. Once, assassins murdered a nobleman at the cathedral in Lisbon, and Anthony's father Don Martino was wrongly implicated. Anthony was living in Padua at the time, a significant distance away. He received a word of knowledge about his father's plight and left on foot to travel to him—a trip of roughly 1450 miles (Note: If we assume Anthony would travel 15 miles by foot per day, a generous travel speed, it would have taken him close to three months to arrive at his father's side.).

Early in the trip, he was suddenly translocated and found himself in Lisbon, the city of his destination. He went to the courthouse where the trial was already in session. When pressed for proof, he told them the murdered man would bear witness as to the accuracy of his testimony. St. Anthony led the court out to the cemetery, where first the grave and then the coffin were opened. Anthony commanded the dead body to tell the crowd whether his father, Martino of Bouillon, was innocent. The formerly dead man sat up, raised a hand, and declared Don Martino's innocence. He requested absolution prayer from St. Anthony, and after the prayer, he then laid back down and died again.

The judges cleared Anthony's father, but pressed St. Anthony for the name of the murderer, at which time St. Anthony refused, saying, "I didn't come to condemn the guilty, but to clear the innocent." Subsequently he left and was supernaturally translocated back to Padua, having been gone for a total of two and a half days, when under other circumstances, the trip would have taken over six months (Hebert 73-74).

Abbess Colette

St Colette was an abbess at a convent in Besancon, France during the 1300s. A contemporary of other miracle workers such as St. Vincent Ferrer, she is credited with a number of remarkable ones herself. One in particular was a miracle that was given to Mr. Prucet, a man whose baby was stillborn. This father was unwilling to believe that his baby girl had died, rushed to the local church in order to have it baptized (Note: For those who are not familiar, in the Catholic tradition it is immensely important that a baby be baptized before it dies, as it is believed by many that the Sacrament of Baptism is what guarantees the child entrance into heaven.). The priest turned Mr. Prucet away as he could tell the baby was clearly dead. Friends encouraged this poor father to visit the Poor Clare Monastery and ask for Abbess Colette to pray for the infant. This father, unwilling to let even a shred of a chance pass him by, took his baby girl to the monastery. When the abbess appeared, he fell on his needs and wordlessly held out his dead baby toward her. Abbess Colette also sunk to her knees and began to pray. The friends and neighbors who had suggested this trip were also present, and everyone knelt down in prayer.

After some time, the Abbess stood and, removing her veil, instructed the child be wrapped in it and taken to the baptismal font at the church. Prucet obeyed and once again returned to the church, insisting the priest baptize his daughter. The priest assumed at first the man was addled in his grief, but quickly changed his tune when he heard the baby crying from beneath the Abbess's veil. The priest delayed the baptism no further, possibly fearing that the child might not live much longer. She was baptized Colette Prucet, and eventually entered that very same convent in Besancon, France, later to become an abbess herself at another Poor Clare monastery founded by her benefactor (Hebert 88-89).

I love this story because it shows the simplicity and ferocity with which a father would pursue the life of his child. This father was not willing to give up for anything, and if even a glimpse of hope was held out to him, he grasped it and ran. I firmly believe that it was both the faith of the Abbess *and* the faith of this tenacious parent who brought his child back to life, and it serves as a reminder and encouragement in resurrection that sometimes we simply have to keep pushing. My wife often says that "Faith is putting one foot in front of the other" and in this case, I have to agree. Faith often looks like very simple actions that we carry out because we refuse to accept any other outcome—Colette Prucet was living proof of this fact.

St. Catherine of Siena

St. Catherine of Siena was a Dominican tertiary in the 1300s and worked hard to bring peace into the church and the world. Her mother Lapa grew ill after Catherine's father died, and eventually she too passed away. Lapa had not paid any attention to the state of her soul during her life, and Catherine was very upset on her passing, knowing that her mother would not confess Jesus as her Lord. There were three women present at the woman's deathbed and during this incident when St. Catherine began to pray—all of whom testified to Blessed Raymond of Capua of this miracle, which he later wrote down.

As it happens, Catherine cried out to God demanding that He return her mother to life. She was quite persistent, stating that she would not leave her mother's side until God brought her back. Catherine continued to pray in faith and declare the promises God had made to her previously—that her entire household would be saved and that her mother would not die against Catherine's will. As Catherine continued to pray, her mother's body eventually began to move again, and Lapa retuned to life and lived many years more, dying at age 89 (Hebert 105-106).

This story is moving both because of Catherine's persistence, but also because she was very clear about God's will and did not hesitate to hold firm to the promises of God in the face of a difficult and trying situation. While circumstances were not in her favor, nothing stopped her from altering those circumstances in prayer, and that is the same opportunity that we, too are given when we seek to raise the dead.

St. Teresa of Avila

One of the more comical stories, if a story of a death and subsequent resurrection can ever be considered comical, is that of St. Teresa of Avila raising her nephew from the dead. It wasn't the situation itself that was comical, but the manner in which she and her brother-in-law addressed it, as you will see.

In 1561 Teresa was helping build a convent when she went on an outing somewhere with her sister, Juana, and Juana's husband Juan. On returning to the house, Juan discovered their six-year-old son Gonzalo dead on the floor. Juana, who was pregnant at the time, was chatting with a woman who had stopped by to visit. Juan, afraid the shock of her dead son would harm the baby, sent a message to the visitor to keep his wife occupied while he carried his son's lifeless body to Teresa, who immediately began to pray. Covering the child with her veil, she asked God to spare the parents this heartache and to bring the child back to life. At that time, Juana entered the room and began to get excited with concern. Teresa motioned for her sister to calm down as though they were only dealing with a minor and inconsequential matter. Within moments the boy Gonzalo began to breathe at which point Teresa gave her nephew back to her sister (Hebert 107).

St Francis of Paola

If anyone thinks that God does not love or care about animals, or believes for some strange reason that they are not deserving of resurrection, they ought to read the story of St. Francis of Paola and his pet fish, Antonella. This fish lived in a pool by the monastery, and one day a visiting priest caught it and brought it home to eat. It is unclear if Francis got a word of knowledge about the matter or if someone notified him that his pet was being cooked and eaten, but at any rate he got word of the matter and sent someone from his Order to retrieve the fish. The visiting priest, annoyed that he was being asked to hand his dinner over, and considering it was already dead, threw the already-cooked fish to the ground where it fell to pieces. The hermit charged with the task returned the broken pieces of pet to St. Francis who then placed them back into the pool and quite simply commanded, "Antonella, in the name of Charity, return to life!" The pieces of the fish formed back together and it was subsequently revived.

This is but one of many stories of St. Francis resurrecting animals, another being the time he raised his pet lamb Martinello, who had been *killed and eaten* by some workmen (Hebert 116). These sorts of stories show us that not only is God in the business of the impossible, restoring destroyed, eaten, and cooked flesh, but also returning dismembered bodies back to their original state, wholeheartedly disregarding whether those bodies were animal or human.

St. Hyacinth

Saint Hyacinth was born in Poland and became known as a miracle-working missionary to many places near and far, including but not limited to Scandinavia, Prussia, Russia, and Tibet. His last miracle prior to his death was a resurrection from the dead—but with a unique and unexpected twist. Hyacinth was invited by the noblewoman Primislava to preach during the Feast of St. James to her vassals. Her son Wislaus was the messenger, and while he delivered the message successfully, he drowned in the Raba River on the return journey and was swept away by the current. Primislava was notified and arrived at the river at the same time as Hyacinth and his associate. Begging Hyacinth to do something, Primislava fell at his feet. Hyacinth consoled her, speaking words of encouragement, then he prayed. As he did so, the youth's missing corpse miraculously appeared in front of them. Praying yet again, he touched the body and decreed life into it, whereupon life returned to the body and Wislaus stood, alive again (Hebert 163-164).

St. Francis Xavier

If the miracle of St. Hyacinth was insufficient to astound, this miracle performed through St. Francis Xavier is likely to do so. St. Francis was a brilliant scholar in his day, but due to circumstances outside his control he was sent on a missionary journey to the Far East. He had a significant hand in bringing many in India and surrounding regions to Christ, and he performed many miracles. One miracle he performed, a resurrection, was while on the ship the *Santa Croce*, sailing to San Chan from another location. A Muslim man was also a passenger along with his family. One day the ship was traveling rapidly with the wind when the man's five-year-old son fell overboard. Given the sailing conditions it was impossible for them to even try to turn around to save the boy. It is hard to fathom the depths of anguish and powerlessness that man must have felt in that moment.

Three days later, he came across Francis on the ship, and somehow Francis had not heard of the tragedy prior. St. Francis asked that if God restored his son to him, if he would convert from Islam to Christianity. The father agreed that if God did this miracle, he would believe. A few hours passed, presumably with Francis praying during this time when the Muslim man found his child running to him on the deck—three days and however many miles away in the middle of the ocean. God had not just resurrected the boy but translocated his body an untold distance. The man was true to his word, and in the face of undeniable proof of God's power, he and his family were baptized (Hebert 182).

St. Francis Jerome

Francis Jerome was a peculiar man, going to lengths to ensure that he almost always had someone else he could blame his miracles on. One such occasion he used a random woman named Marie who had come into his church at the end of a festival for confession. Father Francis Jerome was kneeling a short distance from his confessional and he had her go look inside, instructing that she would find a baby sleeping there. Marie found the baby as he had said, but the baby was dead, as she had been abandoned by her mother there. Marie informed him of the baby's state as she brought it to him, so he made the sign of the cross on it then called the baby's name, upon which it came back to life. Admonishing Marie that the baby was only asleep as he had said before, he then gave it some water. The child had a few teeth, apparently at least a year old. He had Marie return the child to where she found it, then instructed her to open another confessional, stating that she would find the mother there, praying. He told Marie the woman's name, instructing her to send the woman to see Father Francis Jerome.

What St. Francis Jerome knew by word of knowledge that Marie didn't, was that this woman was the mother of that child—and she was crying in the confessional because she was too poor to pay for a funeral, so she had prepared the body and left it in the church in hopes that the priests there would give the baby a Christian burial. He sent this mother to the confessional where she had left her child earlier, and the child called out to her mother, who was shocked and overjoyed to see her daughter alive once again. St. Francis Jerome gave her some money and sent the pair on their way. The situation seems strange, given the Father had to include another woman in the process instead of simply opening the confessional, resurrecting the baby, and handing it back to its mother, but he instead opted for strange theatrics, presumably so he could deny it later. What is clear, however, is that St. Francis Jerome received all of this information—the presence of the baby, the mother, and all of their names, by divine revelation (Hebert 187-188).

This story is maybe not one of the more remarkable resurrection stories out there, but I appreciate it because it showcases God's kindness. This woman's child fell ill, and because she was poor the child was unable to get proper treatment and died. Afraid her daughter would not get a Christian burial, which in her beliefs at the time meant the child finding its place in heaven would be unlikely, she left its body in the confessional. Instead of doing what many of us might do, which is notify the authorities and eventually just bury the child, St. Francis Jerome not only returned her child to her alive, but gave her money as well to help for the future. I believe this is what Jesus would have done if he had been there at the time, and I believe this serves as an example to all of us the level of goodness and love that God would have us display as we pursue resurrection for those around us.

Modern Day Resurrections

In the same way that Jesus and the disciples raised the dead in the Bible, and as we have seen above, other men and women of God have been doing so ever since. I felt it important to share some modern-day stories from men and women just like you and me. Some of these occurred on the mission field, but others happened during the course of normal everyday life having nothing to do with so-called "ministry." And that is in some ways the point—that Jesus raises the dead as part of normal life, not as some special calling for the few chosen elite. I believe these following stories from various men and women will encourage you to believe for the same in your own life regardless of your calling or station: All of these stories were obtained through personal connections and were printed with permission.

Rev. Amy Friend, Divine Connection Ministries

On July 1, 2008 I was traveling to my Doctor's office for an MRI on my broken foot. It was 45 minutes away from my home in Wilmington, Ohio. I was on the highway, over 3/4 of way there, when the traffic ahead of me started slowing down. I could not see what was going on due to a large vehicle in front of my car. As we inched along, I began to see smoke rising up in the air straight ahead. Cars were turning around in a driveway to my left and going back the other way. After the big vehicle right in front of me also turned, I saw why there was a slow-down. Two cars had collided head-on directly ahead of me—later reports said that they were each traveling 55 mph. One car was in a ditch on my right, and the other across from it on the left. I stopped my car and a man ran up to me from the opposing traffic, having stopped a bit earlier. I rolled down the window and said, "I am a minister—is there anything I can do?" He said, "Well -the lady over here is dead (on the left) and the other one (pointing to the right) is hurt bad." I put my car in park and jumped out immediately.

I went over to the crashed car on the left where he said the lady was dead. You could hardly tell it was a car—it was demolished, crushed, smashed. Then I saw her. The window was down and I could see her blonde hair. Her head and neck were twisted in such an unnatural position, as were her shoulders and arms. I felt the spirit of death. There was no life; I knew she was gone. It was like viewing a body in a casket at the funeral home visitation—you just feel, sense and know there is no life present.

The Spirit of God was upon me and out of the depths of my spirit I cried out loudly, "In Jesus' name I bind the spirit of death and speak life to this woman! Life, come back in Jesus' name!" I yelled this a few times and the man who had joined me at her car looked at me like I was crazy, but as we stood there and watched, her spirit suddenly re-entered into her body! We saw her body "jump" as she came back. Then running over to the other side, I found the other lady semi-conscious. She was trapped under the steering wheel and lay face down on her passenger seat, her body twisted. I got down beside her after opening the car door further and spoke the words God gave me. I told her the Lord God said she will live and that He was there with her and that His ministering angels were surrounding her. She responded, "Ok . . . but it hurts so bad." I then spoke a prayer over her asking the Lord to take the pain and touch her body in a special way. As I finished, sirens sounded in the distance. I encouraged her to hold on because help had arrived, and she responded, "Yes, ok" in a weak voice. I discerned a "God connection" from the lady I had just prayed with, later contacting her and discovering her husband was in ministry school and they had a call on their lives.

I went back to the other woman, the one who had been dead, knowing that God had everything in control. Knowing that God was not finished with me yet, I knelt down on the pavement beside this woman's car and begin to fight for her life in prayer as the Lord instructed me. I cried out for the resurrection power and life of Jesus!

Through my voice, the Spirit began to intercede in a heavenly language to save the life of this woman. Although she had been raised from the dead, her body was still badly injured and the need for intercession to keep her alive was very real. Emergency personnel could not get her out of the horribly damaged car, and they brought in the Jaws of Life to cut her out. I prayed for 1.5 hours in the middle of the road in front of her car. There were at least 50 emergency personnel on the scene within a few minutes, but no one asked me to move or stop praying. They frantically worked to insert an airway and an IV. Both lungs had collapsed and she had broken many bones in her body, but she was alive! God had a plan for her life. I found out later after tracking her down (which included another miracle!) that she had borrowed the car from her best friend and was on the way to a funeral. The woman in this broken car was heavily addicted to drugs and had been on her cell phone when she crashed. I cry when I think of His great grace and mercy that afternoon. He is still in the business of miracles and raising the dead—if only we will position ourselves to receive His greater works of His divine glory!

Both ladies know that God was there on the scene of the wreck and that because of Him, they are alive today. The woman who was raised from the dead is making a good recovery and her body is healing. The other woman had a pin placed in her leg and is basically fine, now working through physical therapy. Several emergency workers, friends and the participants' family knew that this was divine intervention. I spoke with the investigating officer, who said, "There was a miracle there that day." I laughed—there certainly was! To God alone be all glory!

D.M.

My friend is a youth pastor. He was visiting South America in preparation for taking a flock of teenagers there on a mission trip the next year. While he was there, he was preaching in a church, and his friend was interpreting. After his message, he offered to pray for the people, but there were so many lining up to have this foreign pastor pray for them that his interpreter started his own prayer line so they could pray for everybody.

He did not speak the language, but he knew how to pray. As each person got to the front of the line, they told him what they needed prayer for, and my friend smiled and nodded just as if he knew what they were saying. And then he'd pray for them, not knowing what he was praying for, but trusting that God knew. Partway through the line, a woman brought her baby boy up and handed him to my friend for prayer. She was animated as she told him what to pray for. He smiled and nodded, wondering what she was saying, then prayed a blessing on the baby, handed him back to his mother, and motioned to the next person in line.

He spent another hour or two ministering, then went home to sleep. The next morning, they got up early and caught a bus to the next town. Partway through their journey, a taxicab frantically pulled up next to the bus, honking and waving and shouting words which my friend couldn't understand. Eventually the bus pulled over, the driver climbed out, and the interpreter got out with him to see what all the fuss was about. There was much shouting and gesticulating from the occupants of the taxi, but eventually they figured out what was so urgent:

Apparently the baby boy the mother had brought up for prayer the previous night needed more than a blessing—the baby was dead, and the incomprehensible story his mother had been telling him was her sharing her immense grief over her dead son. My friend had merely prayed a generic blessing over the child and handed him back, but it seems that something happened in the meantime: the baby he returned was a living baby boy. He had no idea!

That's the kind of story that's easy to blow off: a supposed miracle in an obscure village in a foreign country, and who knows what really happened? Maybe the storyteller was just enthusiastic—except for this. A couple of years later, he went ahead and took a group of teenagers back to that village, and my daughter was one of them. After church the teens were distributed among the church members' homes for the night. My daughter stayed with the family of the resurrected baby—only now he was a very active and curious toddler. She spent a couple of days with the family and they told the story the same way we'd first heard it: "Oops! I raised someone from the dead—I didn't mean to."

Robyn Ngapera

It was God's plan that we were present at our first grandchild's birth. There were complications so we were transferred by ambulance. The baby was born dead and specialists tried unsuccessfully to revive her. We prayed and left it in God's hands. After maybe 15 minutes or so, the time it took for the afterbirth to come away and the mum to be stitched up, the baby took her first tiny breath. She is a miracle—her name Shaneequa means gracious gift of God. She is now eleven and has had many encounters with Jesus. He even took her for a ride on his white horse—all glory to Jesus!

What's more, our one son was a heroin addict for over ten years. One night I was awoken by my son's voice calling me. I rushed to his room—he was on his knees, slouched forward with his face planted in the carpet. There was a lot of froth that had come from his mouth and he was not breathing, nor had any pulse. I prayed "In the name of Jesus, breathe life!" He came back to life at that time.

Another time, my mother called to say she found him dead, sitting in a chair at her house. I drove over, arriving about fifteen minutes later. His face was stone cold, his body a little warm. Yet again he was not breathing and had no pulse. We prayed, and prayed, and prayed. I was feeling and thinking to myself, "Is this how it's going to end, after all the struggles?" Jesus gave me an impression of the man that breathed life into a young boy in the Bible, so I just blew air across his face. As I did this, my son took a huge gasp of air and returned to us yet again.

Another time, I was at work—and I worked at night. I received a call from my mum, she got a call from the hospital to say my son was found dead in a McDonald's toilet and was taken to hospital morgue. I left work and couldn't face going straight to the hospital, so went to my mum's. She said "You won't believe it, he's here." She found him at the bottom of the stairs, wrapped in a sheet. She helped carry him up the stairs. All he could mutter was "Two angels." The hospital had no explanation, but I knew what happened—God had raised my son to life yet again. My son's battle has been long and hard, and many, many people have prayed for him. Our son is now a wonderful Christian man and lives up to the name. Thank you Jesus!

Edward Henne

In 1990 my wife and I moved back from South Carolina to Texas. After 9 months in Texas and not finding any work we moved back to Norman, Oklahoma. I could not find any work as a counselor at the time, so I called an old friend named Tom (Note: the name was changed in this story for privacy). He was a carpenter, and I had grown up doing carpentry work with my father. When my wife and I first were baptized in the Holy Spirit, Tom and his wife were the first couple we met that were also baptized in the Spirit and exploring the gifts of the Spirit.

Tom was just starting a new job with a group of guys who were also Christians, but were dispensationalists—who believed the gifts of the Spirit no longer exist today. The job was putting an add-on in a Methodist Church in Mustang, OK. The very first day on the job, just after lunch, Tom was on top of the 12 foot walls, notching the top plates for the rafters to fit level, and I was cutting. Everyone else was doing something. At one point I turned around and looked at Tom, a tall man measuring over 6 feet, and he was kneeling down. I watched him stand straight up and as he did he began to fall out of the rafters as though he was unconscious, which later I found out he was. Apparently when he stood up the blood rushed from his head and he passed out. Anyway he fell in such a way that his head hit first, then his shoulder and the rest of his body. I ran over to him and saw a pool of blood growing rapidly on the ground. In a flash I saw in my mind his wife Theresa as a widow and this compassion and anger rushed over me. Love for Tom and his wife, but anger at the enemy. The right side Tom's head was split open from his forehead to back corner. Without thinking I pressed my hand over this gash and began praying quite loud in the Spirit which alerted everyone else who were now standing around me looking at me. I shouted orders to call an ambulance. At some point some women at the church came out and joined me in quiet prayer. At another point Tom went limp and I felt him leave his body. It's kind of funny now but I could feel his spirit above us, and I said in a commanding voice,

"Tom, you come back here right now"—and with that he jerked and made a noise that was somewhere between a grunt and a sneeze. His eyes opened right then, and the medics arrived as well.

The next day I could not work and went to see Tom in his hospital room and his wife was there. But as I walked into the room the atmosphere was thick with the Spirit of God, the kind that makes you leak from your eyes. As I hugged Tom, the doctor came in and said, "You are one lucky boy, there's no contusions, no fractures, no swelling, no anything—you can go home." I tell you, I watched Tom hit the ground. His head hit first, falling about 18 feet considering his height and the height of the wall. His shoulder hit second, and it hit so hard that a triangle was broken out of his shoulder blade. They were so focused on his head that they missed a broken arm which Tom had to go back to get treated.

About a week later I spoke with Tom, and he shared what he remembered. He said he remembered floating above his body and seeing two demons fighting over him. One had its hand in his skull where it was open, and the other had its hand in his shoulder where the break was and they were fighting over his body. And he thought, "You can't do that, I'm a Christian." About that time he saw an intense light rise up from behind him, and the demons ran so fast that they hit the horizon in an instant trying to get away from that Light. The next thing he knew he was back in his body.

What I didn't know was that Tom had been very depressed for some time because a real father of the Lord who he deeply loved had contracted cancer and died several months before. While Tom was convalescing he had a vision or dream—he didn't know if he was in or out of his body. But this man appeared to him with a new body and they talked, so a lot of healing took place through this for many people. One of the young men who went to this dispensational church said to me, "I know your prayers saved Tom." Another one of the leaders who had turned away from the gifts of the Spirit years before was questioning his beliefs as a result of this miracle as well.

Brook Magar, Missionary to Nepal

From 2005-2011 I lived and worked among God's beloved poor in Kathmandu, Nepal. I was a missionary and spent most of my days combing the streets for God's treasured ones among the prostitutes, drug addicts, hardened thieves, and pickpockets.

One Saturday morning I was sitting in church and wasn't feeling well. As church services can run for upwards of 4-5 hours, I decided to leave early. I jumped on a bus that would take me a long way around the city and eventually end up in front of my house, but decided instead to get out partway and walk along the Bishnumati River which would get me there faster. The river has crowded, dusty roads lining either side, where slums and piles of trash can overwhelm one's senses quickly, and because I already wasn't feeling well I was in a hurry to get home.

At one point I saw two little boys pointing towards the river saying, "Manche moriyo! Manche moriyo!" which means, "Someone has died, someone has died!" I looked closer and could see a large crowd on the opposite bank of the river, who had gathered to watch a lifeless woman floating face down in the water. I watched for a few minutes as the boys gathered rocks and tried to throw them at the body, like it was a funny game. Tired, and trying to keep a low profile for the day, I decided there wasn't much I could do and continued along the path.

I approached a bridge and decided to cross over, all the while my mind was reeling, thinking of the woman in the river. I knew that if I walked over and asked what had happened to her it would draw an even bigger crowd and would likely end in my having to take responsibility and pay for a funeral! Expectations can be very high as a white American living in such a place, and I had been in the same situation many times. But I just couldn't shake the stir in my heart to investigate. So I decided to chance it.

As I approached the crowd I asked what had happened to the woman, and the response from the crowd was, "Oh she was a poor beggar. She was just a lonely drunk!" They then proceeded to tell me that the woman had jumped in the river to commit suicide; that they had tried to pull her out once but she jumped back in. I had no idea how long the woman had been lying there in the water but I felt uncomfortable with the common occurrence in Nepal where crowds of people gather to gawk at the misfortunes of others without doing anything to help.

So I asked two men to please pull her from the water. As they did the crowd started to look quite amused. *Who is this white girl, and what does she think she will do for this poor, dead beggar? Nobody cares. Let it be. Does she not know the plight of the poor?* So there I was sitting in the dirt, a dead woman's head in my lap, and not quite sure what my next move should be. So I started to pray, "Ok Lord, what do you want me to do?" I heard Him clearly say, "Look around, you have a dead body in front of you and a crowd of people who don't know Me. You can go home or you can do something."

So putting my pride aside, I checked her pulse. Nothing. No breathing. I laid my hand on her forehead and began commanding life to return to her body. I prayed and prayed. The crowd got restless. I prayed in English, I prayed in Nepali, I prayed in tongues and then back to English again. "Surely, Lord you can use this moment" was all I could think. Two young girls eventually brought over a small baby and told me it was the woman's daughter! They held the baby close to the woman's head and slapped the baby to make it cry, telling me that perhaps if she could hear her own daughter's cry it would bring her back, but nothing changed.

What seemed like 20-30 minutes had passed and suddenly the woman took in a deep breath and then coughed. She began to spit out water and gag and then she slumped down to the ground again. The crowd lit up and started screaming at the woman. I had heard stories before of people being raised from the dead in Nepal, only to be beaten to death afterwards because of the deep spiritual darkness in the land. In a predominantly Hindu country the spiritual realm is very, very real and you rarely find a person who doesn't believe it exists and is powerful. But there is no light, no god who would want to help you in this type of situation, so they would kill the person because in their minds the only reason they would come back is if the person was possessed by an evil spirit.

The woman started to shake violently and her eyes rolled back in her head and then she collapsed on the ground again. Over and over demons were throwing her around on the ground and so I continued to pray, this time commanding the evil spirits to come out. After 6 or 7 rounds of convulsing and collapsing she finally sat up. The crowd was screaming and spitting on her, and she was crawling around on her hands and knees like a wild animal covered in dirt and grime from the filthy river. I grabbed onto her and said "Come with me! I live just up the road." She was so confused as if she had no recollection of the previous 30 minutes as we stood up to leave. I grabbed her young daughter and we started walking up the road together, with a huge crowd trailing behind us.

Not feeling very secure in the moment I decided to call a coworker of mine and ask if he could bring a taxi and meet us on the road. Within minutes he pulled up and I handed him the baby so we could all climb inside. As we rode down the bumpy river bank the woman began throwing herself violently around inside the backseat of the taxi, so I held her as tight as I could and commanded the tormenting spirits to leave. We arrived at the children's home that was run by the organization that I worked for and two of our Nepali staff members came out to help bring the woman inside.

We all sat down on the floor and the woman started asking what had just happened? In my limited Nepali language I told her that I had found her in the river and had prayed for her to come back. But as a Hindu she couldn't conceive of a god wanting to help her. So we explained that no, it was not your gods, but the one true God. He loves you. He created you. He knew you were going to throw yourself in the river today so He sent this girl to come and help. She shook her head and simply wept, overwhelmed at the idea of a loving God who would come to her rescue in such a way.

We decided to let the woman and her daughter stay overnight in our guestroom and planned to find a room to rent nearby the next morning so that we could continue to disciple and counsel her. But when we woke up the next morning she was gone. We drove past the area where she was in the river several times searching but never saw her again. I truly believe a seed was planted in her heart and the Lord will continue the work that He began in her because He is so faithful.

The Bishnumati River where this woman was found used to be a beautiful, flowing river full of life, but due to economic and social issues in Nepal it is filthy and full of trash. I lived beside the river for five years and can't count the number of times I saw discarded newborn babies that had been thrown in. Many times, because of social stigma, unwed mothers or women in crisis situations who feel they have no other choice will throw their newborn babies into the river to get rid of them. I even witnessed twins once thrown together who were being eaten by a pack of street dogs. The contrast is so stark when you think of the river of life flowing from the throne of God.

Whenever I tell the story of the woman who was raised from the dead, I like to also tell this one, for the sake of transparency. Two weeks or so after I found her there, I was walking across the same river and saw a large crowd gathered; police with rifles stood in a circle guarding something of interest. As I got closer I saw that once again a new life had been discarded and the tiny body of a newborn baby was lying in a pile of trash beside the filth of the river.

As I passed by in shock, I heard the all too familiar whisper of the Lord's voice in my head. "Go and pray!" Had I not come across the same scenario just days before? Had I not seen what prayer can do? I was frozen in fear, thinking of the crowds and the scorn and the police with their foreboding guns raised. And I didn't go. I, like the people of Israel in the desert, had seen a miracle with my own eyes, but I did not believe. It did not make me a spiritual giant, immune to the weaknesses of the human heart. I simply couldn't muster the courage to go. All it takes is courage, and a mustard seed of faith.

When we step out in faith to raise the dead, we create an opportunity—an opening in the spirit where God can meet us in the midst of the problems at hand. Faith to raise the dead is not the work of full time ministers only, but the right, duty, and responsibility of every follower of Jesus Christ. Step out and enthrone God in your prayers by faith in Jesus, the firstborn of many who will resurrect in the days to come.

Part 2:

Practical Resurrection

Chapter 8

When Someone Dies

Death is not an easy thing to deal with emotionally under any circumstances, which makes it hard to try to raise the dead to begin with. What makes it even more difficult, especially in first-world countries, is that we hide our dead. As a nurse I can tell you that if a body is left for more than a few hours in a hospital room, many nurses start getting antsy and asking questions like, "Why isn't it gone yet?" We have been conditioned to be uncomfortable with death and dying, and as a result, we try to shove it away from us as fast as possible. In the end it means the death-process isn't very open or transparent, and that can be difficult to work with when praying for life.

When someone dies in a hospital in the USA, unless there is a Do Not Resuscitate (DNR) order in place, we medical personnel start doing CPR to try to bring the patient back. We have three-day trainings called Advanced Cardiac Life Support (ACLS) to stay up to speed on how to effectively resurrect the dead through medical and mechanical means. If resuscitation fails, then a series of events begin over which the family have minimal influence, partially due to the speed in which they occur. From the time a person dies to the time he needs to be picked up by a mortician to be embalmed is 24 hours (according to Oregon law, but this won't vary too much in most states in the USA). The embalming process removes the blood and replaces it with highly toxic chemicals that retard the body's internal process of decay. From an aesthetics perspective this helps keep it looking pretty much longer since it slows the breakdown process, and from a disease-control perspective, it kills viruses and bacteria that can readily proliferate inside a warm corpse. The health benefits conferred to those still living are notable and if one wants to have an open viewing it is helpful, but for those of us who believe in raising the dead, we may want to avoid filling the body with significant amounts of toxins that we are then going to have to pray away. In my opinion the best thing we can do when someone dies is to start praying for resurrection immediately, and I believe there are a number of reasons why.

Medically speaking, when someone passes away every cell in the body begins to die due to losing oxygen and other vital resources, but these cells also self-destruct over time. Tiny little membranous globs inside each cell, called lysosomes, are a bit like a cross between a trash compactor and drain cleaner—they have an external membrane that is essentially a bag holding the digestive juices contained inside—and these enzymes are designed to break down the waste products of the cells. While this is normally done within the safety and confines of their special membrane to protect the rest of the cell from eating itself, after death the lysosomes break open, releasing the enzymes which then automatically start to *digest the cell*. This happens in every cell in the body, and is a bit of a problem for resurrection. Rigor mortis, body stiffening, sets in a few hours after death, but at around twenty-four hours the body starts to get soft again. This is caused by the digestive juices in each cell breaking apart the things that hardened up previously, and with those hardening-agents gone the stiffness goes away. Some may find the body rigidity unsettling, but its disappearance is a signal that the body is decaying even further. The sooner we pray, the less repair it needs to sustain life once again, as the number of problems needing healing increase over time.

Immediately at death the embalming process has also not yet occurred, and the body still has its own blood. The Bible alludes to the importance of the blood for life in Genesis 9, but the Lord directly states it first in Leviticus 17:11 and again later in other passages. It says, "For the life of a creature is in the blood, and I have given it to you to make atonement for yourselves on the altar; it is the blood that makes atonement for one's life" (Leviticus 17:11). Scripturally speaking, life is found in the blood, which is why Jesus had to shed his blood—so that his life was a sacrifice to suffer death in our place. From a resurrection-perspective, if a body still has the blood in it instead of deadly chemicals, this is one less thing that will have to be fixed for the body to come back to life. While God is highly capable of replacing it, having it still in the body remains a benefit of immediate prayer. I spoke to a man once who said when the blood is removed the resurrection is over. This is not true, although considering the above passage I can understand where he was coming from. Life is in the blood, but at the point someone is dead, he will still require a miracle to return. If that miracle has to include a miraculous blood-transfusion then so be it—because I happen to know that Jesus is a regular donor and His blood type is "O-Positively-Yes-and-Amen." After a few hours the issue of blood being present becomes irrelevant anyway because it will clot and die. As a result of factors such as these, praying close to the time of death will usually feel easier than it will four days later, regardless of whether it actually is easier or not.

Over the past ten to fifteen years I have read a number of Near Death Experiences (NDEs) and many of them share common traits. Sometimes a person will see angels or Jesus coming to escort him to heaven. At other times he will see demons pulling him out of his body, and I have also read that demons will sometimes stand between the spirit and the body to prevent him from returning. When someone dies a variety of things occur in the spirit realm around him, but one thing is fairly common among almost all stories—that directly after death the spirit is still present near the body, and in some cases it takes a few minutes for the person to even realize he has died. Praying for resurrection immediately means that the spirit just has to move back into the body instead of traveling some further spiritual distance. In saying all of this, I don't want it to sound like I am suggesting the only likelihood of success is if you pray immediately, because that simply isn't true. I do recognize, however, that raising the dead is in some ways a race against time and the above reasons are all good ones to not delay commanding life.

I share many of these keys in my book *Practical Keys to Raise the Dead*, and the following is a relevant excerpt from that manuscript.

If you are a family member present at the hospital, simply ask the hospital staff to leave you alone with your loved one—you can do this for hours if you just let them know you need 'time to say goodbye.' Don't bother telling them what you are doing—while there is a slim chance they would pray with you (I'm a nurse and would be glad to join if it were my patient), more likely they won't be and will think you are nuts—and that won't help. Unless you have already formed a relationship with a staff member and know he or she is on board, just shut the door and do your thing. The nurses can put a sign on the door informing any staff or visitors to see the nurse (and thus leave you alone) before entering the room. It is not uncommon for staff to let a family have a hospital room for hours—possibly up to half a day if the hospital isn't busy and demand for the room to put a living patient in is low. Keep in mind the nurse will probably want to come in and wash the body (it often defecates at death), raise the head of the bed to prevent blood from pooling in the face, and one or two other preparatory things. These are not required but nurses tend to do it as a courtesy, and if they ask to perform those tasks they aren't being rude or anti-resurrection—they are simply trying to care for the body in the way they know how. With that said, staff also understand that each family has its own grieving process, possibly even cultural or religious rituals to perform at time of death, and that visitors will often travel there even hours after death to say goodbye. Use that to your advantage—just don't be loud. The louder you are and the more ruckus you make, the more resistance and interruptions you will get from staff. Louder prayers do not increase the likelihood of resurrection. (King, *Practical Keys* 8-9)

While the above passage is geared toward being in a hospital or with medical personnel on hand, if that is not the case when someone dies, immediately call 911 and begin CPR. Isaiah 11:2 says that God is the Spirit of both Might and Wisdom. In this case what that means is that God has given us both power to raise the dead and wisdom to know how to do the same. We have well-developed medical practices that can bring people back to life if started immediately, of which CPR and calling emergency services are the two primary links in that chain. Don't ever hold back on doing CPR to prove that

God's power will work. God doesn't care *how* someone gets brought to life so long as they get brought back. If you are afraid to put your mouth on someone else's to give rescue breaths, that's okay. As of 2016 (per the classes I have taken), the Red Cross is teaching compressions-only CPR anyway, so just perform steady chest compressions at a rate of 100/minute roughly one inch deep until help arrives, someone can relieve you, or you are too exhausted to continue. While rare, people have been brought back from death even up to an hour after the fact when high-quality CPR has taken place. While this might seem out of place in a book on raising the dead, CPR is one of the many tools God has given us and we should not be afraid to use it.

There are situations where CPR won't help, such as when the person has bled out—which means there simply isn't blood left to move oxygen around the body, or when someone has been dead for some time. Obvious signs of having been long-dead will be the body being stiff, cold, or having insects gather (if outside), but there may be other indicators as well. While all of these sound gruesome, it is because there is nothing pretty about death. If the body has been dead for a while then CPR will be useless. You ought to contact the authorities to notify them, but taking a few minutes to pray first will never hurt. Who knows? Maybe you will bring them back and won't need to notify anyone of the death. On the other hand, pay attention to your surroundings. The fact is that some deaths aren't an accident and disturbing what might turn out to be a crime scene would only implicate you, especially if you wait to contact the police. If nothing happens in a short time, call the police and notify them of the situation.

One of the tricky things about raising the dead, especially in the Western world, is that access to the body is usually difficult and there can be a lot of red tape surrounding the situation. As my friend Tyler

Johnson, founder of the Dead Raising Team says, "In America, we hide our dead" (Johnson, Personal Interview). And it's true. There are legal requirements placed on you such as whether you must embalm, how long the body can remain unburied, and more. Issues such as embalming typically come up if the body is not going to be buried within 24 hours, and let's face it—how many people do you know of who were buried the same day they died? Exactly. This is where knowing state laws comes in handy, but let's be honest: Few people spend time researching state laws to know their legal rights regarding raising the dead. On top of that, as these laws are done state-by-state, there is no easy way to figure out what you are permitted to do in your location. Keep in mind that whether you do or don't embalm, there is no wrong answer and regardless of what you decide, God is with you and able to raise him or her.

To help muddle through the mess that is our legal system, I have provided the names of four organizations below that might be able to help you with laws in your state. As a heads up, they are funeral organizations and have nothing to do with resurrection. I have not contacted any of them to ask for assistance so their willingness to be involved in unknown, but they are non-mainstream so I suspect would be more likely than some to think outside the box if you had questions.

National Home Funeral Alliance (NHFA)
Funeral Consumers Alliance
Green Burial Council
Burial Legal Reference Online

Additionally you can use a search engine to look up "burial laws" and your state's name for other results.

Unfortunately, time is not your friend. When death occurs you have to make decisions or other people will make them for you—and most of the time those people do not believe in resurrection. Even those of us who do believe in raising the dead still have duties we must perform for our jobs, so we may push you to comply with state laws even though we are believing and in agreement with you for life. It is preferable to know what you are getting into in advance, and if you can, make some plans ahead of time. This might sound like strange advice, especially if you are standing in faith for someone's healing. "Contingency plans" might seem like a lack of faith, but I also consider it to be practical, and God isn't going to penalize you for planning for the worst even while you continue to pursue total healing and restoration. If death appears imminent, it is far better to be proactive than fail to prepare and have to be reactive.

Chapter 9

The Risk in Offering Hope

I like to think of myself as a fairly logical person, so when I witness things that don't seem to line up with one another, I always find it strange. As followers of Jesus, the major thing that makes our belief system work is the death *and resurrection* of Jesus Christ, whereby we are also co-crucified, co-buried, and co-raised with Him. Resurrection from the dead is a key component of our beliefs. As such, I find it cognitively dissonant when dead-raising is not an automatic go-to for believers.

Think about it—even atheists who may not have a particular belief about the afterlife will immediately attempt CPR on someone who has just died in an attempt to bring him back. As a nurse, I have been rigorously trained in exactly what to do when someone suddenly dies, and I received this training for one reason and one reason only: resurrection. Medical professionals all across the *world* follow this as a natural part of their daily work whether EMS, Doctors, Nurses, or other support staff. Many companies also pay to have their employees trained in CPR in case someone dies. So why not the church? Why is it an abnormal thing to teach and train people to raise the dead? Why is it unusual when someone wants to spend a few days praying for a corpse to return to life instead of rushing to plan a funeral? Honestly, this boggles my mind.

If restarting a dead person's heart and breathing isn't a form of raising the dead, I don't know what is because at the point their heart stops, they're functionally dead. And while one could technically make various arguments about the exact definition of death in regards to when someone is clinically dead based on brain death or other indicators, the simple fact is this: When someone's heart stops, if we do nothing, he will never live again. Period.

I suggest the Church needs a new way of doing things. As I see it, we are currently far behind even modern technology in our ability (or lack thereof) to deal with death, and for those who are empowered by the Creator of the entire cosmos, this simply shouldn't be so. How do we correct this then? I suggest it starts by recognizing that we are doing something wrong. This isn't a shame and blame sort of thing, but we need to understand that we truly don't grasp God's plans for our lives. When we acknowledge we are falling short in this area, then we can seek an answer. What is the best solution? Learn about abundant life. Learn about God's power to raise the dead. Learn about the will of God to destroy the power of death and destruction. We *have* to realize that we, the Body of Christ, are the *last hope* that anyone has at death.

Just for good measure, I will say that again. The Body of Christ is the last hope people have when someone dies. If you don't step out to raise the dead, there is zero guarantee that anyone else will. Think about it—you may be the *only* person your friends know who believes in raising the dead, or at least who believes it enough to actually do something about it. Sometimes when people get desperate, whether followers of Jesus or not, they will be willing to take a risk for what *you* believe even if they don't believe it, simply because they have little to nothing to lose. As I said before, if you do nothing the dead will remain dead, but if you do something, he may return. Don't be afraid to point out to someone that there is little to lose—but if you do choose to say that, do it with compassion and maybe even a little tact. Keep in mind that from a physical standpoint once someone is dead, you literally cannot screw things up more than they already are, so there is a measure to which resurrection is low-risk.

Before we go any further on this subject I need to share my heart so you can be clear about what I am saying, why I am saying it, and what it means for you. As an author, I recognize that some people take things I write with a grain of salt and look at how what I say fits with what they believe while other people will believe what I say and run with it. The responsibility I feel toward this subject is pretty high because I understand that the words I write in this book may be the deciding factor in some situations between whether someone returns to life or not. I don't say this to make myself sound or feel important; rather, it's a simple fact. When people say things, other people listen to them, which means I have to share all sides of the story as best as I can—and I can't think of a harder place in this book to do that then here, deciding whether to pray for someone to be resurrected or not. The only other place that is equally difficult is the upcoming chapter where I discuss stopping praying for resurrection—because it means someone is deciding whether to stand in faith or basically give up, and in some cases it might be done based on my recommendations. I don't know how it is for you, but it feels weighty to me. As such, I present both my personal practices and the reasons why, along with other options and what they might look like. Thank you in advance for your grace and understanding.

Now that I've said offering resurrection to people is low-risk, let me contradict myself by discussing the actual cost of resurrection and looking at risk versus reward. The truth is that while at first glance there is little to lose when offering to pray for resurrection, it isn't always as low-risk as I make it sound. Imagine you live in a small community and have been part of a church for decades. You grew up in that church and your spouse even got saved there. You were married there, and after your children were born and grew, they were eventually baptized and currently attend high-school youth group, all at this same church. Now imagine your spouse dies. You both served on the board of elders and also own a local business so almost everyone in this community either knows you personally or has heard of you. And while your phone blows up with phone calls, emails, and your doorbell rings off the hook with well-wishers and people from church bringing you casseroles, you are busy trying to resurrect your dead spouse. Oh—did I mention that most of your church doesn't have any clue about raising the dead and neither does the rest of your community? Yes, in case you are wondering you *have* now become the town weirdo. All sorts of rumors start flying around, some of which include the word *necromancy*, and the rest of the elders as well as the senior pastor of the church hold an intervention for you, thinking that they can save you from the fires of hell with this witchery you are attempting.

Two weeks into the resurrection attempt you have been officially removed from your eldership and your business is suffering because the whole town now associates you with strange, strange things. Another month after that your business has to fold because it simply cannot support itself any longer. Even some of your close friends won't look you in the eye much less greet you when you pass each other in the grocery store. All it took for you to become the town pariah was the death of your spouse and a desire to stand in faith to raise him or her based on what Jesus purchased for you.

Some people may think this is over-stretching the truth, but it is a legitimate possibility. In my own case I don't have a church that I have belonged to for decades, I don't have a visible community business, and I live in a city, so the vast majority of people not only don't know me but wouldn't recognize me in a crowd much less in a police lineup. I have friends who also believe in raising the dead and who would gladly stand with me in faith for God's will to come to pass in the situation (which again is *always* for the person to return to life). There are many other people who might not understand, but those closest to me would be standing right beside me with a hand on the body in prayer. Not everyone has been blessed with the kinds of faith-filled friends I have, so what works for me in a situation isn't necessarily what will work for everyone else. A few months back I spoke with a close personal friend who will remain anonymous. This person had just prayed with a man whose child-aged son had died— and this grieving father had literally no one around him who would support him standing in faith. The father was believing for his son to return to life, but he was completely alone. This is real and it happens.

What I don't intend to do through the hypothetical story about the small-town resurrection above is to create fear and I apologize if it has done that for you. Pray it off and keep reading. What I do intend is to demonstrate a sort of worst-case-scenario of what can happen when we start radically going after the promises of God. Call it persecution or label it whatever you like, raising the dead isn't risk-free and Jesus told us to count the cost for a reason. I hope this doesn't so much deter you as it does help you to walk with eyes wide open into the situation. I do know a woman who lives in a small town and everyone knew about it by the time she had to call it quits on her resurrection effort. She is still believing for her husband to be raised, but things were never the same for her after she stepped out in faith believing in God's promise of abundant life. She did lose some friends in the process as well, and while that's a serious shame, it may be unavoidable. As such, my point remains that problems and resistance are a real possibility when pursuing the things of God so we would do well to be aware.

As far as counting the cost goes, I have criteria that I currently use to decide whether to start and/or join in on a resurrection effort. You are welcome to use them as well if it helps you. The first is time: Do I have the time I will need to give a fair attempt at resurrection? Although I dearly love animals, I prioritize humans—and as a result I am willing to rearrange more of my life and cancel other commitments as needed. I will spend far more time praying for humans to resurrect than animals because I believe that time-spent can be an important factor in whether the resurrection is successful or not.

My second criteria is the amount of time elapsed. How long have they been dead? God does not place limitations on dead-raising, but I have practical life-circumstances to consider. At least in the USA, there are laws and statutes we are supposed to follow in regards to the management and burial of dead bodies. Additionally, with regards to our pets and roadkill that I occasionally pick up (yes, I do practice raising the dead on roadkill), I have no intention of keeping rotting animal corpses in a pile in my back yard on the off-chance that one of them will eventually resurrect. As a result I have a three-day policy for dead animals, but with humans it just varies depending on the situation. Why three days? It's a practical number, not a spiritual one. Day 1 is the day I find them and I am interested and engaged. Day 2 I am still pretty engaged. Day 3 my wife is asking me how much more time I am going to give this (she's used to me bringing dead animals home) before I give up, and the body is starting to smell not-so-great. As such, we have worked out an arrangement between us that I don't keep dead animals around for more than three days. As far as humans are concerned, as long as people are engaged in the resurrection effort and God hasn't given me clear instruction otherwise, I am happy to be in it for the long-haul. That said, I also stop praying when they have been buried, which is a time-relevant thing as well. Not everyone feels the same as I do on this, and that's okay, but at this point when the person is buried, I stop praying. I will discuss this more in a future chapter and look at the pros and cons of how to know if or when to stop praying.

This is probably one of the more controversial issues surrounding resurrection. Some people say "But Michael, God can do anything and burial doesn't stop Him! Don't you want to believe him for the impossible?" Yes, I do—that's why I pray for resurrection in the first place. I do, however, have to pay attention to my own time and steward it well. I have a wife, grandkids who are with us every week, I am a nurse with a full-time job, and I am a writer. I keep fairly busy—and adding what I consider to be unfruitful activities for the sake of appearing spiritual seems like poor stewardship to me, not to mention a great way to burn out. God can raise people if we pray from a distance. God can teleport bodies back above ground after they have been buried and then resurrect them. God can take cremated bodies and reform them from almost nothing. God can do all sorts of unimaginable, amazing, abundant, extravagant, and wonderful things! I simply don't feel led at this juncture in my life to spend a lot of time and energy on those "extravagant" versions of resurrection when I have yet to resurrect one of those I have prayed for. I am open to the above ideas in a general sense, but at this point in my life I would need to hear specific instruction from God if they are cremated or buried before I am willing to spend a lot of time to pray for resurrection. If you feel led otherwise, that is perfectly fine—and you know what? God may be calling you to do exactly that and you have my blessing. While that may sound flippant, I mean it—if you feel to go ahead and continue to pray, then do so in faith. At the same time, if I am applauding your faith from the sidelines without joining in, it doesn't mean I don't want God to do it for you—it means I lack the time, energy, or whatever else to get personally involved. As we have discussed before, it is God's will for everyone to be raised, so go for it.

My third criteria is access: Do I have the ability to pray over the actual body? Do I have a family that I can get permission from? People die every day—the thing that separates the ones I plan to pray for from the ones I don't pray for is whether someone is involved in the resurrection attempt and whether that translates into access for myself or others. For example, as the founder of the *Raise the Dead Initiative*, I have run into something I have termed "Celebrity Resurrection." Every now and again some high-profile individual dies. Sometimes they are well-known and other times they might be someone otherwise unknown but whose tragic death-tale has appeared on a local news channel. Invariably one of the members of our social media group (which I moderate) will post a message such as "This person just died. God can do ANYTHING! Let's pray for life!" In and of itself that's a wonderful idea—and yes, God can do anything. Usually, however, praying for that individual is extremely impractical. There is no body access and little to no personal investment with this type of prayer request. Does God require access to the body or "personal investment" to resurrect people? I don't see anywhere in Scripture where it says so, but I believe if we are serious about this we are going to be at least a little invested and usually *someone* involved in the process will be present praying over the body—and I believe as a general whole that we ought to have these two things.

While I have prayed over some of my patients who have died, of the prayer attempts I have taken part in, most of the bodies I have physically prayed over to date have been animals—some were pets or livestock and others were intact roadkill that I pick up from time to time to attempt resurrection. Regardless of how I came upon the body, my heart was involved. I believe resurrection must come from a place of love, not a place of showmanship. I look forward to the day I can share photos with others of a formerly deceased body, whether human or animal, that I have raised to life by the power of Christ, but publicity cannot be my primary goal—I must be motivated by love. My perception is that celebrity resurrection usually lacks a love for the person and his family and is more about the person's celebrity status. If I knew someone had access to the celebrity's family or his body I would be 100% on board with the resurrection, but without even one of those things I typically do not get involved. I do have some good news about being emotionally involved though—it is not difficult to find a heart of love for the person or animal I am attempting to resurrect. I usually start by reminding myself of God's ardent desire for life, then I connect with His love and desire for resurrection, and from there my heart is in it.

Is it possible to be too emotionally invested in a way that can hinder the process of standing in faith? My friend Tyler Johnson, founder of the Dead Raising Teams shared the following in his book *How to Raise the Dead:*

> Once I received a phone call from a desperate man and woman that had just delivered a stillborn baby. They knew the baby was without life weeks before, but went through with the delivery in hopes that God would work a miracle.

The father was crying as he held the baby's body while I was on the phone with him. We would pray together for resurrection life, and he would check the baby for signs of life. To say the least, it was very intense. This man kept saying, "She is so beautiful, so beautiful".

My own wife was due any day with our son Jacob, thus I related to this man's situation very closely. I found myself crying as we prayed, overwhelmed by feelings of hatred for the devil and absolute horror of imagining my own wife and baby in the same situation. The baby wasn't raised, and the parents had to bury their little girl.

I realized later my ability to empathize with the father wasn't any help to him. He had called me because he needed to talk to someone that was full of faith, and I hadn't been that for him.

When people lose a loved one, though they may not say it, they are looking for someone that is militant in faith, someone that will see things drastically different than themselves, someone offensively full of faith. They are looking for someone that is violent in faith.

I am not endorsing a heartless attitude towards families that are experiencing loss. I am communicating that we are called to be a beacon of light and hope for those that are stuck in impossible situations. They are looking to you to have faith, not more sadness. (Johnson 256)

As Tyler shared, we have to look at whether our emotional involvement is helpful or hindering in the situation, but I do think he had one thing right—he cared deeply. In my career as a nurse I have had many occasions where I wanted to cry while at the bedside with a patient, and for similar reasons as above I wait until later to start sobbing over the situation—usually when driving home or after I walk through the door and see my wife. Sometimes quenching our emotions is the most helpful thing we can do for someone else in the moment, but it is also important that we let them out later if we do so, for our own emotional health.

In 2008 and after, God has done a significant work through a move of divine healing in the USA and abroad through the Street-Healing movement, releasing many scores of people and showing them that any believer can pray for the sick and injured and have them recover. The downside of that spike in healing was that for some, healing people became a kind of trophy—a notch in the belt to show all of one's friends how spiritual he or she was. If that is what raising the dead is to you, then your heart is in the wrong place. It is perfectly fine to get excited about what God is doing and pursue it, as well as to keep your own empathy and emotions in check for the sake of helping someone else, but it cannot move too far in either direction.

My fourth criteria is cost: Is it going to be worth it to resurrect this person? This is probably the most difficult pill to swallow for some, and I still have some internal struggle over this one at times, but it's a practical consideration that I believe must be addressed, at least at this point given our limited-but-growing success in resurrection as the Church. Let me give an example. My grandfather died in the beginning of 2015. He lived on the opposite side of the United States when he died, had no grid whatsoever for divine healing, and I never went to pray for him to be healed before he died. Most of my family are believers but very few of them believe firmly in resurrection, and between my mom and her four siblings, my step-grandmother, all of my scores of cousins, second cousins, etc., most of them were present at the funeral. Attempting to resurrect my grandfather would have created so many issues in the family—both with my parents as well as the grand number of other people I just listed, that I personally was not willing to pay the cost for something I wasn't very invested in to begin with. Does my lack of investment or low interest level change the will of God? Not at all. Was God angry or upset with me for not praying? I don't think so. I gladly would have gone for it in general, but under my specific circumstances, it just wasn't worth it to me to put my entire extended family in a tailspin over a resurrection attempt that I didn't consider likely to begin with. Now when it comes to my own parents (who have already both told me they don't want to be resurrected) I don't know that I plan to give them the benefit of the doubt, but we will see when the time comes. As a direct son I have a lot more authority in the situation than as one of a dozen grandchildren—and if I had asked either my mother or any of my aunts and uncles, I can already tell you the answer would have been a hard "no."

Counting the cost is an important part of the resurrection criteria—and in some cases I think it might actually be *the* most important criteria. In Luke 14:28-30 Jesus said, "Suppose one of you wants to build a tower. Won't you first sit down and estimate the cost to see if you have enough money to complete it? For if you lay the foundation and are not able to finish it, everyone who sees it will ridicule you, saying, 'This person began to build and wasn't able to finish.'" It is unwise to consider resurrection if we do not first count whether we are willing to take the potential consequences that come with our efforts. Mind you, we can go ahead without counting the cost, but we may be blindsided on the back end with unexpected negative and/or unsupportive actions from others. Part of the reason counting the cost is so important is that once we get started with the resurrection effort, I believe it is important to see it all the way through. What is the point of stepping out and taking the risk only to back down twenty minutes later after causing a ruckus and not getting results? If we are going to go for it then we would do well to plan in advance so we can be all-in where needed and stand with our faith and determination rooted firmly.

In reading this chapter it could be possible for you to be mentally backing off from this whole resurrection thing as I have made it sound like an awful lot to deal with. The truth is, it can be. I am not sharing these things to scare you off, or in any way to suggest it isn't worth it. If it were my own wife or grandkids who died, I would go to great lengths to resurrect them regardless of the opinions of others, but as I mentioned before, I have a pretty decent support system in place in this area which reduces some of the pressure— although there is always going to be some amount of pressure from someone. Each situation is different, and this is where wisdom and discernment come into play. It is always God's ultimate will for each person to experience abundant life and to never die—Jesus paid for it and stated multiple times in the gospel of John that his will was for people to live forever. In spite of this idealistic and highest reality that we continually strive for, we must walk out the journey with wisdom, which I believe includes counting the cost in advance where possible.

After sharing the depressing things that could go wrong and ways people could take things poorly, I want to remind you of how we started this chapter: that after a death, you are a family's only hope. If we ignore all of the other details for a few more moments, we need to remember that the risk on our side is in some ways negligible for the reward set before us. Jesus said in Matthew 6:33 to, "Seek first the Kingdom and His righteousness and all these things will be given to you as well." And again in Mark 10:29-30a, "'Truly I tell you,' Jesus replied, 'no one who has left home or brothers or sisters or mother or father or children or fields for me and the gospel will fail to receive a hundred times as much in this present age . . . .'" God rewards those who step forward and sacrifice for His Kingdom. Not only that, but there is a separate risk associated with *not* stepping out and trying—the risk that we will wonder for the rest of our lives what might have happened if we had taken that step of faith and gone for it.

Regardless of what we risk, whether we choose to pray or not pray, we will always risk something—it's not a matter of *if* we risk but of *what* we risk. I want to share a personal story with you that I think addresses this somewhat. My family had once found a small litter of mice abandoned in a friend's car. While unclear how the mice got there to begin with, we presumed the mother had run away in fear of humans and abandoned them shortly after delivery. As the scenario went, my stepdaughter bought animal formula and tried to nurse them. I didn't want to get involved at first because I knew the likelihood of three abandoned baby mice surviving was pretty slim, I didn't really want mice as pets (my stepdaughter's family lived with us at the time), and on top of all that, if they died I would feel compelled to try to resurrect them. Did I mention that I didn't want mice as pets? But as things happen, she needed help taking care of them, and after the first two died, I ended up helping feed the third one, named Bub, every few hours for a day or so before it died.

When it died, my heart broke. I was in tears holding it, watching it use accessory muscles in compensation as it mouth-breathed, gasping for air. As a nurse I knew what I was watching, but with a tiny baby mouse I was powerless to fix it. I tried to tap its back lightly while holding it upside down to see if I could help it clear the formula it was suffocating on from its lungs, but after it struggled to breathe for a few minutes, its tiny body ran out of energy. My granddaughters were also present when it died, and the oldest, age 8, began to cry as well. I held Bub's body in one hand and my eldest granddaughter in the other arm for a long time as we cried, both devastated. I spent time over the next day trying to resurrect it, but as you can probably guess, that also failed.

This is an extremely unglamorous story—snot and tears rolling down my red, puffy face while holding a little girl doing the same isn't exactly a reader's dream. I share it because I feel that far too often we tell stories of the nice and happy things in life—especially on social media—except life is filled with not just happy things, but sad ones. So, I share this because anything worth doing involves risk—and in this case it was risk of heartache and loss. The idea of raising the dead is as much a risk-undertaking from an emotional standpoint as from a physical one. When we attempt to resurrect the dead, whether animal or human, we entertain risk, and there is always a price when we step out and take risks, especially in this area. Sometimes it is small—we hazard making ourselves look silly to some stranger we may never meet again when we fail to heal them. Sometimes the risk is much greater—our reputation in an entire town, church, or social circle, the risk of failure, of heartache and heartbreak, and for some even the chance of losing trust in God. Most things in life involve chance, but resurrection is one of those things that is optional. We don't *have* to try to raise the dead—God won't love us any less if we don't. However, I do believe that when we are unwilling to step out and take these sorts of risks, our lives are poorer for it.

I want to encourage and remind you that God has destined you to be a Resurrectionist!! You are the bridge between Heaven and Earth. You are salt and light, and the delivery system of Divine power and presence into this hurting world. Whatever you are facing, whatever sickness or death you are praying over, contending against, dealing with, I exhort you to continue to stand firm in the promises of God. You are strong, you are courageous, and you are beautiful. You are steadfast, you are brilliant, and your best moments are even now coming toward you. I believe God has plans to resurrect those in graves, the cremated, the long-dead, and even those in mass-graves from war and genocide. I am looking to a future where the Church's understanding of resurrection is vibrant and healthy to the point that we are more surprised if someone doesn't resurrect than we are when they return. Greater is He who is in *you* than any life circumstance around you. And remember, even when someone dies it is never "too late" because we serve a God who raises the dead. Go and be the hope that this world so badly needs.

Chapter 10

Access to the Body

There is one glaringly obvious need that every resurrection has to include: a body. It doesn't matter if that body is missing pieces or is scattered in pieces, but without at least some semblance of one you don't really have anything to resurrect; thus gaining access is important. In the previous chapter I discussed some of my own personal requirements in regards to body access, and that is largely again because if you don't have a body, you don't have a resurrection. I firmly believe God can do lots of things above and beyond what I can ask or think (Ephesians 3:20), but that doesn't mean I'm going to spend most of my time there. In my mind, getting access to the body is a pivotal part of the resurrection effort. If you are the spouse, parent, or legal guardian who gets to make the decisions, this isn't much of an issue. There are details involved and hoops to jump through, but once you do that, you can decide much of how things will go during the resurrection effort. Otherwise you have to make a request, and that's where things can get uncomfortable.

First, let's imagine you have legal guardianship of some kind. If you go the funeral home route (as most do) then it will take some time after the funeral home assumes possession of the body before embalming is complete and you can gain access once again. In that time, you may want to activate a prayer chain of some kind, which we will look at in further detail in the next chapter. Once you have access, you can begin to have people come in to pray and declare life.

Either before or after activating your personal intercessory team, contact the funeral home to get an estimate of when the embalming will be complete. Explain your plan to pray for resurrection, as you want access to the body as soon and as often as possible. They may even have recommendations on your options as to how this can best be done. It may be possible to have the body at your home or local church depending on state laws, and if either are possible, you might be able to have the body remain at one of those sites for weeks while staying in prayer. State laws regarding storage and disposition of a body varies but the funeral home should be able to help advise you on some of these laws. Just remember, what you are suggesting is historically uncommon, and resistance is a real possibility. You might consider researching state laws in case the business gives you the run-around, but continue to pray for favor in the situation and hope for the best. Death is the industry of the mortician, and funeral homes deal with death and dying every day. You might not be the first person they have met who will try to raise the dead, and then again, you might. It is entirely possible that your act of faith will open the door for the gospel and even pave the way for future success in resurrection at their business. Who knows, the funeral home may even be sympathetic to your cause. One woman I interviewed had immense favor with the funeral home—it turned out that not only were the owners followers of Jesus, but they also believed in raising the dead (Gladney, Telephone Interview)! You never know what kind of divine appointments God may set up for you, so pray for the best and walk forward with your head held high.

If the body is at a funeral home, you will have to define hours of access for prayer and viewing, and rooms tend to rent at a daily rate. While expensive, the funeral home will probably be willing to store the body as long as the money is rolling in. A church (if even agreeable in the first place) may charge a fee for renting a room although it is likely to be far less, and I suggest this is a far less common option. They won't have any sort of refrigeration on hand, which if you aren't doing 24/7 prayer is a consideration to keep in mind. If it is your home church you may be able to get a key to the building for the duration of the prayer effort. It will vary from church to church based on the discretion of the leadership. If you own your own home or property and keep the body there, you have much more flexibility in regards to access for prayer because you make the rules, ultimately depending again on state laws.

If you are not the guardian and/or a close family member who can arrange for prayer, then you will need to get in touch with the family to gain access. Unless they are a close personal friend, this is a bit like a cold call from a telemarketer—and even if you know the person, it may be awkward to ask for permission to resurrect him. I helped a friend do this once and we actually wrote out a script of what she was going to say before she made the phone call. Writing it out helped her to know what she wanted to say, what she felt comfortable with, and helped reduce the awkwardness on the phone. We practiced it a few times together, prayed, and then she made the call. I share the full story in Chapter 14, but I personally felt the practice was helpful and you may feel the same way.

Before going further, I feel it important to point out that asking for permission to pray for someone's loved one is essentially a sales call. Having worked as a telemarketer for a short time and having had jobs in various sales positions, I discovered that you will get what you ask for much more often if you actually ask for it rather than beating around the bush waiting for the other party to figure out what you want them to agree too. If what you want is access to the body, clearly state as much in your conversation. Also, I have found that sometimes when I ask people if I can pray, especially when I pray with random people on the street for healing, they seem to think I am asking for general permission to pray about them in my life as I go on my merry way. I don't really need permission to do that, so sometimes I have to specify that I mean to pray for them right then and there. Resurrection is no different. People may thank you for offering to pray but not realize you are wanting to stand physically in the presence of the body and command life back into it, so make sure you are clear up front about your intentions—just don't be pushy.

To help with all of this I have provided a sample script of what you might say. This is not meant to be the single "right" way to do it, but provide a base for you to develop your own method. Keep in mind that regardless of what you think you should say, it is going to vary in every situation based on the relationship you have, what you already know about his or her beliefs, and how you feel led by the Holy Spirit. Keep in mind that while the script is written as a monologue for the sake of this book, it is actually best if you leave room for dialogue. People are much more open when in a two-way conversation.

Hello [Insert their Name],

This is [My name] and I want to express my condolences over your family's loss. I know this must be a very difficult time for you and your family and I am praying for you all. I keep thinking about your situation and am reminded of the Bible stories where Jesus raised the dead and commanded his disciples to do the same. I believe God wants to do a miracle in this situation. Would you be willing to let me come to [the location of the body] and pray over the body/him/her and believe for Jesus to raise [the deceased's name] back to life? God wants good things for your family and I don't believe it was [the deceased's name]'s time to die.

*Note: You can *always* say that last line with faith as it is *never* anyone's time to die.

From there, let the conversation play out. You have asked for what you want and they will either say yes, need time to think about it and/or discuss it, or say no. If they say yes, you will want to discuss the details of what that is going to look like. Don't be rigid in what you expect although it is perfectly appropriate to suggest what you feel is the best option. Ask for what you want and take what you can get. If all they will permit is ten minutes of privacy to pray over the body, then take ten minutes and thank the Lord for favor. If they need time to think about it, keep in mind that time is of the essence and set a time to call them back or see if you can answer any questions right then and walk them through it with discussion. Whatever you do, *do not wait* for them to call you. Why? If there is one thing I have learned from my experiences in both sales and evangelism, the burden is on the person who finds the matter more important. If they aren't sure, they clearly don't consider it important enough to keep in touch and you cannot expect that they will give you a call back in a timely manner. That, or they are drowning in grief and really don't have the presence of mind for one more thing on their plate. Set up a time to get in touch with them and make sure you follow through. They may be stalling for time without realizing how to say "no" and hope that you will go away if they stall long enough. If they don't give you a hard no, you have nothing to lose by reconnecting a few hours or a day later. In the end, be sure to let them know that you aren't pressuring them to say yes, and unless you can tell they really want to say yes but need convincing, just take it easy. Not only will coercion make them more likely to say no, it adds additional tension to the already stressful circumstances.

If they say no, don't just drop them like a bad habit. They are dealing with a horrible situation and most likely have immense grief. See how you can pray for them, bring them some food, watch their kids for an afternoon, or do something *else* in the situation to sow some of the life of Jesus Christ in the circumstance. While we all want body access, if that isn't what *they* want, forcing the issue, arguing with them, or anything similar is not only completely inappropriate, it is totally unhelpful. Be the love of Christ in the situation even if that doesn't look like what you were hoping for. Reassure them that you are praying for them and make yourself available to meet another need they may have. If it is a coworker, consider donating a day of sick time to them or work extra so they can have another day off. Do something else other than pray that visibly demonstrates your love and concern because you might be the only Jesus they have ever met and the only Bible they will ever read.

I had a situation once where a mother contacted me to join her in prayer in resurrecting her dead son. Another woman from the group I run got in touch with her and wouldn't leave her alone, nor would this woman accept the mother's answers when the mother told her how things were going to go. This other woman also contacted me and began hounding *me* about the situation as well—all in an effort to try to move the resurrection forward. The crazy part? We were *already trying* to raise the young man! It's not like anyone was dealing with opposition from the family, who were completely on board—they were the ones who contacted me! That kind of behavior was a big surprise to me at the time, and I ended up having to remove the woman from the group. If you are serious about raising the dead then you will need to openly display the fruit of the spirit in your interactions with the family, acting and speaking with love, kindness, grace, and honor.

I believe honor is a major key in this area because as someone once said, "No one cares how much you know until they know how much you care." Honor is how we treat people when we want them to feel valued. It is how we treat those who are struggling and may not be emotionally able to respond in like kind. It is how we respond because if we were in their situation that is how we would want others to treat us. If your goal is to come in and act like the man of power for the hour with an attitude to take control and fix everything, you've missed the boat. Faith and power don't look like manipulation and control. They look like radical service in love, knowing that true faith flows from our walk with Christ, not our circumstances or outward appearance.

The one final thing to keep in mind is that even if they say no, that doesn't necessarily mean you cannot pray at all. What it does mean is that you need to be wise about it and a little sneaky, all the while generally respecting their boundaries. In other words, if you plan to go to a viewing of some kind, there is no rule that prevents you from praying for the body for a minute or two while "paying respects." I'm not talking about praying loudly in front of people, but more of a quiet-under-the-breath command for him to return to his body and be made whole. Regardless of the family's wishes, God's desire is for that person to return to life, so if you gently ignore the family's refusal and give it a respectful and *quiet* last-ditch effort while at the funeral, there is nothing wrong with that. What would be a *serious* problem in such a scenario is making a scene. While the idea of ignoring a family's wishes might sound offensive to some, I'm not talking about trespassing on funeral home grounds in the middle of the night, interrupting the service to shout prayers while standing on a pew, or doing anything else distasteful or illegal. I am talking about respectfully attending a funeral like everyone else, but with a different agenda in mind, exercised in an inconspicuous, peaceful and non-offensive manner. I even heard of one woman who was visiting funerals of people she didn't know for that very reason—to quietly pray for life. While that's not a method I choose to engage on my own, I have to applaud the woman's tenacity that is mixed with reverence and a certain level of tact.

In summary, you have a variety of tools at this stage. First, pray and ask God to give you favor. Then, figure out what you want to say. Ask respectfully, giving honor to the family in their time of pain. Regardless of their response, act with demonstrations of love, and if nothing else is available, you can always throw out a ninja-level prayer at the funeral during an appropriate time. Remember, ninjas are never seen or heard.

Now that we have looked at how to approach the situation, in the next chapter we will look at what to do when it is time to pray over the body. What do we do and how do we pray? Read on.

Chapter 11

The Hour of Prayer

Where the rubber meets the road when raising the dead is when it comes time to actually pray. Unless you have just pulled up to a traumatic car accident or something else completely unexpected, you may have time to contact other people before standing in front of the body needing to pray. You may want to contact your local church if you are part of one and activate a prayer chain if resurrection is something they believe in. While a growing number of ministries believe in it, there are a limited number of groups out there who are specifically available in a sort of on-call basis for raising the dead. The only ones I know of at the time of publishing are the *Raise the Dead Initiative*, *Dead Raising Team*, and *Dead Raising Campaign*, we and they can be contacted via website or social media to join in prayer as well. The contact information is as follows:

Raise the Dead Initiative:

http://www.thekingsofeden.com/raise-the-dead-initiative/

https://www.facebook.com/groups/124203581018584/

Dead Raising Team:

http://www.deadraisingteam.com/

https://www.facebook.com/groups/57430291805/

Dead Raising Campaign

https://www.facebook.com/groups/1772840282986299/

You may be able to locate people in your general area who can join with you in prayer by way of maps located on the websites. These groups are good options for anyone who lacks a support system and/or who wants more faith-filled people on board whether they can physically attend or not.

The one caveat I will give as you seek assistance in prayer is that more is not necessarily better. When Jesus went to raise Jairus' daughter, he kicked some people out of the room (Matthew 9:23-24). The more people who know you are going for resurrection, the more naysayers, skeptics, and doubters you will alert, and let me tell you— the enemy will mobilize them in full force. This does not necessarily mean you should be secretive or keep it from your church, family, and friends, nor does it mean you should shy away from posting on social media. What it does mean is that you want to use prayerful wisdom and discernment whether to do so or not, and when you select your resurrection team. Many followers of Jesus are what I would call "unbelieving believers" and while they might be your closest friends, there is a good chance they're not going to help the cause. Try to differentiate between good friends and faith-filled ones, and if you find both in the same people, you are blessed!

When it comes down to actual prayer, the ministries who have the most success worldwide have one thing in common: 24/7 prayer. I'm not talking about general 24/7 intercession but rather having someone with the body at all times praying over it. In some places and with certain cultures they don't hide their dead like we do in the United States so someone can actually sit with the body for days on end as it is sitting on a table in a hut somewhere. In the United States that is more difficult, so arrangements have to be made. As covered in the previous chapter, see if you can get the body moved to a local church or your home (if you are the guardian) and hold the sessions there so you can guarantee round the clock access. If that is not possible, then work within the constraints of the funeral home and ask them to give you as much access as you can get.

If full-time ongoing access to the body isn't possible, that by no means will prevent resurrection as proximity to the body and constant prayer aren't required. I am simply sharing what appears to be best-practice based on collective past experience from those who see regular success in this area. Thus, if you have the time and ability, and hopefully other people to relieve you as a team, pray around the clock in the presence of the body and if you can, lay hands on it as you do so. This process can go on for as long as you are able to sustain prayer and the body is available—God does not put time limits on resurrection.

One of the hard parts about praying over a dead body is that after about an hour or two you have run out of every single thing to request, prophesy, decree, and declare that you can think of. You will have prayed through every resurrection scripture you know and spoken every unique prayer you can think of . . . and if the person hasn't gotten up yet, what do you do next? This process isn't a formula, or I would share the formula and be done with it instead of writing a full-length book on the subject. So you're out of interesting things to pray—what then? Spend time worshipping and refocus back on God and step back into a place of rest. Get a drink or go to the bathroom, then return and try again. Put on some worship music and enjoy His presence for a bit while you rejuvenate (this is especially helpful if you have been at it for hours).

In reality, prayer is much more about what we intend in our hearts than it is about any words we say, so you can always stand there and simply release your intention for the person to return. When I say this, I don't mean that you are forcing him to return by your will, but that you extend toward God your desire for him to return, just without words—God hears even the unspoken prayers of the heart. In fact, while I am usually a loud pray-er and like to pace up and down as I do, some people can pray quietly for hours while kneeling in a single spot. I'm not sure how they keep from falling asleep, but I've seen people pray like that for lengthy periods and it is impressive. I certainly can't do it like that. Regardless of the "method" you use to pray, the key is persistence. Ask and keep on asking, seek and keep on seeking, knock and keep on knocking. Be as repetitive as you need provided you understand it's not a formula. Cycle back through praying life-related Bible verses again and again if it keeps you going. Most of all, stay encouraged in faith.

Now it's easy to say "stay encouraged" but when you have a dead body in front of you, it is a bit more difficult to just "keep your faith up." Not only that, this isn't like when someone asks you to pray over their marriage—where they expect God to do something in the future long after you pray. This is the kind of thing where you expect results right then and there, and in reality, you need to have the miracle happen pretty quickly. Mind you, after you leave the person could very well come to life and get up. That has happened before too, where after the person praying leaves then life returns to the body, much like people who sometimes get healed hours or days after getting prayer. I can't explain why that is, but do know it can happen. Either way, the goal really is results-based on this one, so it's a bit difficult to keep a high level of faith all the time especially if going for hours (or days) with no clear results. One thing you can do is try checking the person's pulse. Strange as this may sound, I have felt heartbeats before—irregular and sporadic, but it felt like there was an occasional heartbeat as I was praying as if the body was trying to jump-start back up. If you do check, be careful to use your fingers and not your thumbs, as you are more likely to feel your own pulse through your thumbs and mistake it for his. If it were me praying for a human, I might even bring my stethoscope to listen directly to the chest, so that's another option you can use if you have one and want to bring it along.

If you run out of prayers and feel low on faith, what can you do to get reinvigorated? How does one stir up faith to continue praying? How can you effectively push aside the nagging and negative thoughts the enemy is throwing at you? How can you put the force of faith to work for you? The enemy will whisper in your ear the entire time, trying to derail you, telling you that the person is dead beyond repair, that he will never come back, that you don't have the faith it takes, that he wants to stay in heaven so you should just stop praying, and much more. All of these are lies designed to stop you from persevering in order to keep the person dead. This is literally life-and-death, and demons play for keeps. They do *not* want you standing in your authority as a son or daughter of the Most High God and successfully commanding that spirit to get back in the body and for the breath of life to return. If the demons can keep you off-target, in low faith, and discouraged, they will do their best because it means he stays dead—and their goal is always death—yours, mine, and everyone else's.

As such, staying encouraged is a super-important part of this process. When I feel my faith going down and my levels of worry and doubt rising, I usually refocus back on how good God is and how utterly kind it is that He gives us the ability to raise the dead. I begin to recite, out loud, the many promises and provisions in Scripture about raising the dead. If you need an easy-to-find list, you can reference Appendix II at the back of this book. I literally go through and pray scriptures back to God as a reminder to my own soul and simultaneously as a prayer to God asking Him to do what He has said He will do. I must point out that this is not a form of spiritual blackmail whereby we can force God's hand. I have heard people preach the absurd notion that when we pray scripture back to God He is *forced* to perform it as though we are reciting an incantation that God is bound to obey—it doesn't work like that. I find that as I pray scriptures and focus on what God has said He will do, I can literally feel my spirit rising up and encouragement well up within me. This is one of the best ways to keep encouraged while praying over a body. Other things you can do, as mentioned above, are to get back into a place of worship or to soak in His presence. Any and all of these methods should help rejuvenate you. If you have a handy set of testimonies of either historical or modern resurrections (much like those conspicuously located in Chapter 7 of this book) you can recite them out loud to remind yourself that God is not a respecter of persons, doing things for one and not for another (Acts 10:34). He will do what He has promised again and again and again—and He will do it for you.

Fasting is another tool in the arsenal. While I don't believe fasting does anything specific to convince God to move, it releases power through our personal sacrifice that shifts *us* and the atmospheres around us, which make room for angelic activity, enhances our prayers, and overall helps us to partner with God on an entirely new level. The thing I have found while fasting is that while sometimes it can make me feel more spiritually alive; at other times it feels like it deadens my spiritual senses—it really just depends. Some of that may be a matter of having low blood sugar, also common when fasting. As a result of consuming almost no calories when juice fasting, or consuming zero calories when water fasting, people get tired much more easily. Metabolism slows down which accounts for the lack of energy, and it explains why people get cold more easily. If you plan to fast, have warm clothes on hand. You will likely get sleepier, more irritable, and may even get dizzy or have your vision grow dark if you stand up too quickly, a temporary condition caused by a momentary lack of oxygen in the brain. Sit back down, wait for the dizziness to pass, and stand up again—but slowly this time. Juice fasting is easier on the body than water-only fasts, and it may help alleviate some of these symptoms. If you haven't fasted before, you will want to re-read everything I just shared above, since you may experience one or all of the above symptoms and it is best to prepare. Fasting has good benefits overall and can help you to connect better spiritually with God, so you may find it to have been a very wise choice—in this type of situation I generally recommend fasting over not-fasting provided you don't have any conflicting medical issues that prevent it.

As you pray, don't be afraid to command demons to leave and pray to break the power of darkness over the deceased. Demons are involved in each and every death, and especially in suicides. I have read multiple death-experiences people have had where upon returning to life they reported seeing demons at their bedside trying to either take them away or prevent them from returning to their bodies. We are in an incredibly real spiritual battle over life and death where demons actively oppose us. Bind them and command angels to break their power. Sometimes people die because curses have

165

been placed over their lives, cutting life short. Consider breaking curses and powers of witchcraft over the individual as you pray. You may feel led to do identificational repentance—where you apply God's forgiveness over the problem through prayer as though it were your own issue. You are acting as a stand-in for the person and pray as a representative in heaven on his behalf.

Sometimes people will feel led to do what are known as prophetic acts. All throughout the Old Testament the Lord told prophets to do specific actions, often strange ones but that influenced outcomes. In fact, one king lost a battle because when he performed a prophetic act at the instruction of a prophet, he didn't hit the ground with an arrow enough times (2 Kings 13:18-19). It is possible the Lord may be showing you to stomp, clap, take communion, anoint something, or do another specific action that has spiritual significance in the circumstance.

Keep in mind that even though you may feel you are hearing God, you need to test the word you receive. While the radical-faith part of me says "Obey God," the wisdom part of me realizes that we are fallible and sometimes hear God incorrectly. Sometimes we hear Him just fine but interpret incorrectly which ultimately has the same outcome. If the prophetic act involves destruction of facility property, that is called vandalism and is a crime. At the risk of stating the obvious, getting arrested will probably slow the resurrection effort. If it involves personal property of the deceased, or the action is going to be disruptive to others present, you should get permission from the family or person in charge at that time (if it isn't you) before moving forward.

Oftentimes, especially in the Charismatic churches, at the point where someone tells another person to ask permission is when some people say, "I obey God, not man." Well, I have news for you: If it isn't your family member or your property, I don't care what you think God says—it's ultimately not your choice, it's theirs. I've met people who are willing to ruin relationships in order to obey God for something that truthfully might not even be God to begin with. That's not called obedience; that is foolishness. Test the idea with other believers to make sure you are hearing God. It's not a matter of majority-voting, but group discernment in accordance with the principle laid out in 1 Corinthians 14:29. Asking the family for permission shows them honor and deference, which is appropriate under the circumstances, especially since the item in question may be theirs to begin with. If the word is from God, He is going to confirm it through other people present, and waiting a few minutes to double check isn't disobedience—it's wisdom. If everyone present decides that it really isn't God, you need to lay it down or do it back at your own home. If for some reason it was God, He will work out the details. The whole thing about using prophecy in a group setting is that it's not an anarchy-parade with every man for himself. We need to work together toward a common goal, and that means sometimes we sit one out. There is something else I have learned in this process—something highly practical that I believe applies to this situation. A friend once told me, "Being right about the facts but being wrong about the relationship is complete and utter failure." We have to keep in mind that relationships are key, and God already knows that—He's a relational God who created us in order to enjoy life together with us and each other.

I should also point out that just because something is done in the Bible doesn't make it a good idea for the resurrection. For example, in 2 Kings 4:32-35 Elijah lays on top of a child's body three times to bring him back to life. While laying on top of a decaying corpse already sounds super-cool to begin with ... some people will feel the urge to do so anyway simply because it's in the Bible. Well, guess what—walking around town naked for a year and cooking with poop are both scriptural too, as is wiping mud in blind peoples' eyes to heal them, but I don't see any of those things happening regularly in spite of their "scriptural" nature. We must use wisdom here too. If it's a bad idea, then it's a bad idea—and laying on dead bodies seems like a pretty bad idea to me in most cases. Think about it—if the funeral director or a family member, or really anyone else for that matter, sees you lying on top of a dead body because "it's Biblical" you may still end up in jail depending on state laws. At the very least you could seriously offend the family and be asked never to return—there goes your resurrection effort, totally in the toilet with some poisoned relationships to boot. If you decide to go forward with that, you had better be 3000% sure you heard God, and another 5000% sure that He will back you when it comes time for the deceased to get up.

Another aspect of praying for resurrection involves who is and is not present at the prayer meeting. While this might seem mundane, it is practical—and part of practical includes asking people *not* to be there. The fact is that some people really don't belong at a resurrection, and even Jesus didn't let doubters into the room with the deceased (Luke 8:51-52). More is not better. When people pray faith-less prayers, such as, "God, if it be your will to bring so-and-so back then let him return, but if it not be your will then keep him in heaven," they need to go. This isn't a heavenly popularity contest where he with the most prayers gets to go back to his body—faith is key. If someone is praying doubt-filled prayers he or she clearly does not believe God wants to raise the deceased and is just as likely to hurt the attempt as help it. Faith and doubt are both like yeast that spread through an entire loaf of bread. If you let doubt-prayers go unchecked, it has the potential to poison the faith of everyone else present, but if you politely have the person leave and spread words of faith, you can bring everyone present back to center and refocus on the fact that God *wants* this person resurrected.

One thing you might try before asking someone to leave is have a conversation—talk to them privately. Sometimes it's a simple matter of education. Many people have been taught that we must pray according to God's will, and they're not wrong. The problem is they don't understand that God's will is for resurrection, so they are praying the best they know how. What they know *is* a faith-less prayer, so if you explain what they don't know, they may learn something and be willing to change how they participate. If not, politely asking them to leave seems completely reasonable to me.

As you go through this process, you will also need to determine who your friends are and locate your adversaries. While we struggle against spirits and not physical people (Ephesians 6:12), some people will speak and act in agreement with the enemy without even realizing it. Some will simply spread doubt, and others will actively oppose your efforts. This is an attack of the enemy sent to destroy faith and keep your loved one in the grave. Considering the enemy killed them to begin with, don't put up with it. Those people who oppose you and the resurrection effort need to go. Make firm boundaries and ultimately shut them out of the prayer effort if necessary. We are talking life and death, and now isn't really a great time to have to deal with peoples' pettiness.

I have addressed this somewhat above, but it bears repeating. If you are the one leading the prayer—presumably a family member or the designated person who is leading the effort on behalf of the family, people really should show you some deference during the prayer. When I say deference, I'm not talking about a twisted control-thing like you will find in some churches with a pastor or other leader trying to dominate everyone. It is ultimately about honor and respect, and if you are in charge, people need to listen. They do not have to agree with your decisions, regardless of what those decisions may be, but as long as it is legal, within reason, and related to the resurrection, they really should respect your choices. If they can't do that, they don't need to be there. By the same token, this goes both ways. If you aren't leading this particular effort, show the people in charge the respect you would want if you were in their position.

Think about this from another perspective. The family has lost a loved one and is getting bombarded by stressors on all side. If you can reduce the stress level instead of increase it, then find ways to do so. If you feel the person in charge is a significant part of the problem, then take the high road and kindly invite yourself to leave peacefully and pray at home. In any situation, aim to be the solution, not the problem. This isn't about manipulation, control, or a power trip—it's about raising the dead through the power of Jesus Christ. If things are going poorly overall, pray for God to open peoples' eyes and for both human and angelic reinforcements to shift things heavenward. God is not limited and He can bring the right people at just the right moment to turn things around. Shift frustration into prayers and refocus your difficulties by praying from heaven in a place of victory, not from a place of defeat. Do your best to emulate the fruit of the spirit, giving grace, mercy, and kindness to all. Offer support and attempt to serve wherever possible. Extend extra grace to everyone under the circumstances because many people are likely to be a bit on edge, especially if they are fasting, tired, and dealing with grief and the stress of a potential impending funeral at the same time. The enemy will prowl about looking for whomever he can devour (1 Peter 5:8), so don't be the one to give the devil a free lunch.

Chapter 12

Practical Considerations

As airy-fairy as this subject may sound to some, raising the dead is actually extremely practical. It stops grief in its tracks, brings families back together, and produces healing in what is otherwise an irreversibly damaged body. Let's face it—dead people have a host of health problems: heart failure, total renal failure, apnea, brain inactivity, liver failure, circulatory problems, endocrine issues, thermoregulation problems, and more. Raising the dead is extremely practical, but did you know that there are physical actions you can take during the effort that are equally practical? If the resurrection succeeds, some of these things will also help the recovery process go a bit more smoothly. The following list is taken from my book *Practical Keys to Raise the Dead*:

- Keep the room temperature low, preferably 60 degrees or lower, as bodies decay more slowly when in cooler temperatures. This is especially important if the body isn't embalmed and it might keep the smell down for a slightly longer period. If prayer continues for weeks, the effect on the person's appearance will be significant. While not necessarily impacting the resurrection attempt, an air-conditioned body is more pleasing to the eye and may be more comforting to those present.

- Ancient cultures used myrrh and other highly aromatic spices after death for a reason. Essential oils may be used as a perfume to help cover the smell of decay, but you may need several bottles. An essential oil diffuser could help with this.

- Any and every body is eligible for resurrection even if embalmed, cremated, organs removed, burned, missing limbs, etc. God is a creator and will make everything new. It's not based on percentage of body present but on the power of God. Don't let missing parts turn you away from your goal.

- Bring a change of clothes with you—for the deceased, not you. Funeral homes cut the clothing down the back to dress the body easily, so clothing is usually like an apron—only covering the front. When he or she awakes, it will get a bit windy back there and probably be rather embarrassing. Yes, at that point he or she is no longer dead so a little embarrassment at that point isn't a big deal in comparison, but if you're going to go for it, you might as well come prepared with at least a robe. More preferable is a full change of clothes: shoes and socks, underwear, bra for the women, pants/dress, shirt, and sweatshirt or coat if the weather calls for it. I can't imagine being dead and then waking up only to be absolutely freezing—that sounds pretty unpleasant.

- If the body is at a church or person's house and you are going to be there for days without leaving, you might consider bringing a toothbrush, change of clothes, deodorant, etc. for yourself as well.

- Bring food and water to have on hand for the newly-resurrected person. From the stories I have heard, and even from Jesus' example in scripture (Mark 5:43), it is appropriate to give the person food and water upon his return, and he will often ask for it. Having it on hand not only makes things much easier, but it is an act of faith. If you think about it, having food (and clothes) on hand are what someone who is expecting results is going to do. Engaging in simple acts of faith that the person will be raised can help. Consider neatly placing the food and clothing near the casket, if one is used, as a visual reminder of the end-goal. Go expecting success and keep in mind that faith looks like something—then go and do whatever that looks like.

- If your spouse died and you have children, they will need a lot of love during this process. You may need to take a few hours away from praying to tend to their hurting hearts. This isn't a lack of faith on your part, even if it feels like it. It's loving your family through a really, really difficult time. And no one is going to pretend that it is easy—you are hurting as well and trying to stand in faith. It's a battle—but children don't always understand that, and they need what they need. Work to balance their needs with the ways the enemy may try to use them to drag you away from the resurrection. You have to be spirit-led on this—there is no easy answer.

Chapter 13

Should I Stop Praying?

One of the most difficult questions to try to answer in regards to raising the dead is knowing when to stop. This is hard because the answer is so situational, but also because the God of the Bible is the God of the living, not the dead (Mark 12:27) and thus it is always His will for everyone to be raised from the dead each and every time. Period. Yes, this brings up all sorts of issues about overcrowding on earth, how we can go to heaven if we don't die, and more—all of which I will address in the next book in this series which is about immortality—physically living forever. Those are legitimate questions and not something I have room to speak to here, but what I have shown in the first half of this book is God's will and provision for abundant life. Death rails against His will in that area, and thus is anti-God. If death is anti-God then life is always the answer. Because God always wants us to live (such that 1 Thessalonians 4:14-17 speaks of the dead in Christ eventually all being resurrected anyway), there is no theological "right time" to stop believing for resurrection. At the same time, we also have to keep living our lives and from a practical perspective cannot simply put life on hold forever to bring someone back. The best I can do is give some guidelines and ask questions to bring out the wisest decision under any circumstances.

First, do you have the time to keep going? Time is a legitimate issue here. If I were going to seriously go after a resurrection for a close friend or family member, depending on my schedule I might need to call off from work. At some point in time I would either run out of sick time or be in danger of losing my job from not appearing there when scheduled. If I stop other things in my life to make room for resurrection, how long can I keep that up until it causes problems that will be hard to recover from later? Regardless of whether the resurrection attempt succeeds or fails, losing my job could also mean losing my house (and making everyone in it homeless), which all together would put me in pretty hot water, on top of having lost a loved one. I am married and have life responsibilities including helping raise young ones—so I am not the only one who suffers if I lose my job. On the other hand, if losing my job was what it took to get my loved one back, it might well have been worth it. If it were my wife or grandchild and all I had to do was give up my job to get them back, it would be an easy decision to make. The problem is that we are not given any guarantees, so that isn't something we can know with surety—and as such can't make wise decisions based off of "what if."

There may be a legal option available to help us all as we pursue raising our loved ones. Depending on the relationship you have with the person who died, the Family Medical Leave Act (FMLA) may allow you to take unpaid time off and keep your job legally protected on your behalf. Human Resources at your job would have the information on that. If you have sick time you can use during your leave, so much the better, but that is one option that may be available. I recommend you speak with wise counsel and get advice on the best way to approach this issue for your unique situation.

Right up there with time is the issue of money—and whether or not one has the money to keep going is a very real matter. In most cases, at least in developed nations, the body will be kept at a funeral home, and this costs money. Essentially you are renting the space for the body to be housed, and unless you have significant wealth behind you, the money may run out sooner than later. In some cases you may be struggling just to find the money to get him buried. If you have to borrow to keep paying for funeral home services to continue a resurrection effort, how long can you keep that going? How long is it going to take you to pay that debt off? I don't recommend you gamble all-in on the "if it works I will be fine" option. I suggest wisdom makes a plan keeping in mind both the worst *and* best-case scenarios to develop a plan.

Sure, if everything works out and he is raised in a day or two that would be great—and we all want it to take far less than that. The problem is that if it doesn't work and a few weeks later you have blown through enough money that it will take you a decade to pay off at your current income-level, that is a bad idea. At that point your attempt to walk in faith has put you under significant financial bondage. On the other hand, God might tell you to do it anyway, and then miraculously pay off the debt. He is not threatened or limited by our financial lack, and we can learn to transcend those limitations, but money is still a very real issue and there is no shame in deciding you need to stop for financial reasons. As I said before, seek wise counsel for your particular situation because the one who will have to live with the outcome is you.

The next thing to look at is our emotional state. Are we actually standing in faith, or have we moved out of a place of spiritual rest? Are we striving to force the person to return to his body? Because not only will that not work but it will make things worse. There is a very real emotional danger that can come when we use "faith for resurrection" as a way to hide our denial. Sometimes in our difficulty coping with loss, we shift away from believing he will return but keep up an act of praying to keep the grief at bay. The longer we try to resurrect him, the longer we can avoid the grieving process, and this alone is a good reason to stop. If we recognize resurrection is no longer being done in faith but is actually an emotional crutch, burial may be the best choice. When I say this, I am referring to people who have been going after resurrection for weeks or longer, not people who have given it a day or two. The presence of grief in and of itself is not a reason to move on, but if it is coupled with denial behaviors and one has been at it a while, it may be time to call it quits—at least until one can move into a healthy place and try again, although yes, that would unavoidably be some time after the burial.

This may sound a bit harsh to some, but I have met people who are emotionally tied into resurrection in really unhealthy ways. I know of multiple situations where people continue to stand in faith even years after burial, and that's okay. In these situations it is simply that they know the will of God for their family is to have their spouse back with them and they refuse to accept anything less than His best. In and of itself there is nothing wrong with that, and when done with a right heart approach that approach can be perfectly fine. On the other hand, I have seen it become detrimental— an unhealthy obsession that completely shortchanges the grieving process. Let's face it—if our loved one dies, grief is normal. I also think it is normal to thrust grief aside when pushing for resurrection, but if it is months later and we are still after it, at some point in time we need to grieve the loss and get some emotional healing. If we are in the same place years later, that is particularly harmful to our emotions, and ultimately to our physical health as well. Continuing to pray long after burial is fine provided the emotional state is a healthy one, but bottled up grief will literally speed our own demise.

Where is the body located? This is again one of those things one has to decide individually. Personally, if it were my family member and I decided to bury them, I am planning to stop praying. While this sounds like strange advice from someone who is all about raising the dead, I simply cannot put my entire life on hold forever. For me, at this point in my life, burial is an end point. And if that isn't where you are at, that is fine provided your decision to keep going is not based on denial and emotional paralysis. The truth is that there are demons of grief who want to keep you bound. If you are so focused long-term on bringing someone back such that you don't live your own abundant life, you are in bondage. This doesn't bode well for your future, and I have seen people in this predicament.

Practically speaking, after burial the body is underground, usually in a coffin inside a sealed vault in the middle of a field. To have a successful resurrection, the body will either need to be legally exhumed (which if you went ahead and buried him, it is unlikely you will do this) or it will need to be supernaturally translocated out of the earth and simultaneously resurrected. What I just stated is not too hard for God—after all, in Matthew 19:26, "Jesus looked at them and said, 'With man this is impossible, but with God all things are possible,'" and again in Chapter 7 I share historical testimonies where God has indeed translocated the bodies. Yet, in spite of this, sometimes we just have to move on. I am very much pro-resurrection but my advice is also to use some wisdom, which for me means when I bury, I stop praying. If someone else is in charge of the body and you are praying from the sidelines, when they put the body in the ground it seems reasonable to me to move on. Mind you, if that is the case, go ahead and pray until the last moment available as you never know when the breakthrough could come. You might opt for cremation and simply keep the ashes on hand for similar purpose—to keep praying. Again, nothing is wrong with this provided an appropriate emotional state, but the issue of regenerating the body still remains post-cremation. It isn't too hard for God, but that may serve as a clear end-point for some to cease resurrection efforts.

If you can hear God, ask Him for clear guidance on the matter of when or if to stop. If you don't know how to hear God, you might ask friends who do, but if you go this route then don't blame them afterwards if you don't like how things are going if you follow their guidance. At the end of the day we are humans and humans are fallible—even in our ability to hear God speak to us. If they gave you the best they had, it is up to you to decide what to do with that information. God is very kind, infinitely so, and will even make things clear to us if we don't know how to hear His voice—and will do so usually through signs or using basic wisdom in the situation. While it is important to learn to hear God speaking to us, a moment of crisis like this isn't the best time to start learning. If you are reading this and don't know how to hear God, or cannot hear God well, I highly recommend you make that a priority in your life. I cannot tell you how many situations I have been in where hearing God speak to me has been helpful—to the point of making significant life decisions based on His direction. Hearing God's voice is not a prerequisite to raising the dead, but it certainly helps in the process.

For some examples of how hearing God influences the situation, I know two women who live in different parts of the United States, both of whom have prayed for God to resurrect a family member. In each case, as they were in prayer the Lord gave them specific dates (weeks after death) by which either their family member should be raised or they should stop praying. Again, let me reiterate that while life is always God's highest will, He also knows our circumstances and there may come a time when we need to stop. God in his boundless grace gave them clear direction on how to proceed forward, and though I am certain it hurt their hearts immensely, when their family members did not return by those dates, they had them buried. The one then had a divine encounter shortly afterward where the Lord brought much inner healing in place of the grief she had in the situation. If you don't know how to hear from God, then look at the situation with the recommendations and questions shared here, speak with wise counsel, and make your best decision possible. At the end of the day you can't really make the "wrong" decision if you do your best, regardless of the outcome.

Having said that, I want to contradict myself a little here. As I have repeated over and over, God is always about life. He doesn't have special timeframes by which people must be resurrected or else it would never happen. How can I say this? I mentioned it earlier in the chapter, but let's look at 1 Thessalonians 4:14-17 again:

> For we believe that Jesus died and rose again, and so we believe that God will bring with Jesus those who have fallen asleep in him. According to the Lord's word, we tell you that we who are still alive, who are left until the coming of the Lord, will certainly not precede those who have fallen asleep. For the Lord himself will come down from heaven, with a loud command, with the voice of the archangel and with the trumpet call of God, and the dead in Christ will rise first. After that, we who are still alive and are left will be caught up together with them in the clouds to meet the Lord in the air. And so we will be with the Lord forever.

The Bible says that everyone who has died in the Lord will rise first, and then everyone else will join them. So when Martha was talking to Jesus in John 11:24 about a "last day" resurrection, not only did he agree, but he took it a step further in v25 saying, "I am the resurrection...." In other words, yes, there is a last-day resurrection, but there is also an *everyday* resurrection available to those who believe in Jesus. While we continue to pursue the everyday resurrection, there is a "last day" resurrection, whatever that looks like, whereby we will eventually see them again anyway. What does that mean for us? God is always ready, willing, and able to resurrect our loved ones. We don't actually *have* to stop praying for them ever, but I suggest that after we bury them we have moved from what I will refer to as an "active" resurrection phase to a "passive phase".

The active phase is obvious—it is what we have discussed so far in this section, where we actively and intentionally pray for someone to return to life. The passive phase is where we are no longer actively pursuing resurrection. Most likely we have buried the body already and are working to move on with our lives, but we still hold out that sliver of hope because Jesus died that we might live. This phase is where we generally believe that God wants him or her to return but we aren't really seriously praying toward that end. This can go on indefinitely, but there is a measure to which even that has its limits. Tyler Johnson shares his thoughts on this subject in *How to Raise the Dead*.

Families are sometimes eager to pray for their loved one's resurrection after they have been cremated or buried. There is nothing wrong with this. In fact, it is the radical will of God. At the same time, the family needs to govern their emotions and know when it isn't healthy to continue to pray for resurrection. For example, my mother still has my father's ashes, and though I know that God wants me to have a father, I do not pray over my father's ashes for his resurrection. Why? Because there is a sneaking suspicion in my heart that it would be unhealthy for me to do so. I have painfully embraced a paradox, and in doing so continue to stand in faith." (Johnson 249)

While there is nothing inherently wrong with continuing to pray and believe for resurrection long after burial or cremation, each person has to decide individually whether this is a healthy pursuit or not. And believe me, I have been in contact with people who fall into both categories. This is part of why inner healing is so incredibly important in the Body of Christ as a whole, but especially when we come across significant painful situations such as a family member's death. The unhealed wounds of our hearts leave room for the enemy to come in and wreak havoc, and as with most situations, if we give an inch they will take a mile. Regardless of whether you feel led to continue praying after burial or to cease, you need to get healing. God is not going to penalize you or look at your prayers as somehow being "lesser" because you pray to get healed from grief while still standing in faith for resurrection. God isn't abusive—He is kind and loving and good. He already knows your hurting heart needs His loving touch, and by no means will He withhold His love from you in your time of need.

One final situation that isn't very common, but does exist, is in any situation where your own life is in physical danger. I spoke about it in my book *Practical Keys to Raise the Dead* but feel it is important to reiterate here. I learned years ago as both a Boy Scout and a lifeguard that my life was a priority in any emergency situation. If I become a victim, not only am I unable to help the current casualty but I have compounded the situation, doubling the number of people who need rescuing. If you are trying to raise the dead and it is physically unsafe for you to be there, you need to leave. The dead body cannot possibly get deader than it already is, but you on the other hand can go from living to dead if you remain somewhere dangerous. The wisdom choice is to get to safety and if possible, return and try again later. I might remind you that in 2 Kings 13:21 a man's body got thrown into a tomb because his friends' lives were in danger when they were trying to bury him. What did God do? The moment the body hit Elisha's bones the dead man came back to life—and I am guessing he probably ran to safety with his friends. God isn't bound by what we see as limitations. Prioritize your own life over that of the deceased and I believe that God will honor the intention of your heart one way or another.

Men and women of faith have raised those who have been long-dead (years and even decades) so time is not a limiting factor to God. Yet, the sad truth about raising the dead is that sometimes the resurrection does not occur. We are the ones who live under limitations, and that is why when or if to stop praying is incredibly situational. To be honest, at least in the USA, it seems to fail far more often than it succeeds at this point, although to be fair it is difficult to measure. Failure comes with the territory, and the next chapter addresses what we do and how to move forward if we are unsuccessful in raising the dead.

Chapter 14

When They Don't Want To Return

The single most common question I have ever been asked about raising the dead is "What if my loved one doesn't want to return—what if they want to stay in heaven?" Hard on the heels of that question is the notion that if they don't want to come back we should stop praying to resurrect them. This is the most common question not just for me, but of other ministers I have spoken to who minister on resurrection. Many different ideas exist out there, but I will be honest, most of them aren't scriptural at all—to the point that I am devoting an entire chapter in this book to cover this topic alone. The issue is very straightforward to me, but I will attempt to address this question in its entirety. If you read nothing else but this paragraph though, let me give you the short version: *under the circumstances, a dead person's will is of no import—raise him anyway.*

I have a strong reason for this position. The Church is extremely unhealthy in its understanding of resurrection, and questions like this strike at the very core of our faith in who God is—a God of life, light, and love. People freak about raising animals, about whether to bring someone back or not, and about whether or not we *can* even bring people back against their will. Well, let's take a good look at that—what about their will? How involved is their free will in the resurrection process? Is it cruel and mean to bring people back when they die? I see lots of people say things like "If I die, then don't bring me back. I just want to stay in heaven." Even some of my own family members have asked me not to try to resurrect them if they die. You *must* understand that this mentality is a massive, big, large, serious, enormous, major, and gigantic problem. We have a collective rapture-ready escapist mentality that says we need to get away from the earth and get to heaven as soon as possible when Jesus in John 17 said the exact *opposite,* and then there's the Lord's Prayer which says it is our job to make earth like heaven, not leave here and go there!!! "To *live is Christ (emphasis mine),* but to die is gain" (Philippians 1:21). What that scripture means is if you die, well, that's manageable and okay since you are a believer, but to *live* is Christ and that's God's best plan. Comparing "Christ" and "gain," "Christ" is the better of the two by far, and that means life. I will attempt to answer many of the questions I posed above in the following chapters, but I share these above to point out just how little people understand the goodness of God, that He doesn't kill, and that life is the only thing He has to give us. If God is a God of life, why would He condone letting people stay dead? The truth is He doesn't—we do. Jesus was very clear in Matthew 10 when he told his disciples to raise the dead. He didn't make special provisions for whether someone wanted to return or not—Jesus simply commanded them to go and do.

Sometimes we are so inconsistent with our spiritual beliefs that we don't think in depth about what we are actually asking—so let me spell it out. Even atheists who may not have a particular belief about afterlife will immediately attempt CPR on someone who has just died in an attempt to bring them back. As a nurse, I have been rigorously trained in exactly what to do when someone suddenly dies, and I received this training for one reason and one reason only: *to bring that person back.* Let's face it—if restarting a dead person's heart and lungs isn't a form of resurrection, I don't know what is because at the point his heart stops, he's dead. As stated before, we can argue the minutiae of the exact moment that death occurs based on brain death, cell death, etc. but it is an undeniable fact that if we do nothing when the heart stops, he will never live again. On the other hand, if we do something, he may yet return to life.

As mentioned in previous chapters, medical professionals worldwide are trained in resuscitation measures, as do many companies. Why do we think it strange in the church that one might actually step out in faith to believe in the promises of God that the world is better about pursuing than we are? Church people can get freaky when we start discussing this stuff. At least the world has an excuse—all they've ever heard of are zombies, so that's what their mind immediately jumps to, but the Bible is very clear about this. *Twelve* different Bible stories address someone being resurrected. It is a pivotal part of our beliefs, without which we have *no Christianity.* You literally cannot separate Christianity from Resurrection—the two go hand in hand because no resurrection means no risen Jesus and no risen Jesus means no hope. But because we have this hope, we need to *do* something with it! Paul had to address this same thing in 1 Corinthians 15:12-20 (New Living Translation), saying:

> But tell me this—since we preach that Christ rose from the dead, why are some of you saying there will be no resurrection of the dead? For if there is no resurrection of the dead, then Christ has not been raised either. And if Christ has not been raised, then all our preaching is useless, and your

faith is useless. And we apostles would all be lying about God—for we have said that God raised Christ from the grave. But that can't be true if there is no resurrection of the dead. And if there is no resurrection of the dead, then Christ has not been raised. And if Christ has not been raised, then your faith is useless and you are still guilty of your sins. In that case, all who have died believing in Christ are lost! And if our hope in Christ is only for this life, we are more to be pitied than anyone in the world.

But in fact, Christ has been raised from the dead. He is the first of a great harvest of all who have died.

Are things really no different now than they were 2,000 years ago when Paul was preaching and teaching? Why is it that we still have to prove to the Church that Jesus is in the business of raising the dead? Paul even stated in verse 20 above that Jesus is "the first of a great harvest of *all who have died (emphasis mine)*." A great harvest of everyone who has died isn't a suggestion that one or two should get raised, but that it is God's will for everyone to return—and that means anyone who has asked me not to bring them back is actually outside the will of God as stated in scripture.

God is clear throughout the entire Bible that His desire for us is life, not death. Death is the work of Satan, not God, and Death is an enemy who is to be destroyed and placed under Jesus's feet. Since death is the opposite of God's will, and we as believers are supposed to be submitted to His will in both this life and after death, then it seems entirely irrelevant to me whether the deceased wants to return or not—God's will is for them to live.

I do not see a single place in the life of Jesus, much less the entire Bible where it shows or suggests we should inquire of the will of the dead before attempting to raise them. On the contrary, as I said above, in Matthew 10:7-8 Jesus instructed his disciples to go all throughout the nation of Israel healing the sick and raising the dead. He didn't give them advance instructions about which ones wanted to stay in heaven. He didn't tell them to go into a trance and interview the spirits of the deceased to make sure they want to come back. Jesus kept it really simple—if they were dead, bring them back to life. If you think about it, when people start talking about the "free will of the person who died" the various options above are ultimately what they are suggesting, whether they realize it or not.

With this in mind, I don't consider the will of the dead when I decide to resurrect them or not. The Lord spoke to me once and said, "No one who comes and experiences the glory of heaven wants to return to life on earth." That makes sense because from what we understand, Heaven is a pretty amazing place. It's peaceful, easy, and filled with God's rapturous glory—what's not to like? However, our mandate isn't to die and go to heaven, but to bring Heaven to earth. As such, the will of the deceased has no part in our decision-making process because we can understand that anyone who dies will want to stay in heaven. If they all want to stay in heaven but God wants them all to come back to earth, why bother attempting to discover the will of the dead? Theoretically, if one is a believer he should be submitted to God's will anyway. Instead of wasting time on nonsense, just follow the will of God and command him to return.

Now that I've said it's a waste of time and that I don't care what the deceased want, let me explain a bit more. Typically, the next thing people come at me with is that I'm callous, uncaring, and not honoring their free will. I care about this far more than one might imagine, which is why I am tackling this subject to begin with, so I will tell you a story—only one of many that I and those like me have experienced. I hope this will show you why seeking out and honoring the will of the dead over obeying God grieves me so. I think it grieves our Heavenly Father as well.

My grandfather, whom I told you about before, died in the beginning of 2015. At the end of January that year I flew from Oregon to Virginia to attend the funeral. God set me up with a divine encounter a few days prior that revealed to me a great deal about how unhealthy the Body of Christ is in regards to our understanding about resurrection. Two days before the funeral, I borrowed my dad's truck and drove up to Pennsylvania to look at the contents of a storage facility my wife and I had so we could clear it out later that year. I had brought a few books with me on the flight to Virginia, and I brought one book up to Pennsylvania with me, *How To Raise The Dead* by Tyler Johnson. I spent the drive up listening to messages on the topics of immortality and abundant life from WOW Ministries in Sri Lanka, and my faith was flying high—all in all it was a fantastic drive for me. I was blessed to have a 4+ hour lunch with my good friend Will, much like the old days when we lived in the area and would chat at a restaurant from lunch until dinnertime. While I enjoyed the time with my friend immensely, I didn't know that God was actually using it to prevent me from driving 3.5 hours back to my parents' place in Virginia until much later that evening.

We ended our lunch meeting around 5:30 pm as per our usual and I had just started the drive back to VA when my wife called from back home in Portland, Oregon to tell me that our friend "Jenna" called her. Jenna lives in Myerstown, PA, right down the road from where we used to live. She called my wife to tell my wife that her son's friend had died the day before from either a clot or hemorrhage in the brain; the woman was 25 and engaged to be married. My wife had me call Jenna back—who was blown away to discover I was less than an hour away from her instead of on the other side of the United States. She wanted to raise this woman from the dead, but had never tried it before and needed some help and encouragement. I plugged her address into my GPS and an hour later was at her house to pray, talk, and walk her through the process.

My philosophy on resurrection (and actually most Kingdom-related things) is this: If I do nothing, nothing will change. There is no hope. If I do *something*, there is still the chance nothing may occur, but there is hope where before there was none and a whole lot of chance that a miracle *will* happen. After all, let's face it: how many people do *you* know who will plan to resurrect you if you die? If you can count more than one person, you are a minority. If more than five, consider yourself both extremely rare *and* blessed.

My advice to Jenna was in keeping with my philosophy, and as she was nervous I had her sit down and write a script of what she wanted to say before making *that* phone call. We started with condolences, then moved to the part where we tell them we want to pray for resurrection, what we want from them (access to the body), and then ask for their assistance—the same as on the script in Chapter 10. Mind you, this was done very respectfully and not at all as callous as this could sound on paper, but you will have to trust me when I say that words on the page don't convey the same heart as if one was there in person.

Jenna dialed and asked for permission to pray for resurrection in the most kind, heartfelt, and loving way possible. The family was even looking at pictures of their daughter and Jenna's son when she called, so there was favor at the time of the phone call. What the family said was that they "felt peace" about her death and felt that God giving them peace was Him telling them to let her remain dead. That was that—resurrection attempt over.

While I was blessed that God was releasing measure upon measure of His grace on this family in the midst of this life-shattering event, I was deeply grieved in my heart. Hosea 4:6a says, "My people are destroyed from lack of knowledge," and in this case it could not have been truer. This woman, only 25 years old, had a good life—with a fiancée who was about marry her, a career, possibly children and grandchildren in her future, and a family of parents and siblings who loved her dearly, but in a freak moment her life suddenly and abruptly ended. Yet when the *only* people they knew who had *any* hope at all extended a hand to offer that hope, it was graciously-yet-firmly refused, and all because they believed God wanted their daughter dead.

I have been accused before of lacking compassion for the dead and the dying in regards to my beliefs about death and resurrection, but that couldn't be further from the truth. As I think about it again, even while composing this chapter, I had to stop and sob on my wife's shoulder for a while. I was in tears when I first wrote this, and I am in tears again now as I write. You have to understand that it pains me deeply even now to know that this woman could be alive right now, *today*, if her family knew what Jenna and I know. Jesus said it best to the Samaritan woman at the well in John 4:10: "If you knew the gift of God and who it is that asks you for a drink, you would have asked him and he *would have given you (emphasis mine)* living water."

If only they had understood that God's resurrection power is alive and well and that Jesus still raises the dead even today, they might have reached out their hands to take hold of the hope Jenna and I offered them. If only they had known that God sent me across the USA, then three hours north of my destination to meet with Jenna, complete with a book on the very subject of need sitting with me, full of faith and ready to go, and this very same God had kept me from driving home for hours after I had planned to leave, they might have relented and she most likely would have been raised. People truly do perish for a lack of knowledge. Death is a horrible thing. It causes pain, loss, grief, and a host of other really bad things. It uproots lives, destroys families, and is as demonic an attack from the pit of hell as anything ever was. When I say that someone's free will is irrelevant from the earth-side of things when they die and that God's will is for them to return, it is not because I am heartless, callous, or uncaring. It is because I understand God's heart on the subject and feel it quite deeply.

When I said at the start of this story that God revealed to me the state of the health of the Church, I am sad to say that it was bittersweet then and continues to be now. I am encouraged that God is moving and at work among His people, but it does upset me at times to know that many are living with grief and problems that simply don't need to be there. I am reminded through this event that part of my job, our job, as believers is to extend the abundant life that Jesus promised us in John 10:10 to all who are in need, and that the first place it must start is the Church. The Body of Christ *must* reach a place of health in our mindsets and beliefs where we understand that when God says in Revelation 20:4 that, "He will wipe every tear from their eyes. There will be *no more death (emphasis mine)* or mourning or crying or pain, for the old order of things has passed away," that God meant what He said.

This isn't a far-off heaven-when-you-die reality for a day yet to come. We are called *now* to burn as bright flaming beacons of light amidst a world that is filled with broken, hurting, and even dying people and to destroy the power of death in and through our actions, placing it under Christ's feet. The Old Order of things passed away 2000 years ago on a splintery wooden cross on a hill in Israel when the Savior of this world gave up his spirit and died in his body so that we wouldn't have to, then rose again, and that the power and authority to extend the life he purchased for us would flow in and through us to dry the tears of this world. I will not stop proclaiming this Gospel of Life that Jesus purchased for us, so that the Church may be revived into fullness, and through, it the world might live again. Resurrection from the dead is a key part of this life, and to miss out on that is to fall far short of God's will for us.

To get back to the idea that I believe scripturally we don't have to worry about honoring the free will of a dead person, we have to remember that the will of the dead carries no earthly weight whatsoever. Truly, even in court, someone is required to have a pre-designated legal document in place, known as a will, to decide what happens to their belongings after they die. If no will is present, then it's up to whomever is left to decide, and the dead person doesn't get a choice. The court doesn't hold a séance to contact the dead person to discover whether the aquarium should go to Cousin Judy or Cousin Marge, and which son should take the baseball card collection. In medicine it is the same way—if you don't have an advanced directive or Physician's Order for Life Sustaining Treatment (POLST), you don't get a say in what happens to you after you die. Ultimately it goes like this: the moment you lose your body, you lose the right to decide what goes on in the earth.

From what I have been able to gather, it works that way in the spirit too. Enoch and Elijah never died, and yet they still went to heaven. Moses died, but later on Michael grabbed his body and brought it back to him (Jude 9). And when Jesus went up on the Mount of Transfiguration, two of those three men appeared and directly interacted with him. Why doesn't this sort of thing happen more often? How many people in history do you think went to heaven without dying? Not many—so in reality I suggest there aren't all that many people who are able to come and go from heaven and back to earth as they please. If we want to have spiritual rights to make choices in the earth, it requires a body. I don't find it coincidental that of the many people throughout history, the Two

Witnesses in Revelation possessed the same powers that Moses and Elijah did, both of whom have retained or regained their bodies. My understanding is that when we die and abdicate our bodies, some things we consider as "rights" go out the window. Why do you think Satan was so eager to get Adam and Eve to die? He wanted to take over. No body, no rights, no earth.

So then, do the dead get to decide whether to return or not? Is it possible that some people refuse, which is why they don't return when we pray? I suppose so, but let me go on to explain why that doesn't matter. The Bible says in 1 Thessalonians 4:16, "For the Lord himself will come down from heaven, with a loud command, with the voice of the archangel and with the trumpet call of God, and the dead in Christ will rise first." The Bible says that everyone who is dead is going to be resurrected. Jesus alluded to this truth when he spoke with Martha at Lazarus' tomb (John 11:21-26). Martha stated she knew Lazarus would rise again at the last-day resurrection, and not only did Jesus not deny that this was true, He went on to express further truth about Himself as the one who raises the dead. In other words, even if dead people don't come back now, they will be literally incapable of remaining in heaven when Jesus brings them back at some future point in time—so whether they get to stay there for a little while now is in some ways irrelevant.

Most people who have died don't return whether anyone prays for them or not, so what we know from the heaven-side of things is based entirely on the experiences of those who have returned, whether through prayer or physical resuscitation. Most near-death-experiences (NDEs) that involve heaven are pretty similar. Someone dies, goes to heaven, and at some point in this process they are asked to return to earth. Some people agree readily and others hem and haw, but ultimately when they ask God what He wants them to do, He tells them to return. Occasionally someone will be given a choice without being forced to return, but they are also shown the negative difference it will make on earth if they choose to remain in heaven, and so they rightly choose to return according to God's will as well.

This is a fairly common narrative especially for Christian NDEs, but there are a few things I want to point out. First, even if God asks for the person's preference, He usually also states that His will is for them to return—which only confirms my point that we already know the will of God regarding life and death and don't need their input. Second, there are many NDE stories that turn out differently than one might expect—God completely ignores their will and forces them to come back anyway! The prophet Bob Jones, who died in 2014, had also died once before—in 1975 (LeClaire). At that time, he was told by God to return even though he wanted to remain in heaven—and God didn't give him a choice. For those who say that I am ignoring dead people's will by trying to bring them back if they don't want to return, it seems that in this type of situation, God prefers to ignore their free will too. If God doesn't have qualms about ignoring the free will of the dead, I'm not going to lose any sleep over it either. If I am able to bring the dead back to life, they can argue with God about respecting their free will later. Additionally, when they are dead, whether God respects their free will or not is between them and God in heaven. I am not part of that conversation, and it doesn't change the fact that God has told us to command life. If I am praying for them to return and God wanted them to remain dead anyway, or if He was willing to honor their free will over my prayers, then at that point it wouldn't really matter now, would it? And since the vast majority of people who die remain dead at this point, the argument could be made that a lot of people are getting their way—so I'm not going to feel bad if someone comes back kicking and screaming because, as I said before, God told me once that literally no one who tastes heaven wants to return. God, in His infinite wisdom and mercy, knows this full well yet has told us to raise the dead anyway.

On the other hand, if we consider the idea that we should not pray because it may be the dead person's desire to remain in heaven, we have to think about what that actually looks like when put in action. There are a number of problems with this idea. First, someone has to get a revelation at some point in time about whether that person wants to come back or not. When do we decide to start praying to resurrect him—before or after we get this super-special revelation about his free will? If we're going to subscribe to this "honor the will of the dead" theory, then we need to be consistent and take all the time we need to truly, thoroughly, and deeply discern the dead man's will before we bother to be obedient to God and pray for him to return. He might even be buried before we find out for sure. After all, we wouldn't want to offend dead people—it's better to be disobedient to God instead.

Second, even if the person doesn't want to return, how do we know we heard correctly? Prophecy is fallible because the people who hear God (all of us) are fallible. I have made tons of mistakes in my life as I have learned to prophesy, and from time to time, I still make mistakes. While I am far more accurate than I used to be when I started out, I can't ever say with surety that I'm hitting 100%. Likewise, when people say they heard God tell them the dead want to stay dead, how do we know it is God? If we "test the spirit," it automatically fails in regards to keeping in line with God's will in the Bible, so that doesn't work. If we try to rely on our proven track record, well, again, we all can still get it wrong. So how do we really know? Multiple confirmations? Could be. But then again, a whole group of people could be under a spirit of delusion, and when we test the spirit against scripture it is going to fail ten times out of ten. In fact, 1 Kings 22:22 and 2 Chronicles 18:21 speak to the fact that spirits can give us revelation that is a lie—to the point that they can do it to an entire group of prophets. It has happened before, so there is nothing stopping it from happening again. We certainly could travel in the spirit to heaven and hunt our deceased loved ones down to find out what they want—but while that is certainly possible, it doesn't change a single things about the fact that in reality there is *no actual way to verifiably test and know* if the person truly wants to remain dead or not, so we just need to be obedient and pray.

The third problem, and possibly one of the biggest problems with this whole "dead person free will" subject is that it erodes faith, plain and simple. As the founder of the *Raise the Dead Initiative (RDI)*, I have spent *years* talking to people and helping them pray to bring their loved ones back to life. The most common thing I hear: "I had a dream/vision/word-of-knowledge/audible-voice/angelic-visitation/singing-and-dancing-bear/talking-horse/imaginary-friend/whatever, and God (or your loved one) showed me they want to stay dead." Great. So now that you have told the person standing in faith for their loved one's return that their family member wants to stay dead, what do you think happens to their faith? Right—unsurprisingly, it drops through the floor. And how could it not? We speak death as much as we speak life—and in situations where people are believing for resurrection, we have to work hard to make sure we are speaking only encouraging words of life. Telling someone that their loved one wants to stay dead is the opposite of life-giving, and if we understand that sowing death and discord is the work of Satan, do you really want to become Satan's messenger? He should have to work a bit harder at it than that, but it would appear that the Church seems to think that giving Satan freebies is our job. I eventually had to make a rule in the *RDI* that the one thing we do *not* do is tell someone their family member wants to stay dead—and I am not big on making rules. If someone wants to do that in their own free time via private message, phone call, or meetup in person, I have no power over that, but I will never permit that kind of demonic discouragement under the guise of well-meaning spirituality in my organization.

While that might sound contradictory given that I shared in the previous chapter that the Lord spoke to women and told them a date by which their family member would either return or not, you need to understand the difference. In those instances they were standing in faith for resurrection, and the Lord gave them wisdom in that moment to know how to proceed further as things continued and the resurrection was not taking place. In one of those cases it went on for over a *month* before the Lord gave the instruction. That chapter and those examples were designed to illustrate how to figure out when or if to stop praying, and this discussion we are having here is not that. In this section here I am talking about using the so-called "Word of God" to speak death into a situation and discourage people from even trying when the command of God is *for* us to raise the dead.

So there you have it—multiple reasons not to bother seeking the will of the dead to know if they want to return, and then three significant problems that arise even if we do decide to go on a revelatory wild goose chase. One final nail in this "free will post-death" coffin, and one that may help you get a larger picture of this situation, are stories that show us God honors our choice as humans when we pray. I have come across two stories while writing this book that I believe demonstrate this point quite well. The first is about a man who died sometime before 600 AD and is recorded in Pope St. Gregory the Great's work *Dialogues*.

As the event happened, there was a righteous man named Marcellus who lived in the city of Todi, where Fortunatus was the Bishop. Shortly before Easter he fell sick, and on Easter-eve he died.

He wasn't able to be buried that day because the distance his body had to go was somewhat far, so his sisters, having some reprieve, went to track down Bishop Fortunatus.

When the sisters asked the Bishop to come and raise their brother back to life, he asked them to leave, stating that it was God's pleasure to receive Marcellus' soul and that no one can avoid death. Yet, even though he was saddened to hear of Marcellus' passing, he was still troubled by it, and the next day, Easter morning, he took two of his deacons to the man's house and prayed for him anyway. When he finished praying, he called Marcellus by name, and life returned as the man sat up and talked to him. Marcellus shared that when he died, two beings, presumably angels, came and took his soul out of his body and carried him to a pleasant place. Then, as Fortunatus prayed, another being went and told those two to carry Marcellus back to his body *because Fortunatus was waiting at his house for him.* Right after he shared that, his sickness was healed and he lived for many years after. The Bishop stated that God wanted Marcellus dead, but because Fortunatus prayed, he returned to life—something that would not have happened if he hadn't prayed. Because and only because the Bishop was faithful to pray, the man rose to life regardless of what one perceived the will of God to be in the situation (Gregory 46-48).

Then there is the story that Bobby Connor, a current-day prophet and well-known Charismatic minister, shared at the Experience God Conference in July of 2016 in Portland, Oregon of which I was in attendance. He shared publically how he raised his mother from the dead twice, and the second time he did so, the Lord told him this: "It was my intention to keep her the second time, but your prayers overrode my will." While I can't say I understand the part about it being God's will to keep her (as that doesn't match with anything God has revealed about himself in Scripture), the underlying point remains—that originally she wasn't going to come back but God made her return anyway because Bobby stepped out in faith. While this is a striking testimony about the power of our will (the will of those still *living*) and the preference that God gives it, the point can be made that even if God were to choose to keep someone in heaven, which I still maintain He doesn't, we can change the outcome and bring them back anyway. In other words, regardless of whether it is God's idea to keep them or the will of the deceased to stay behind, it doesn't really matter—our job is always to be obedient to God's commands to raise the dead, and leave the rest of the extraneous, hyper-spiritual revelatory details to Him.

In the following chapter we are going to look at the personal cost associated with failed resurrections—because like it or not, many resurrections do fail, and we must be prepared for the baggage it may bring.

Chapter 15

The Price of Failure

Regardless of how upset or unsettled people might get over praying for resurrection, a lot of that is likely to go out the window if the loved one in question returns to life. The miracle has a way of shutting up the dissenters all on its own. With that said, the one major risk associated with raising the dead is the possibility of failure. The current facts are that more resurrection attempts fail than those that succeed. I do not believe it will always be this way, but that has been Church history and seems to be at the present as well. Those who try and fail usually pay a price, whether emotionally, relationally, or otherwise. Someone once said that faith is spelled "R-I-S-K" and the thing about risk is that it is a gamble—if it weren't, it would not be risky. There are downsides to failing to raise someone from the dead, but they are really just tradeoffs from never having tried to begin with. As mentioned in a prior chapter, you are the last hope someone has when he dies, and the price someone pays from never trying is hopelessness and a guarantee he will never see his loved one again until he gets to heaven or at the last-day resurrection.

The thing about failure is that it can do a lot of things to a person. My brother-in-law told me a story once of a guy he knew many years ago. As it goes, this young man had recently joined Teen Challenge and was getting his life together. He was a new believer and coming out of a lifestyle of significant alcohol abuse. His mother died shortly after he joined the program, and he prayed for her to return to life. The attempt failed and the young man turned his back on God at that point, unable to deal with his anger, grief, and disappointment in a constructive manner. I will add that alcoholics and drug addicts often have poor coping mechanisms so he probably wasn't well-equipped to handle the problem, but the story is a good example of what can happen if our hearts aren't rooted and grounded in God's goodness regardless of the outcome.

So let me ask you: What will you do if your loved one doesn't return to life? Will you get angry and turn your back on God? Will you get embarrassed and blame God for making you appear foolish in front of others? Or will you continue to believe God's promises and stand in faith for the next one as though you had never failed before? We don't get to decide whether resurrection will take place or not—what we get to do is step out in faith and pray and see what happens. If we remember that God is good and His desire is for life 100% of the time, then we will remember that failure to resurrect means God's will wasn't being done as well, and while He isn't blaming you, the outcome didn't go as He wanted either.

This idea messes with some peoples' view of God's sovereignty, but as discussed in Chapter 2, God being sovereign doesn't mean all of life goes His way—it just means that as the King of Kings and Lord of Lords, He is the highest authority in the universe. The devil and his minions are lawbreakers and set themselves in opposition to

God's will, which is a large part of why I believe resurrections fail. Failure doesn't mean God doesn't love or care about you, and it doesn't say anything about your level of faith, purity, holiness, or anything else. A failed resurrection means that possibly hundreds of things took place in the invisible realms that we simply don't know about—witchcraft, word curses, lack of faith, demonic resistance, and maybe even more things we don't know about but that halted the attempt anyway. One of the best pieces of advice my father ever gave me was that when bad things happen, don't change anything. Whatever happens, do not change your beliefs about God and His love and goodness based on the results of a failed resurrection.

There is something else you need to consider in regards to failed resurrections—there are two ways to look at it. The first kind of failure means that the effort didn't succeed and the person did not return to life. That is how I have been expressing the idea of failure so far, but there is another kind of failure—the kind where you *didn't even try*. God has commanded all of us to raise the dead, but I personally lack the power to accomplish that on my own, as do you. The only way we can raise the dead to begin with is the resurrection power of the Christ who lives within us. We pray and they will either return or not, but if we have stepped out in faith and prayed, then we have done our part—the rest is God's job. Far more people engage the second kind of failure rather than the first; after all, some have never seriously considered praying for the dead to return prior to reading this book. If you have made an honest attempt to resurrect someone, regardless of whether you felt that you did it right, said the correct things or not, or feel you could have done better, you are a success in God's eyes. Let me say that again: If you have tried to raise the dead and failed, you are a success in God's eyes. You have passed the test, won the prize, and moved on to the next level. We all know that hindsight is 20/20—it's called reflection, and it is one of the ways we learn from our experiences and improve for the future. How do you think I felt able to write a book on this subject without having yet been successful? I have prayed for almost two dozen dead in person between animals and humans, and God has taught me through each and every failure, as well as through my job as a nurse and in conversations and interviews with other believers who have had their own successes and failures with resurrection.

In spite of your success as someone who has stepped out and tried, picking up the pieces of a failed attempt can be harder than if you had never tried to begin with. People have lost friends for standing in faith on God's promise of resurrection—friends who probably would have stuck around if the loved one had returned. If you are a parent and your spouse is the one who died, your children will need a lot of your time and attention during this period. Not only will they have needed you during the prayer attempt, but they will need you even more afterwards, and possibly even help to maintain their own faith in God during this tough time. One of the things I learned years ago is that when we get radical for the things of God and go against modern convention, even many of our Christian friends may desert us. The only thing we can do in those cases are to give time and attention to the few who are most important to us during the process, knowing that those closest to us are likely to be the ones supporting us if the attempt fails, and even then some of them may not remain. Hopefully none of this will happen to you, but I share this because unfortunately, it does end up that way for some people.

The other major downside of failed resurrection is the grieving process gets delayed, which is even harder if a child or spouse is the one who passed away. After the prayer has ended you will need to take time to grieve—time that you simply couldn't spend doing so before. This is vitally important. Stuffing or medicating your difficult emotions is a short term solution that will cause long-term health problems in your future. Your whole family needs to take time to go through the grieving process, and God is as much a healer of broken hearts as He is a resurrecter of dead bodies. Give your pain to Him during this process and He will heal your broken heart. Continue to draw near to God in this time of immense pain, as you will need Him all the more. A simple prayer you can pray, adapted from Praying Medic's book *Emotional Healing in 3 Easy Steps* is as follows:

> God, I don't want this pain (grief, suffering, etc.) anymore. I give you my pain and ask that you heal every wound that caused it. In place of pain I ask you to give me your peace (hope, love, strength, grace, etc.) and I receive it now in Jesus' name.

That prayer won't fix everything, but it is a good starting point if you don't know where to start to seek inner healing. There are many ministries out there who work with healing the wounded soul, and some are far better than others. Another helpful book I have used is Karol Truman's book Feelings Buried Alive Never Die. In the end, whether you seek nonreligious counseling or go to a prayer minister of some kind, your emotions need tending to, and there are often simple prayers such as the one above that can help.

During this time, be gentle and do not blame yourself. Hindsight is 20/20 and if you had been a different person in the past you would have done things differently. We all start out with the hand we were dealt, and while God helps us grow in and through our life experiences, we can only grow from where we are right now—and God knows where you were at when you set out on this oftentimes-unpleasant journey of resurrection.

In the end, I am utterly sorry the resurrection failed. It is horrible, it is hard, it is an unfathomable loss, and I do not envy your position. If you need help, please reach out to someone. As you grieve, talk to friends and family, even see a counselor if that would help. Dealing with grief doesn't mean you are lacking faith or doing something wrong—it means you are a human whose heart is hurting because someone you love died. That's normal and you are awesome. I am sorry for your loss and I pray God's grace touches you even now.

Chapter 16

Betrayed by Prophecy

In the previous chapter we looked at what to do when a resurrection fails, but something I didn't address was what to do with the many messages people received from God about the situation. I and many of my friends hear God somewhat easily and are familiar with Him speaking to us in visions, dreams, and in His still, small voice. When we pray, it is common that the Lord shares things with us about His will in a situation, and praying for resurrection is no different. What sometimes happens is that when we hear things from God and share them with others, it encourages them in the short-term to keep believing for life, but if a week later the body is buried anyway, then almost none of those words the Lord has spoken to us come to pass. Some people have a lot of difficulty with this because it gets their hopes up and later they are disappointed; in fact, some people feel downright betrayed. This is understandable because Proverbs 13:12 says, "Hope deferred makes the heart sick, but a longing fulfilled is a tree of life." When we get our hopes up because of something God shares with us and it falls through, it can be easy to blame God and get angry or disappointed with Him. What makes this even more difficult is that some then struggle with what to do with *any* prophecies they may hear, as in their minds, if prophecy doesn't work when it matters most, does it really work at all? The short answer is "yes," but there is a much longer answer.

Prophecy is usually conditional. When I hear God tell or show me something, it is not a guarantee that it will come to pass. It is actually an invitation to experience an optional reality, and I have a part to play in whether that reality occurs or not. A good way to think of this is that science now theorizes that time is not just linear, but with billions of potential timelines and realities cropping up every second. It's almost like a one-way maze that has limitless roads to travel down, and each time we come to a fork in the road we have another billion choices of which path to take. In the majority of those timelines, things will be largely the same—gravity will still be in effect, the sun will still rise and fall, and we will still have to pay taxes. Some of the things that change, however, are ones that can be decided by prayer. Does someone pray through to get that new job? Does the child get divinely healed of cancer? Will that lost puppy be found before the storm hits? When God gives us a prophetic word, He is showing us a *potential* reality, and it is our job to pray it through until it becomes the *only* reality.

Using this analogy of a billion paths in a maze, imagine that they all have varying levels of light on the path. The brighter paths represent God's will being done and the dark paths represent turning from God's will and the enemy having their way. As we pray, half of those paths disappear, and most of them are dark ones. Just the fact that we chose to turn to God in the situation removes a large number of potential negative futures. The longer we pray into the situation, the more of these darker paths blink out of existence and the collective glow of the ones that remain only shines more brightly with the glory of the Lord. Eventually, we reach a place in prayer where regardless of which reality is left, all of them contain the outcome we have pursued in prayer. Oftentimes, the Lord will show us at that point that we do not need to pray any longer. While I wish that every time I prayed it was as simple and clear as watching paths disappear on a road before me, it rarely is that simple. I am usually unsure if I have partnered enough with God in prayer to obtain the desired outcome until it either happens or doesn't. I have had definite times where I knew that I had pressed through in prayer to obtain my answer, but with things like raising the dead, you really only know you have the answer when he or she awakes. Until then, it is our job to partner with God to pray into the potential realities where the resurrection occurs.

What I believe often happens when someone does not return to life is that we failed to partner sufficiently with God. The devil and his minions are in the business of death, and whenever they can prevent someone from returning to life, they will—and they oppose our prayers, which is why we must persevere. This is often where people make the argument that the reason someone didn't return is because he didn't want to, but you already know where I stand on that. There is so much that goes on in the unseen realm that we must continue to walk in faith, believing our prayers are procuring the desired effect—and we must continue to push forward until we see the answer manifest. The purpose of prophecies from God in these situations is to help us because it encourages and engages our faith to continue to pray the desired reality into being.

When prophecies fail it means that either someone misheard or that between the positive and negative unseen forces at work, it did not end in the desired result. What it doesn't mean is that someone is a false prophet. We don't stone people anymore, and we live under a different covenant than the Old Testament where someone who got a word wrong was killed for it. The fact is that we all make mistakes. We mishear God from time to time, and occasionally get either the revelation wrong or we hear the revelation correctly and misinterpret it. What makes someone a false prophet is, in my opinion, the motivation to misdirect people (Matthew 24:24), not simply mishearing God. If someone is guilty of over-encouraging or hoping really hard and thinking it was God speaking to them, then they are simply someone who needs to mature in the prophetic—and don't we all have room to grow? As I explained about potential reality, I suggest that more often than not someone *did* hear God and things simply didn't turn out.

Confession time: I once gave someone a prophetic word during a resurrection effort that in three days they were going to see significant change in the situation. I felt fairly certain that God told me exactly that, as I pay a lot of attention to clearly discerning prophetic words I give, so I shared it with them. They were praying and believing for a friend's son to be raised, and not only was there no resurrection, there was no significant change in three days either. I am now unclear as to whether I heard God or not—though at the time it seemed to be so, but what I did next was something I believe is not just appropriate, but highly necessary: I apologized. I consider myself to be moderately seasoned in the prophetic and experience over time has shown me that I am fairly accurate, so while I was surprised that I was wrong I don't think it changed the need to correct my mistake. Some could suggest that we steer away from giving dates and times in regards to the prophetic simply so we don't run into these sorts of situations, but I disagree. I believe we simply need to walk in wisdom and discernment, fess up and make things right if we do mess something up, and continue to learn and grow. When it comes to giving dramatic words about people being resurrected, I suggest those are the sorts of situations where we need to use maturity and wisdom, but that doesn't mean we shouldn't speak. I forget who it was, but I once heard a prophet share a story where the Lord told him to tell a married couple they were going to get pregnant and have a baby. When the prophet told the Lord he didn't want to say it, do you know what the Lord said to him? "If you don't say it, it won't happen." There is a time and a place to make prophetic decrees, so shrinking back won't help anyone— getting really good at discernment will.

Not everyone understands that most words are partnership-based, not immutable fact. It is fairly uncommon to hear a word that is essentially "because I said it, the word will come to pass." Prophecies are designed to be partially self-fulfilling, as self-fulfillment is a significant part of how and why they have value. However, while each prophetic word carries with it a measure of divine power, not every word contains the power needed to complete the entire task. It is better to assume that a prophecy must be prayed into and interceded for than to expect the results will come without personal involvement. If there are things in the natural that need to be done to make it happen, then take those steps. Failure to do practical things to walk a vision out will likely result in poor outcomes. For example, if God gives you a vision and in the vision you see yourself laying hands on a body and it being raised, and you not only never go to the funeral home to visit the body but just assume that because you had a vision of that person being raised that it would be so, don't be shocked when they get buried a few days later. If you go to the funeral home and lay hands on them and pray and they aren't raised, then it doesn't even mean that you heard wrong—it is again most likely that more prayer was needed. It is possible that another person was given the same vision and God had set it up that you would have been at the funeral home at the same time and prayed together, but because only you obeyed the prophecy and he didn't, the resurrection didn't occur.

Back when I was an assistant in a campus ministry, I had gone to a retreat center early the day of our fall retreat to spend hours in prayer over the event before the weekend began. During my time of prayer I had a vision of an oven dial--and the very moment I had that vision my right hand involuntarily twitched at my side as if it were turning the dial. Assuming this was a vision of what God was wanting to do over the weekend, proverbially "turning up the heat", I began to pray into that. What I didn't find out until dinnertime was that the actual physical oven in the retreat-center kitchen was basically broken—and had I turned it on hours in advance when I received the vision from God about turning on an oven, it would have had six hours to pre-heat. And while no normal oven needs a quarter of a day to heat up, this one apparently did. It took *hours* to bake the evening meal to a sufficiently edible level because I failed to rightly discern and then *act on* the word the Lord had given me.

The thing about the prophetic is that we can second-guess ourselves all day long. Either a word was correct or it was not, but whether it came to pass doesn't actually tell us whether we heard God or not. In truth, that makes prophecy a bit confusing because we can't even rely on something happening to show us whether we heard accurately or not—and this is just one of the reason that many pastors and priests really don't like the revelatory gifts. If it were simple and straightforward, we wouldn't need a Counselor and Guide to counsel and guide us.

If you were on the receiving end of prophecy that didn't come to pass, I am sorry, and even more so if it was related to a failed resurrection. You may be disappointed, and that is understandable.

However, God is in the business of encouraging and probably gave you words of hope to keep you praying in this time of trouble, even if they didn't all pan out. God does not casually give prophetic words to make us feel good with no hope on the back end—if He says something it is because He is making His will known so that we can pray that will into existence. We have to remember that God did not betray you and it's not His fault—it is Satan's. God wants nothing other than life for you and your family and friends, and the enemy wants nothing but complete and utter destruction for all of you. If death, loss, and devastation are your experience in this moment, I encourage you to remember that God is not the author of that encounter and only He is capable of bringing you out of it. Continue to turn to Him, continue to give grace to others, and don't let yourself be swayed off the path. Grace and peace to you.

Chapter 17

Intimacy Versus the Occult

In the past I would have said that there is not a single religion other than Christianity that can raise the dead, but in researching for this book, I no longer believe this to be true. Even if we ignore the mythology of various religions, a number of which include some sort of resurrection of a god or gods (Odin, RA, Persephone, and more), there are actually testimonies of people, in some cases practicing occultists or witches, who have performed blood rituals to resurrect people. As strange as this may sound, and as outlandish as it may seem to some, I think it is important to look at the differences between these other so-called resurrections versus the power of the Living God. Followers of Jesus ought to be aware of additional facts as we pursue God's resurrection life. To discuss this thoroughly we will need to get a basic understanding of the tenets of how occult magic works, the means by which such resurrections occur, and then discuss both the similarities and marked differences between the occult and our practices as believers.

Before continuing further I feel the need to make a disclaimer. I will be describing the basics of magic, but this is as a result of revelation the Lord has given me from a number of my questions that the Lord has answered over a period of years as I have sought to understand and therefore better teach about the miraculous. I do not practice nor do I condone practicing magic or sorcery of any kind, including but not limited to spells, incantations, hexes, magic circles, magic potions, or anything else. I should also mention that occult resurrection is exceedingly uncommon.

To do magic it requires three things—power, focus, and effect. There are, in fact, some parallels between performing magic and how miracles work, but that is a conversation for another time. Take a lamp as an analogy of this process. The electricity is the power, the electrical cord is the focus, and the bulb is designed with one specific effect in mind, which is to give off light. The focused power has the effect of increasing light as a result of a lightbulb that was designed to help reach the end-goal. In magical practice, when one focuses enough power toward a predetermined end-goal, he will end up with something close to the desired result. Oftentimes one will use some type of magical artifact—a crystal, blood sacrifice, or other object that is meant to collect or help harness power, oftentimes at a time and location that are beneficial for the same purpose; a wand, spell circle or other means designed to help focus the power; and some sort of spell, rune, verbalization, intention, or other means by which the desired effect is expressed so the energy involved is sent toward making that come to pass. Regardless of the exact method, most magic involves some variation on this theme of power, focus, and effect.

It has come to my attention recently that I had been missing an additional yet crucial component: a contract. The purpose of the contract from the demonic side of things is to force humans into sharing their power with the demon on an ongoing basis, but on the human side this contract allows them to access the demon's power as well. While it might sound mutually beneficial to those who engage in these practices, demons don't generally do "mutual benefit" and any contract is designed to ultimately place the human under further demonic bondage.

We followers of Jesus can be considered to have signed a permanent spiritual contract with Jesus as well—having traded our lives in for His. The Bible shows that God has ratified this contract and marked us with His mark of ownership via the Holy Spirit. Romans 6:22 says that we have become slaves of God. Ephesians 1:13 says that when we heard the gospel of Jesus Christ and believed, we were marked and sealed with the Holy Spirit, and verse 14 goes on to refer to us as God's "purchased possession". 2 Corinthians 1:22 says that God has put His mark of ownership upon us and put his Spirit in our hearts as a deposit for the fullness that is yet to come. While sharing all this in a chapter about magic and demons might sound creepy, the key difference is that we have bound ourselves to the Being of Purest Goodness and Love, while demons' most pure emotion is that of hate.

In occult practices, the contract is part of what defines the relationship between the human and the demonic, and the interaction with the demons helps aid in the process of casting magic through demonic manipulation of power and focus to reach the desired effect. Nothing about demonic resurrection is healthy, and it is dangerous. Because all spiritual engagement is transactional by nature, this has a significant effect on the outcome of an occult resurrection ritual—and the resulting aftereffects. Before going further, consider that even godly spirituality is a form of transaction. Prayer can in some ways be likened to a business deal between us and God, whereby we send out our spiritual request and God releases an answer. Faith is the key component, although not the only one, as to whether our prayers get answered because it is the mainstay of the deal. It would not actually be wrong to look at faith as a sort of currency. Faith is a force, and when we exert enough of that force or power toward heaven, the transaction is fulfilled and God sends the answer back down to us. At times the answer to our prayers may be hindered or prevented by demonic powers, but the initial interaction of getting a prayer answered is a transaction between us and God.

Magic is really no different, specifically in this regard. When something needs to get done, there is a trade that takes place, usually between the human supplicant and the demonic forces they work with. The humans supply some source of power—in the case of resurrection it is likely to be blood sacrifices or something of equivalent spiritual power-value. The demons then engage and help create the desired effect. There is, however, a catch. If a demon is doing to do some level of heavy-lifting such as a resurrection, there is a higher price than normal. Why? Because unlike God, demons don't do things for free, and this is where things can get dicey.

When an occult resurrection takes place, the people involved will have to pay a price to make it happen—and that price is going to be putting themselves under further bondage. While they may be doing it willingly, that doesn't change the fact that binding oneself more closely to demons is foolish, and those who play with fire eventually get burned. Occult resurrection is a horrible idea, but that doesn't make it impossible. Consider Revelation 13:15, which states, "The second beast was given power to give breath to the image of the first beast, so that the image could speak and cause all who refused to worship the image to be killed." That word *breath* is the Greek word *pneuma* which is the same word used for Holy Spirit, the human spirit, any spirit-being including angels, and/or the breath of life. I suggest in this context that the word is being used to say that the breath of life was breathed into the statue, but regardless of interpretation the fact remains that if it is possible, it is possible. There exist legends of the *golem*, typically a construct of clay and sticks or similar earth-matter, which were animated through Kabbalism, a set of Jewish mystical teachings. I mention this here simply because there may be some truth behind the legends. If the enemy can animate statues in the Bible and Jewish mystics can do the same through arcane (presumably demonic) means, then why not in real life? And if a statue can be animated, is it really a stretch to say that a human's body can be reanimated as well? The devil has no power to create a soul or spirit, which means any spirit that would have been used is one God created and the enemy stole—but in this case the plan is to use the person's actual spirit to reinsert it into the body.

This entire process involves the power or action of transference—whereby one thing is transferred or shifted onto another. This is actually a very biblical concept, and the Hebrew people used it regularly in the Old Testament. Each year the High Priest would transfer the sins of the people onto a goat that was then sent out to wander in the wilderness, keeping everyone safe from the effects of sin for yet another year (Leviticus 16:20-22). When an occult resurrection occurs, this same process of transference is at work. When a blood sacrifice is made, the power of the life in that blood is transferred from one body to another, and the spirit is then brought back into that body and the person resurrected. While this might sound far-fetched to some, it's really not. In the Old Testament, Saul consulted with the Witch of Endor in order to speak to Samuel and consult him on God's will. 1 Samuel 28:12-16 shows us that the Witch was indeed successful in bringing Samuel's spirit back to speak with Saul—presumably against Samuel's spiritual will. If the occult has the ability to draw the spirit of a man of God back even in death to consult with someone, and we know from Revelation 13:15 that the enemy can put a spirit in inanimate objects, it is not really much of a stretch to think that with enough power, through the process of transference someone could be brought back to life.

Christian resurrections involve a measure of this power of transference as well. Think about it—we have received life in Christ because we traded our lives for his. Romans and Galatians both cover this concept in depth. When we go through baptism we die and are buried with Christ, and when we come up, we step into new life with Him, in Him, as Him. Galatians 2:20 states, "I have been crucified with Christ and I no longer live, but Christ lives in me. The life I now live in the body, I live by faith in the Son of God, who loved me and gave himself for me." 2 Corinthians 5:17 says, "Therefore, if anyone is in Christ, the new creation has come: The old has gone, the new is here!" Romans 6:3-4 says, "Or don't you know that all of us who were baptized into Christ Jesus were baptized into his death? We were therefore buried with him through baptism into death in order that, just as Christ was raised from the dead through the glory of the Father, we too may live a new life." These three verses are just a taste of the many things the Bible says about this death and resurrection—but what is clear is that we are trading our lives for His—a transaction by which our life is transferred to him and His life is transferred to us. In fact, the entire purpose of the sacrifice of Jesus on the cross was to use the power of His perfect blood to pay for our sins once, for all time, and through the power of that blood give us new lives. On some level, whether occult or Christian, blood is the medium by which resurrection occurs, although the life of Jesus Christ is on an entirely different level than whatever the enemy does through blood sacrifice.

As mentioned earlier, when a demon is involved in a resurrection, there is a cost attached—all magic comes with a price, regardless of whether one realizes he is practicing it or not. It is possible to engage in a contract with a demon without realizing it, and in doing so make a trade that, were we aware of the price, we would not be willing to pay. Imagine that as a Christian you have such desire to raise the dead that you pursue it with all you have. Suppose that you have moved so far beyond a place of rest and intimacy into a place of intense striving whereupon you are going to *force* someone to come back to life. Given that you lack the power to actually do that, and given your heart position in the situation, there is a good chance you are operating in pride. As you continue to engage this pride, subconsciously exalting yourself to the point where you are actually trying to make yourself equal with God in regards to resurrection, you form a contract with a spirit of pride who then empowers you to resurrect someone. At the time you raise the dead person, you don't actually sense the Spirit of God at work because in your pride, you also aren't operating in discernment—else you would have recognized the spirit at work within you was not Him. Because you were successful you only continue to feed into that demonic snare, but what you don't realize is that your choices and actions have cost you far more than you ever dreamed. Within two days of raising that person, your spouse inexplicably drops dead. What you did, albeit unknowingly, was trade the life of your loved one for whomever it is that you raised—all because you engaged the *wrong spirit*, and demonic spirits don't care that you didn't *mean to*—they just care that you created room for them to gain access, and took advantage of the opportunity (Anonymous, Personal Interview).

This is a pretty scary thought, actually, but it's not outside the realm of possibility or I wouldn't bother including the idea in this book. While I suggest this situation is exceedingly rare, we face a very real potential danger when we get into striving. If we try to force creation to bend to our will, which is essentially a form of witchcraft, we are much more likely to form a demonic contract that allows us to focus power and get the effect we desire—which is, as I have explained, the very definition of magic. The good news is there is a way to avoid this pitfall entirely—through intimacy and rest.

Intimacy is about staying connected to Jesus. John 15:4-8 says:

> Remain in me, as I also remain in you. No branch can bear fruit by itself; it must remain in the vine. Neither can you bear fruit unless you remain in me.
>
> "I am the vine; you are the branches. If you remain in me and I in you, you will bear much fruit; apart from me you can do nothing. If you do not remain in me, you are like a branch that is thrown away and withers; such branches are picked up, thrown into the fire and burned. If you remain in me and my words remain in you, ask whatever you wish, and it will be done for you.

Jesus is clear that it is only as we remain within Him that we are fruitful and our prayers are answered accordingly, such that we can ask whatever we desire and have it done. It is key to remember that Jesus always dwells within us by the Holy Spirit, so it's not that we sometimes have Jesus and sometimes don't—it's a position of the heart as well as a matter of focus. I am on intimate terms with my wife—she is my best friend, my lover, and as a whole I enjoy spending time with her. Whether we are engaging in some form of intimate behavior or are simply talking on the phone, my heart toward her is one of openness and engagement. In this sense she is always "in my heart" regardless of whether we are near each other or not. On the other hand, we also purpose to spend time with one another. Intimacy is not just a heart position but an action. In our relationship with Jesus we must have an inner posture where our hearts are always turned toward Him, but from time to time we need to focus on him in our deeds as well.

Before I was married I used to spend an hour or more on most days in prayer, worship, and soaking, spending time with the Lord. After I got married that lessened significantly over time, and in the ten years since I have struggled at times to feel like I was "spending enough time" with the Lord. This is not my wife's fault, and in many ways is the natural result of joining my life to another—my time is no longer entirely my own. While I have not gotten it all figured out, I have realized that God isn't necessarily looking for quantity of time on a daily basis, but for ongoing and regular engagement. Brother Lawrence's *The Practice of the Presence of God* and for that matter the practice of many of the Christian mystics, are all about focusing our hearts toward Jesus regularly throughout the day. While there were certainly dedicated times of devotion, the majority of life was lived *in* Him, not necessarily praying or thinking about God or doing some other spiritual activity. The goal of intimacy was to learn to dwell in Him and have Him dwell in us—abiding love. That is why in John 15 above the word *remain* could easily be translated as *abide*—because it isn't about working really hard to think about Jesus every second of the day—literally no one can do that. It is about having an underlying understanding that whether I think of Him or not, we are one, and when I do think of Him I let my heart overflow with my love and enjoyment of Him, so that we share a special moment together.

This sounds all well and good on paper, but in real life it often doesn't feel that fantastic. I don't feel like I am super-great at being intimate with Jesus, but I have been told by numerous friends and have received many prophetic words that speak to the contrary—I would be willing to bet the same is true for many readers as well. We are usually harder on ourselves in introspection than we are with other people, and I believe it is important to recognize and understand that. Although I don't feel like I do a great job regarding intimacy with God, the things the Lord says to me reflect something else entirely. Certainly there are times I sense or feel Him tugging at me to come away and be with him, but that's not an indictment about my failures. My wife tells me many nights I leave for work that she misses me and wishes I could stay home that night, and to be honest I usually feel the same way. The Holy Spirit nudging me that He wants to spend more one-on-one time with me free of interruptions and distractions isn't Him saying I am not doing it enough—it is Him expressing both how much He enjoys me and that He wants me to continue to make special time for Him on a regular basis. Only when I misinterpret the loving affection of the Lord drawing me near do I get into condemnation about not doing "enough."

The significance of this in regards to resurrection is where we get back to John 15. Apart from Him we really can't succeed at anything. Intimacy is the wellspring from which all of the rest of our life is supposed to flow, and it is where His power is made strong within us. Samuel was intimate with God, and it was out of that relationship that God caused all the things Samuel said to come to pass (1 Samuel 3:19). Intimacy is also how our identities are transformed so we can operate strongly and confidently in the authority He has already given us. Intimacy is the anchor, and it begins as we step into His rest.

The Bible speaks a number of places about this. In Genesis 1 God rested from his labors on the 7th day. Hebrews 3:19 explains that the Israelites were unable to enter God's rest in the Promised Land because of unbelief. Hebrews 4:9-11 says, "There remains, then, a Sabbath-rest for the people of God; for anyone who enters God's rest also rests from their works, just as God did from his. Let us, therefore, make every effort to enter that rest, so that no one will perish by following their example of disobedience." This Sabbath rest exists for all of us, and it is accessed through faith. When we are able to trust God for who He is and what He says He will do, we are able to exist in a place of rest in our hearts. It doesn't mean we lazily sit there, but that our hearts are positioned in a steadfast and unshakeable place where we don't have to worry or be in fear. It is only from that place that we can be most effective in prayer.

This concept of rest, as I said, isn't about doing nothing, but about staying in faith and letting the ability of God flow through us without striving. This doesn't mean that we cannot target that flow, praying for the things we desire, but we do not let the focus of our prayers get us anxious and stressed. When we are praying for resurrection and discover we have stepped out of that position, we must make a shift in our hearts, re-engage our faith in God's goodness, and move back into that place. Rest is how we remain well-connected with God and don't cut off the flow. Rest is where we keep ourselves in that place of peace in God. Rest is the means by which we let Christ move through us.

The difficult thing about this concept is that it seems at odds with being results-oriented, where we have a goal and are aiming toward it. To address this dichotomy, I will share with you some poignant teachings found in the book *The Isaiah Effect* written by author and speaker Gregg Braden. This man was formerly a senior computer system designer and earth science expert, who eventually turned his pursuits toward things spiritual, and has spent decades delving into what he considers sacred mysteries of the ancients. While not necessarily Christian, per se, he has studied a wide range of spiritual beliefs and has some stunning revelation about prayer—what he calls the "fifth mode of prayer", I call praying from a place of rest.

Braden shares a story about an encounter he had with a man named David, a Native American who was either a shaman or maintained native shamanic practices. He watched as David prayed rain in a sacred circle one day. That was not a typo—he did not pray *for* rain, as David noted if he had done that it would have further cemented the lack of presence of rain. Rather, he prayed into the current existence of rain even though it was not present yet. Whether he knew it or not the shaman was engaging a similar method to that Abraham used when he trusted what God said about a nonexistent reality; in so doing He became the father of many nations. Romans 4:17 says that God is the one who "Calls things that be not as though they were." When we engage our faith to create a new reality instead of engaging that faith to focus on how bad a current reality is, we are more likely to shift things toward that which we seek.

Much of our conditioning in Western traditions has invited us to "ask" that peace come to pass in specific circumstances of our world. In asking for peace to be present, for example, we may unknowingly be acknowledging the lack of peace in our world, perhaps inadvertently reinforcing what may be viewed as a state of non-peace. From the perspective of our fifth mode of prayer, we are invited to create peace in our world through the quality of thought, feeling, and emotion in our body. Once we have created the image of our desire in our mind and felt the feeling of our desire fulfilled within our heart, it has already happened! Though the intent of our prayer may not have appeared in full view of our immediate senses, we assume that it is so. The secret to the fifth mode of prayer lies in acknowledging that when we feel, the effect of our feelings has occurred somewhere, upon some level of our existence. (Braden 168)

This notion that we can essentially feel our way through prayer is fascinating and matches up with what I have found—when our thoughts and emotions line up, we are best prepared to release faith and see prayers answered. This alignment is impossible when striving and can only be done from a place of internal rest. Gregg Braden goes on in his text to explain that our current-day understanding of scriptures is largely skewed due to twelfth-century translations of Aramaic texts based on translators taking liberties with meaning and sentence structure, and he shows how new translations can shed new and more accurate light on what the Bible actually says and means:

> This fragment of our lost mode of prayer invites us to "ask" that our heart's desire come to pass and we shall "receive" the benefit of our prayer, as in the familiar admonition "Ask and you shall receive." A comparison of the expanded Aramaic text with the modern Biblical version of the prayer offers powerful insights into the possibilities of this lost technology.
>
> The modern condensed version:
>
> *Whatsoever ye shall ask the Father in my name, he will give it to you. Hitherto have ye asked nothing in my name: Ask and ye shall receive, that your joy may be full.*
>
> The original, retranslated Aramaic version:
>
> *All things that you ask straightly, directly . . . from inside my name, you will be given. So far you have not done this. Ask without hidden*

motive and be surrounded by your answer. Be enveloped by what you desire, *that your gladness be full. . .*

Through the words of another time, we are invited to embrace our lost mode of prayer as a consciousness that we embody rather than a prescribed form of action that we perform on occasion. In inviting us to be surrounded by our prayer and enveloped by what we desire, this ancient passage emphasizes the power of our feelings. In the modern idiom, this eloquent phrase reminds us that to create in our world we must first have the feelings of our creation already fulfilled. Our prayers then become prayers of giving thanks for what we have created, rather than of asking that our creations come to pass. (Braden 170-171)

Gregg Braden rightly expressed that our feelings are a powerful means by which we can access God's power in our lives. When we settle into a place of rest, we can more easily pursue what we seek in prayer.

In my own life I have found that this concept of rest is almost entirely emotional in nature. My wife and I get into discussions at times, especially with finances, and on rare occasion it gets downright overwhelming, to the point that I can feel my heart getting heavy with a sense of impending doom and I can feel a panic starting to rise up within me. When that happens, I have found that I have to shift what I am thinking about, or at least *how* I am thinking about it. When I purposefully change my perspective, I am able to shrug off the crippling fear and redirect my emotions back into a place of rest. As I do this, I empower myself to move forward and be productive, knocking out the tasks ahead of me step by step. Rest, in my mind, is more directly ruled by our emotional state, but as our feelings are significantly influenced by our thoughts, rest is best found when both are settled and at peace.

As I stated previously, it is difficult at times to try to have goals and seek results when the pursuit toward something has the potential to exacerbate the fact that we have not, in fact, reached our goal. I believe the apostle Paul understood the confusing nature of this paradox, saying in Hebrews 4:11, "Let us, therefore, make every effort to enter that rest ..." Where rest fits in this baffling dichotomy is that we are well-able to pursue a goal—we simply have to have the right internal perspective. No one is denying that we pray for things we do not already possess, or else we wouldn't need to petition God for them. However, when we can enter into a stable emotional state, we let ourselves exist inside of a result we have not already obtained, and in doing so we change things on a quantum level—shifting our experience from one timeline to another, thereby bringing our life into alignment with the results we seek in prayer. This notion is a bit in contradiction to the prayer of command that Jesus prayed when raising the dead and healing the sick, as quite often Jesus would simply flat-out command a result to occur. Both forms of prayer are valid and good, but Jesus was at rest in his authority—who he was and what He was permitted to do. I suggest that even Jesus' prayers of command did not come from a place of striving, but from someone who has truly and fully identified within himself that he has the right and ability to command that which he is speaking forth. Thus, even in the prayer of command we can use our authority from a place of rest. The opposite is to try to force the outcome, which as was mentioned above is self-limiting and negates effectiveness.

While this might seem all well and good in general, how does it connect to raising the dead? When I have prayed for resurrection, at times I have tried to experience and sit in the feeling of that person or animal being raised—envisioning the moment they return to life, what it feels like, the joy and pleasure I feel and that I know God feels at their return, and enjoying and sitting in the experience of God's goodness in that situation as well. It is yet another way that I can actively pray for life in the middle of a very dark and horrible circumstance—pushing back all the worries and concerns, the questions of "what if he doesn't return" and other niggling fears.

The occult is all about forcibly creating and managing a result based on our own power and influence or contracting with whatever supernatural power will create the desired effect. As stated at the beginning of this chapter there are definite similarities between how magic and prayer function because they are all based off of unchanging and impassive spiritual laws. However, the ones who serve as a source of power to engage and enact those spiritual laws are as different as night and day. One is evil and creates further bondage and dependency whereas the other is life-giving and creates freedom because it is His nature to do so. When I engage God through this experience of my prayer already-answered, my faith rises to another level, and at the same time encourages me that God is still the One who raises the dead. I encounter God intimately in these moments, much like one might imagine David did when he wrote in Psalms 23:5-6, "You prepare a table before me in the presence of my enemies. You anoint my head with oil; my cup overflows. Surely your goodness and love will follow me all the days of my life, and I will dwell in the house of the Lord forever." May the rest and peace of the Lord fill you, carry you, and guide you as you step out in faith to raise the dead.

Chapter 18

Common Questions

It is my desire to bring both further wisdom and clarity to you as you walk this journey to apprehend and release resurrection power. While I have attempted to address all questions in topic-relevant places throughout this book, this chapter is made up of some of the ones that just do not fit into a tidy category. In speaking with other leaders who minister on the subject of resurrection, I have found these questions are pretty standard across the board.

✗ How do I know if God wants me to pray for someone to be raised?

This subject was covered in some depth in Chapter 5 when discussing the difference between *huios* and *teknon* children of God; I recommend you go back and review that chapter first. If still unclear, consider what Jesus said when he was training his disciples. In Matthew 10 he sent his first disciples out on a sort of immersion-based internship: "Jesus called his twelve disciples to him and gave them authority to drive out impure spirits and to heal every disease and sickness" (Matthew 10:1). Just a few verses later, he said, "Heal the sick, raise the dead, cleanse those who have leprosy, drive out demons. Freely you have received; freely give" (Matthew 10:7-8). Jesus was very clear to his disciples that if they saw dead people, they were to bring them back to life. He didn't specify which ones should be raised because any and all dead people were fair game, and they still are now.

Ultimately, if it is in your heart to pray for someone, go ahead and do it. The same life of Christ is available to anyone in any situation, and God is anti-death 100% of the time. If you step out in faith, you can know with complete certainty that God wants that person resurrected. Reread the story about Bobby Connor in Chapter 14 and how his mother was resurrected—even when God said that at first she wasn't coming back! We serve a permissive God, so you can't really go wrong.

Can animals (or plants) be resurrected?

People can get a little strange about this question and get into all kinds of debate about whether animals have a soul, whether they have a spirit, whether they have the same kind of soul/spirit as humans, and whether Jesus' resurrection paid for humans only or if it applies to other living creatures. While geared toward animals, the answers in this section equally apply to dead plants.

Anyone who wants to do an in-depth Bible word-study on the topic of animals' souls is welcome to do so, but the study is likely to be inconclusive because the Bible doesn't clearly address the matter—and any inferences I have ever read were based on assumptions because in spite of going back into the original Hebrew, the lines of reasoning used to reach a conclusion were illogical at best. I personally believe the matter is simple. As mentioned ceaselessly in this book, Jesus, the Father, and Holy Spirit are all about life. Regardless of the type of spirit or soul that plants or animals may possess, God was capable of creating them the first time, so keeping a soul from dissipating on death and/or reforming it or recreating it or whatever you believe would have to happen is well within God's abilities. If you have an animal (or plant) who has died and you want to resurrect it, go for it—God is behind you! Death, regardless of what dies, is upsetting. Our pets are no less part of our families than our children, parents, or spouses, and when they die, it hurts. God wants to remove that pain as much as any other pain, and Jesus came to restore *everything* that was lost, which means animals aren't supposed to die any more than we are. If you want to pray to raise your animal, go ahead. I pray you meet with rapid success!

⍥ How do I know if it is someone's "time" to die?

Only two verses in the entire Bible say there is a time to die, and the second one doesn't even count because in context, it doesn't even mean that. The first verse, Ecclesiastes 3:1-2a says, "There is a time for everything, and a season for every activity under the heavens: a time to be born and a time to die." Solomon was writing an entire book about how there was literally no point to life other than to serve God because he had watched everything repeat in cycles. Truthfully, the man had so much insight into the natural world that he sounded downright depressed due to sheer boredom. He was observing and expressing what he had seen *so far in life*, not mandating a rule for the future that we who live under a greater covenant would be bound by. Jesus' sacrifice destroyed the power of death—there is no longer a "time to die." Solomon in all his wisdom had no way of knowing what Jesus Christ was going to do thousands of years later, and that is clearly reflected in the hopeless tone of Ecclesiastes. The only *other* verse in the Bible that suggests we all have a time to die is so badly misquoted that I sometimes wonder if people actually even read their Bibles—because it isn't really about us dying at all.

Hebrews 9:27-28 says, "Just as people are destined to die once, and after that to face judgment, so Christ was sacrificed once to take away the sins of many; and he will appear a second time, not to bear sin, but to bring salvation to those who are waiting for him." Wait—so verse 27 that is so often quoted as saying we all are destined to die has a *second half* of the sentence that totally changes the meaning? Turns out it does. The above verses in context, especially if we add in the verse or two before, is *actually* saying that because we all had a date with death, Jesus died once for all of time and for all people as a replacement for us. Colossians 2:12-14 explains this as well:

. . . Having been buried with him in baptism, in which you were also raised with him through your faith in the working of God, who raised him from the dead. When you were dead in your sins and in the uncircumcision of your flesh, God made you alive with Christ. He forgave us all our sins, having canceled the charge of our legal indebtedness, which stood against us and condemned us; he has taken it away, nailing it to the cross.

In simple terms, you were co-crucified with Christ, co-buried with him, and co-raised with him. The death he died, you died. Galatians 2:19-20 says, "For through the law I died to the law so that I might live for God. I have been crucified with Christ and I no longer live, but Christ lives in me. The life I now live in the body, I live by faith in the Son of God, who loved me and gave himself for me." Wow! Isn't that amazing? Reading the second half of a verse in context totally changes everything, and incidentally, it matches up with other verses that talk about what Jesus did.

If you are a follower of Jesus you have already died with Him, which cancels the legal code of death that is against you. Thus, death no longer has a hold over you and there is no longer such thing as a "time to die." If you *want* to die you certainly can, but I don't understand that line of thinking. I might add that it's not really our job to decide when someone's time to die is, and quite honestly, we all lack the spiritual authority to make that decision. Give a read through Job Chapters 38-41. The answer is basically the same— which in summary God says "Who are you? Are *you* God to be able to make that decision? I thought not." There is no such thing as a "time to die," and even if there were, it's not our right to determine that. So ultimately, no—just pray to raise them, or heal them if they are still alive.

✍ I only believe in raising people if they died a premature death. How do I know if their death was premature or not?

As with the last question, we have to remember that scripturally speaking, there is no such thing as a *time to die*. Thus, the term premature death is complete fallacy. It has been used in Christian circles to spiritualize resurrecting young people instead of the elderly. Scripturally, there is *no such thing* as "premature death" as opposed to "normal death" because *all* death is abnormal. We *have* to get that term out of our collective vocabulary! It is demonic as ever a demonic teaching comes, and is designed to keep people dead. Hell, comma, NO!

✍ What if they weren't a Christian—does God want to raise them?

Yes, yes, and yes. The Bible says in Revelation 13:8 that "Jesus was the Lamb who was slain from before the foundation of the world." A better, or possibly more accurate translation of that verse is "The Lamb who was slain before the moment of conception of time and space." In other words, Jesus was slain in Eternity as well as at a moment inside the flow of Time. If he was slain in Time for us in Time, who then was he slain for in Eternity but those in Eternity? What is my point here? God is not willing that *any* should perish but all come to repentance (2 Peter 3:9). God wants non-Christians to be resurrected and saved just as much as anyone else. In fact, I personally know two men in unrelated situations who died and were in hell and cried out to Jesus to save them and He brought them back to life and they became believers. At least one of those two had no one praying for him to be resurrected at the time because no one even knew he had died! Yet, God is faithful to his word in that "all who call upon the name of the Lord shall be saved" (Romans 10:13). While it goes against a more recent historical understanding of the text, nowhere does it actually specify that they have to be alive to call on Him and receive salvation—and this doctrine, called apokatastasis, is actually the one held by the early church fathers (Murray 9-12).

Before you get your feathers ruffled and your pants in a bunch, let me be clear. This is not universalism, I didn't say that there is no hell, nor did I say that people don't go there. While it might seem to some like splitting hairs, there is a very key difference between what is taught as Universalism today and what I suggest here. Hell is very real and those who choose to reject God go where they choose. God doesn't send people to hell—they condemn themselves. The Bible is also clear that Jesus was slain in Eternity and that anyone who calls upon Him can be saved. Ephesians 1:4 says that God chose and predestined all of us in Eternity (again properly translated as "before the foundations of the world") to become adopted as His children alongside Jesus. What this means is that what God predestined in Eternity, He also made provision for. John 3:16 tells us that God's love for us was so great that He sent Jesus so we would not die. Resurrection power is a manifestation of God's great love for us—whether believer or pre-believer—because in the end, everyone is destined to come to know God. His love is so undeniable that I truly believe even if it takes eons upon eons of time that God will eventually woo all mankind to Himself with His immense, inevitable, inescapable love. I personally like to call it the Doctrine of Eternal Courtship, and a thorough study of the theology of the early church shows that they, too, held this belief. It was the common understanding of the day until pagan converts who didn't understand Greek came in, mistranslating and misrepresenting Bible passages to demonstrate God's fire as punitive instead of refining out of love (Murray 12-13). Nevertheless, if someone doesn't know Him and has died, the best thing you can do is to try to bring him back. It is God's mercy and love to bring him out of self-exile and torment in hell into the glorious freedom of Jesus Christ, and this is best done through raising the dead and sharing the gospel with them while here on earth.

✍ What if the body is incomplete—can he still be raised?

Yes. The same God who created people's bodies to begin with and who is able to restore missing limbs for those who are living, can do the same for those who are dead. Missing body parts, whether due to trauma, organ donation, or other means, is not a hindrance to God. If the body is in pieces for some reason but the parts can be brought together, you might as well do that and then pray. I have read stories of saints of old whose captors cut the bodies into pieces and buried them separately because if they didn't, the saints would just resurrect shortly thereafter. The persecutors' solution was to try to prevent resurrection by splitting the body up, but even this wasn't always able to stop it. God spoke the entire cosmos into being with just a few words. Is a missing body part hard for Him? God is not bound by such things; our faith must not be either.

✄ What if they committed suicide? Will God still let them come back? Should I even pray?

If there is any one time you *should* pray, it is if someone commits suicide. I do not believe a single suicide is ever committed without significant demonic assistance. Said another way, God has put a desire to live within each of us. For that internal governor to be overridden to the point that someone takes his or her own life, demons have been *hard* at work. Additionally, the individual may have been assisted by chemical imbalances in their brain that literally drove them to do it. None of these are their fault, and at no time should blaming the dead person over his suicide prevent you from praying, nor should it diminish your faith that God wants him to return. The whole mess about suicide being somehow different than any other sin because "he was unrepentant at death" is a big load of crap. Can I say crap in a religious book? Well, I'm the author so I guess I can. Let me repeat myself—it's crap, doo-doo, poop, refuse, dung, offal, scat— a smelly material only meant for a latrine, septic system, or fertilizer for your flowers.

Why? A core tenet of the gospel message is that *while we were still sinners* Christ died for us (Romans 5:8). If we were able to solve the problem ourselves, Jesus would never have had to die and rise again. Since we never could have fixed the sin problem, Jesus took it upon himself to address the issue for all people for all time. The highly inaccurate Catholic view of absolution having something to do with saying verbal confession to an earthly, human individual is not actually how the Gospel works. Jesus' death forgives our sin. Period. The Bible doesn't differentiate between when that sin occurs, or even if it hasn't happened yet. Hebrews 10:12 says, "But when this priest had offered for all time one sacrifice for sins, he sat down at the right hand of God... ." Jesus, the high priest, offered himself as one sacrifice for *all* sins for *all time*. Jesus *is* the only absolution you will ever need or can even obtain. If you are in Christ there is ultimately no such thing as an unrepentant sin because even the sins you haven't committed or repented for yet are still forgiven already because God forgave them in Eternity which is outside of this Time-realm!

Looking at this logically, no one actually even *really* believes that unrepentant sin keeps us out of heaven. How can I say this? Easy—people don't believe that Christians who die in car accidents are in hell. They don't believe that Christians who die in bombings, plane crashes, earthquakes, heart attacks in their sleep, or any other situation where someone died unexpectedly are in hell. Although, by rights, if someone holds that belief about suicide, remaining consistent with his beliefs instead of being a hypocrite, he *has* to believe the same about these other situations simply because there is *no way* a person could have properly repented in advance from whatever random sin he might have committed earlier that day due to not knowing the day or hour of his death.

The underlying issue behind this question isn't really about suicide at all, but is about the goodness of God and whether we are once-saved-always-saved. I have news for you—believe whatever you like, but if we are going to condemn people in our beliefs and actions over suicide, we need to realize we are totally and royally *screwed*. As I said above, if suicide sends us to hell then so does basically everything else, and the gospel of Jesus Christ is actually no gospel at all and our hope in salvation through His name is absolutely worthless. This isn't one of those sit-it-out-and-figure-it-out-later beliefs. Either we believe Jesus paid for our sins once for all time when we were incapable of doing so, in alignment with the scriptures, or we don't have a gospel of salvation at all. Take your pick, but if you choose the latter, then this book is irrelevant because in your belief system resurrection and heaven simply don't exist anyway.

✍ What if my loved one died a long time ago? I didn't know anything about raising the dead back then. Is God mad at me? Should I try to bring them back now? *Can* I bring them back now?

God doesn't blame you for things you didn't know and He most certainly isn't mad at you. After all, He doesn't condemn you, ever (Romans 8:1)—the enemy does that. If you are feeling regret, remorse, disappointment, shame, or any other negative emotion from not having prayed for resurrection before, that isn't coming from God. It is normal that you could be upset because of missed opportunities and from things you didn't know. Honestly, how you feel is

243

understandable, but don't beat yourself up about it as it won't bring your loved one back. God isn't upset at you, so why should you be? If you feel led to try to raise them now, go for it—you really lose nothing by trying. As for whether you can bring them back, certainly it is possible—but I cannot say whether it will or won't happen. All I know is that God has done many bizarre things in this world and resurrecting long-dead people isn't new for him. Matthew 27:52-53 says, ". . . and the tombs broke open. The bodies of many holy people who had died were raised to life. They came out of the tombs after Jesus' resurrection and went into the Holy City and appeared to many people." If Jesus' resurrection brought many others back to life—some of whom presumably were long-dead, how can time-spent-dead be a limitation? In fact, I once heard someone point out that Abraham, Isaac, Jacob, and Joseph all were buried not far outside of Jerusalem, so it is entirely possible that the Patriarchs, dead for thousands of years, roamed the city after Jesus rose again. That puts a significant spin on the whole long-dead idea. St. Patrick was known for raising the long-dead as well. In other words, it's not too late on the one hand, but it might not be the best plan either depending on where you are at with the matter. Pray about it if you are unsure, and as I said before, you can't really go wrong by giving it your best shot.

If we raise people from the dead, how will they get to heaven? Don't people go to heaven when they die if they believe in Jesus?

Technically, yes—believers go to heaven when they die. However, last I checked, Jesus didn't say that death was the door to heaven—He said that He was.

> "And if I go and prepare a place for you, I will come back and take you to be with me that you also may be where I am. You know the way to the place where I am going."
>
> Thomas said to him, "Lord, we don't know where you are going, so how can we know the way?"
>
> Jesus answered, "I am the way and the truth and the life. No one comes to the Father except through me" (John 14:3-6).

In context, Jesus told his disciples that he was leaving them but that they could come join Him. When they asked how to find Him, Jesus told them that *He* was the way. Jesus is the path, the door, the gateway to heaven, not death. In fact, he says roughly the same thing four chapters earlier in John 10: 9-10. "I am the gate; whoever enters through me will be saved. They will come in and go out, and find pasture. The thief comes only to steal and kill and destroy; I have come that they may have life, and have it to the full." Jesus was clear that He and He alone is the gate, and that those who enter through Him will not only be saved, but find pasture—a picture of paradise, peace, and rest, reminiscent of Psalm 32. On the other hand, he juxtaposes His job as the doorway with that of the thief who brings death. You cannot have both Jesus and death be the door to heaven—they are mutually exclusive and you will have to pick one. Ultimately, if Gods will is for us to not die, then death cannot be our solution to get to heaven. Enoch and Elijah didn't die and yet we still understand they are in Heaven. Has God changed his plans? Since the answer is clearly no, you will need to look to Jesus to get to Heaven instead of treating death as though it were your savior. Thus, the issue isn't a matter of whether someone is in heaven after they died, but is it God's will for them to return to life—if they died, the answer is yes. From there, Jesus will handle the rest of the details about getting to heaven.

✆ If I raise someone from the dead once, what if they die again? How many times should I raise them? How many times *can* I raise them?

This hits on more of what I discussed in the last question, and thus I will answer your question with a question. How many times should you raise them? Well, how high can you count? In all seriousness, because it is never God's will for us to die, there is no limitation on the number of times God will allow someone to return. I suggest a large part of it is how many times are you going to pray for them to return? If you bring them back once, and a second time, do you really have any reason to believe it won't work a third, fourth, or fifth time? This question hits on the main topic of the next book in this series, titled *The Gospel of Life and Immortality*, but I will give you a little taste. 2 Timothy 1:9-11 says:

He has saved us and called us to a holy life—not because of anything we have done but because of his own purpose and grace. This grace was given us in Christ Jesus before the beginning of time, but it has now been revealed through the appearing of our Savior, Christ Jesus, who has destroyed death and has brought life and immortality to light through the gospel. And of this gospel I was appointed a herald and an apostle and a teacher.

Get that—the apostle Paul actually says that God appointed him an apostle, messenger, and teacher of the gospel of life and *immortality*. Jesus said many times over that if we believed in Him we would live forever. Look at what he said to Martha in John 11:25-26: "Jesus said to her, 'I am the resurrection and the life. The one who believes in me will live, even though they die; and whoever lives by believing in me will never die. Do you believe this?'" Good question. Do *you* believe this? If we die we can live again, which is to be bodily resurrected, as he demonstrated with Lazarus within the hour he spoke that to Martha. If you aren't dead already and you believe in him (which if you are reading this, applies to you) then you are able to never die. The question really is whether you are willing to believe it or not. I'll let you think about that.

Chapter 19

The Future of Resurrection

Having pointed out a few times in this book that resurrections currently fail more often than they succeed, I think it is important to address where I see this heading. What is the end-goal of raising the dead—or rather the end-goal that Jesus has in mind? Are we ever going to do the "greater works" that Jesus promised in John 14 that we would do? After all, if he did a group dead-raising during his resurrection (Matthew 27:52-53), shouldn't we be seeing people in mass-graves from terrorist attacks and genocide come to life? Keep in mind that in order to do mass-resurrections, one has to be at the site of mass-tragedies, but yes, God does have mass-raisings planned for us. In fact, that is just the beginning. I see this dead-raising thing going a whole lot further than some might imagine.

First, let me give some encouragement for those who have yet to see a single resurrection come to pass. As I was preparing the manuscript for this book, I read back through a number of old files and notes I had written to myself, and found a journal entry with a scripture verse that goes along with a prophetic word the Lord gave me on October 24th, 2011, the same month I founded the *Raise the Dead Initiative.* I have shared the journal entry and prophecy here:

"Now Elijah said to Ahab, 'Go up, eat and drink; for there is the sound of the roar of a heavy shower.' So Ahab went up to eat and drink. But Elijah went up to the top of Carmel; and he crouched down on the earth and put his face between his knees. He said to his servant, 'Go up now, look toward the sea.' So he went up and looked and said, 'There is nothing.' And he said, 'Go back' seven times. It came about at the seventh time, that he said, 'Behold, a cloud as small as a man's hand is coming up from the sea.' And he said, 'Go up, say to Ahab, 'Prepare your chariot and go down, so that the heavy shower does not stop you.' In a little while the sky grew black with clouds and wind, and there was a heavy shower. And Ahab rode and went to Jezreel. Then the hand of the LORD was on Elijah, and he girded up his loins and outran Ahab to Jezreel" (1 Kings 18:41-46).

I was driving home from school a week ago and praying about the *Initiative.* I was driving toward a very large hill in front of me, and a small cloud was just starting to peek over the crest of the hill. I felt Holy Spirit nudge me that he was speaking to me in that moment regarding "a cloud as small as a man's hand." I began to listen to what He wanted to tell me, and was pondering the above scene in scripture. He then said to me, 'Many prayers that have been prayed are coming to fruition.'

God is speaking to us about breakthrough in this season we are stepping into. It is not just some tiny, measly thing where we are hoping that God has something else planned for the future and hoping that this isn't 'it'. Well, it *is* it, but it's just the beginning.

I know that things have been up and down in this group since it opened Oct.7, and we have been working through trying to figure out the best way to structure things as well as having some interesting clashes of personality and maturity levels in the group. However, God is taking us into a place where we are not only calling the rain of God's spirit to come, but He is empowering us to run *ahead*. Everyone in this group is participating in a trail-blazing effort in the spirit and in the natural. God is empowering us to run ahead of others who have been busy "eating and drinking," which represents paying too much attention to the needs and cares of this world. These same people are unable to understand what God is doing because they need another person to tell them what God is saying.

In 1 Kings, Isaiah led the way to Jezreel, whose name means *God sows* or *God will sow*. Because we are both hearing God *and* responding to Him in this hour, we are being positioned to lead the people of the church and the world (in this area) to the place where God will sow his love, poured out through his Son's blood, into their lives so they may reap abundant life. Even if you haven't prayed for a single dead person, it doesn't matter. You are in line to reap the blessings of the promise of God.

As I re-read my journaling above it was incredibly encouraging to me, and I hope it is the same for you. This prophecy says that as we respond to God, we will be able to lead others into a place where they can receive the abundant resurrection life that Jesus promised us. God lives in the realm of eternity, outside of the confines of time. Five years have passed since I wrote the above journal message, and it will be later still as you read this book, but this same word applies to you just as much today as it did in October of 2011. If you are willing to step out in faith to grasp this, you will reap the blessings of this promise from God. The future of resurrection begins in the now—and right *now* God wants to use you to raise the dead, as well as in the days to come. As a deeper revelation of God's abundant life grows, more and more of us will see this miracle with greater frequency. This is just the beginning!

My good friend Praying Medic published the book *Divine Healing Made Simple* back in 2013. We talk regularly, and a few months before he finished the manuscript, we were chatting on the phone. The Lord gave me a vague prophetic word at that time that God had more information that He wanted the Medic to include in the book. A few weeks later he had a dream that became the final chapter of the book, titled "Greater Works"—a chapter that he wrote to give a clear vision of the future of healing. While the entire dream is revelatory, I believe part of it most clearly defines the future of resurrection. Praying Medic has graciously given permission for it to be shared here, though I recommend you read the original book and the dream in its entirety.

The third and final scene brought the four of us to a countryside dotted with small villages. We weren't in the car any longer. And we weren't walking. Something had happened to us. We had the ability to travel wherever we wanted, merely by willing ourselves to go there. As soon as we decided to go here or there, we quickly went in that direction as if we had no physical body. We were very much like angels. The bodies we inhabited has a luminescence and transparency to them that was similar to the bodies people have reported seeing in heaven.

We traveled quickly to the nearby cities and encountered many people in need. Some needed healing, some deliverance, some were poor and others were hungry. As we encountered each person, we released the resources of heaven that met their need. I would gesture toward a person with my hand and a brilliant flash of multi-colored light exploded above them. As soon as this happened, their need was met and I would find another person in need and do the same for them. The four of us scoured the cities in what seemed like a few minutes, finding everyone in need and taking care of them by releasing the resources of heaven. A brilliant light flashed each time one of us released something from heaven. Nothing was delayed. People and their circumstances were changed in the blink of an eye.

We moved like the wind—without caution and without resistance. We never asked permission to do these marvelous works. As we met one person then another, we immediately knew what had to be done. There was no thought involved. We never questioned whether God wanted to bless them or if it was right to heal them or cast out an evil spirit. We instinctively knew that everything we did was in perfect harmony with the will of the Father and was well-pleasing to Him.

We encountered no enemies that I was aware of. If there were any, they must have been invisible or hidden. The light and glory of God that accompanied us made it impossible to see the presence of darkness or evil. All we could see was the

constant release of the light and power of God as it flashed
before our eyes everywhere we went. This was how the
dream ended. (Medic, 247-248)

This is one of my favorite dreams, not because I gave a prophetic
word prior to it coming forth, but because I believe this dream is a
visible demonstration of the plans God has for us. When I read the
Bible I see something very different than the rapture-ready preachers
out there with a doom-and-gloom "hold on 'till He comes because
we're barely going to make it" gospel. The Jesus I read about even
in Revelation is a victorious one. Even in death He was in control,
laying his own life down and taking it up again (John 10:18). He isn't
sitting in heaven wringing his hands in worry over whether we will
be able to get it together or not—He is sitting there gloriously pleased
with where He is taking us! The Bible says in Philippians 2:15 that
we will shine like stars as we release the gospel. It says in 1
Corinthians 15:53-54 that we will take these mortal, death-filled
bodies and clothe ourselves with *immortality*—and that when we do
that, we shall have truly conquered death! After all, isn't defeating
death what resurrection is all about?

We are in a war over life—in our bodies and our health, our
finances, our marriages and families, our cities, nations, and world.
Every area must be infused with the life-energy of the Risen One, the
Christ, Jesus of Nazareth. He has given us both power and authority
to destroy works of darkness in every aspect of life, and even now
we are coming into a greater understanding of what that looks like.
The gospel is the literal "good news" and this amazing news is that
God has a good plan for our lives, which is to remove death from
everything we touch and experience! The dream that Praying Medic
had is just one example of what this life will look like. Every sickness
and disease healed every time. No lack, no loss, no poverty, no pain,

no oppression, no sickness, no disease or infirmity, and no demonic power strong enough or capable enough to stand against us. We must understand that we are the Crown Princes and Princesses of the Kingdom of God. Romans 8:32 says, "He who did not spare his own Son, but gave him up for us all—how will He not also, along with Him, graciously give us all things?" There is literally nothing in the Kingdom that God will not do for us and through us—and that is the future of resurrection!

Through raising the dead, God is giving us a brief glimpse of what it means that we can literally live and never die—a promise that Jesus gave over and over in the Bible. Many people are troubled by that notion because we have been taught to believe in a far-off heavenly reality where we have eternal life, but only after we die. Jesus is the door, not death, and He has destroyed the power of death and the grave. Is not living forever a natural outcome of those who have been transformed by His life? I will discuss this subject in great depth in the next book in this series, *The Gospel of Life and Immortality*, but the future of resurrection is quite plainly reaching a place where not only does death and corruption not ever touch our lives, but where the life of Christ is so overbearing through us that we force the Kingdom into every area in both our lives and those around us.

The *Amplified Bible* says that, "From the days of John the Baptist until now the kingdom of heaven suffers violent assault, and violent men seize it by force [as a precious prize]" (Matthew 11:12). There is a holy forcefulness that we as believers must use to release the Kingdom into the earth. I am not talking about forcing our viewpoint down other peoples' throats or disrespecting their will to choose (living people, that is), nor am I speaking of invading peoples' personal space or violating their own personal rights to their body. I mean that we live in such a way that the Kingdom infuses us in a measure that wherever we go, Heaven is there at a level so it doesn't matter anymore if someone wants to get healed or not. It doesn't matter if they like their pet demons, their marital dysfunction, their emotional insecurities, addictions, or whatever other life-crutch they have developed—wholeness and restoration come because greater is He that is in us than anything that exists outside of the Kingdom realm.

We have become accustomed to praying the way someone wants to be prayed for, such as for a surgery or chemotherapy to go well instead of a hip miraculously restored or having the tumor evaporate into thin air. As a nurse, while I am all about God using people and giving us wisdom, at the end of the day He isn't interested in surgical repair—He is interested in wholeness by His grace. If someone wants to keep their sickness or disability, it shouldn't really matter. God is growing us to a point that not only will we be able to fix their disability, but we will also be able to provide the solution for a job, a new living situation, and all of the other changes that will come into play when someone who has been incapacitated for over a decade suddenly is about to lose their disability check. Some people think that in so doing we would be "overriding their will" and that God doesn't do that. Well, I hear your opinion, but I have to disagree. God loves us so much that He will usually let us have things go our way for a time, but in His relentless love, He will ultimately remove everything that hinders His goodness in our lives anyway, whether we like it or not. The Kingdom is all about fixing things, and while sometimes there are difficulties in a transition, ultimately the Kingdom appearing means *everything* gets better.

The future of resurrection is the true vision of the Church—and if it isn't, it needs to be. After all, if we're not fighting for things to become better—for them to become here on earth the same way they are currently in Heaven, what are we doing? What are we actually believing? What is a gospel that says it's all going to burn up in the end so we best just hold on? That is no gospel at all! Things are going to get better, brighter, stronger, fuller, and more amazing. God is releasing His Spirit on the earth in increasingly unprecedented levels, and "of the increase of His government and peace there will be no end" (Isaiah 9:7a).

I pray that your life is radically changed by the message of the true gospel. I pray that your heart and mind are filled with a revelation of the limitless potential God has placed within you, and of the power and authority He has given you. Even as Paul prayed in Ephesians 1:18-19, "I pray that the eyes of your heart may be enlightened in order that you may know the hope to which he has called you, the riches of his glorious inheritance in his holy people, and his incomparably great power for us who believe." I release the light of the Kingdom of Heaven upon you to break off every darkness, every doubt, and every fear. I decree that you are a dead-raiser—a Resurrectionist who is made in the image of the One who is Bright and Radiant, King Jesus. I pray that your hands will raise the dead back to life and will heal every sickness and every disease you come across. I decree that blessings flood your life, family, ministry, job, and that everything you touch prospers. I pray that every hindrance to the goals and dreams of your life falls away and that obstacles are crushed in the light of heaven over you. I decree that new destiny is being released to you even now, and I release angelic hosts from heaven to carry those gifts, mantles, and new assignments to you. Even now, God is upgrading you and making you a greater force to contend with against the darkness. Even now, opportunities will begin to flood toward you in greater measure to release the light of the King into the lives of others. You will not fail as you walk forward. You will stand tall and be successful in the things you set your hand to. God is sending angels before you to make the path free of obstacles as you shine like a star and hold out

His life to those around you. I decree and release an impartation of the life of Christ to heal the sick, cleanse the leper, cast out demons, and raise the dead. You ARE Christ in this world—now go demonstrate Christ-in-you to the nations!

Excerpt from *The Beginner's Guide to Traveling in the Spirit*

S pirit Travel has gradually become familiar to me since I first tried it in 2005. I was in a period of intensified spiritual growth, and spent a lot of time practicing and engaging the prophetic. I discovered that on rare occasion I would have visions that felt much more real than I could otherwise explain—as if I was just a thread away from actually tasting, hearing, and smelling the things that I encountered.

One of these was during a Wednesday night membership class at my church. My good friend and mentor Diane led the class, one of a months-long curriculum that covered the theological basics according to that church. I don't recall when or why it happened, but we were on the second floor of the education building and I had a vision of a dark stone room. There was a light shining through a doorway across the room, but the room itself was in shadows. I could see a raised circular platform in the middle of this chamber with what looked almost like a large stone vase or chalice in the middle. I stepped up to it and found it was filled to the brim with water— making the whole device much like an ornate baptismal font, or a fountain but without cascading water.

This vision felt more real than normal to begin with, but as I looked at this water, a scene began to form in its depths. I watched three horses with riders on their backs charging across a desert, and I could literally feel myself pulled somehow into this water and into this scene. I heard the shriek of a hawk or eagle coming from it as well. It was odd because I was acutely aware of the class being taught around me but I was trying to ignore it to focus on this unexpected vision, and while that was happening the sounds in the vision were so real inside my spirit that I could almost hear them with my physical ears. The sensation itself was like something was trying to get sucked out of my body to dive deeper into the waters to get to the desert.

As this was happening I simply couldn't understand what was going on except that I assumed God was advancing me in the prophetic—moving me from having visions to prophetic experiences. Eventually, I lost my focus and continued paying attention to the class, visionary experience over—but thirteen years later that event obviously stuck with me as I have not, to my recollection, ever written it down prior to now. I didn't realize it at the time but I believe that was the first time I ever consciously was involved in spirit travel. During that period of time, God was drawing me deeper in things prophetic, which would eventually be played out when I took my first trip to the heavens on purpose.

During this phase of my life God would invariably drop little hints my way about things. I would listen to preaching messages and the strange things were usually what stuck with me. It was a little bit like playing a game of connect the dots, or how people draw constellations out of the stars. One isolated comment doesn't mean anything, but when strung together with a series of other data points a bigger picture would emerge. Traveling in the spirit was like this for me.

I remember one preaching message I heard by Todd Bentley where he quoted Ephesians 2:6 saying, "And God raised us up with Christ and seated us with Him in the heavenly realms in Christ Jesus."

Todd shared that he believed there was supposed to be an experience to go along with that statement we usually read as positional theology—and if there was an experience to have, that he wanted to have it. I heard a message by Patricia King once where she told a story. In that story, she, Bob Jones, and someone else were meeting together. Bob took their hands and simply said, "Ascend," and up they went in the spirit! I am certain that I heard these messages months apart from one another, but those factoids stuck with me—and revealed to me something deeper. Another time Todd Bentley shared how he was ascending in the spirit and was stopped by a demonic entity—but the fact remains that he was indeed traveling in the spirit. Here I was wanting to learn how to prophesy better and see angels (and I still want all of that even though I am more experienced now than I was then), but these people were talking about taking trips to heaven—and they made it sound like this was entirely normal! David Hogan preached a message many years ago where he spoke about how one of his pastors was killed by a principality that walked into this man's hut in the form of a four-foot hoot-owl—and how the man's spirit was carried from his body to a gathering of local black-magic warlocks. The wife prayed and he was resurrected, but not before his spirit-man had already seen the identities of these warlocks—men and women who had been living among them and keeping their satanic practices a secret. All of these stories only served to further cement inside me that spirit travel was not only possible but that it was something God designed for us to experience. After all, why talk about it in the Bible as a scriptural promise if it is unavailable to us as believers?

I have a habit of pondering these sorts of things, gleaning insights and uncovering deeper spiritual truths within them as I do so. As I meditated on these disconnected and seemingly unrelated messages, I realized that these different Bible verses all suggested a higher spiritual experience than I was having—and like Todd Bentley, if there is a spiritual experience to be able to have, I want it just because it is something God has for me.

Ephesians 1:3 says, "Praise be to the God and Father of our Lord Jesus Christ, who has blessed us in the heavenly realms with every spiritual blessing in Christ." These spiritual blessings are from God to us, but the only way we can access them is in the heavenly realms—so if I want to receive these blessings I need to head to the heavens to get them! Ephesians 2:6 says that, "And God raised us up with Christ and seated us with him in the heavenly realms in Christ Jesus . . ." If we are seated with Jesus in the heavenly realms, then I'd very much like to have the experience of being seated to go along with the theoretical position that I already am now in Christ. Colossians 3:1 says, "If then you have been raised with Christ, seek the things that are above, where Christ is, seated at the right hand of God." This verse directly tells us to seek spiritual things and to do so by going to where Jesus is seated in the throne room right next to the Father. Yet again, Hebrews 4:16 tells us to "approach God's throne of grace with confidence, so that we may receive mercy and find grace to help us in our time of need." If we are to appear before God's throne, then we have to actually be in His throne room—and the Bible tells us to do it with boldness!

After a while of pondering these verses, along with the stories these preachers and prophetic teachers were sharing, I couldn't help but sense there was something more—something I was missing. As I would consider these things I started to wonder how I could choose to go into the heavens. If Bob Jones could grab peoples' hands and say the word "ascend" and then go up, it means this is possible—but how did he do it? And how can I experience being seated in heavenly places like the scriptures say I am?

This led me on a journey, but a covert one. You see, I suspected, and as time went on I realized I suspected rightly, that if I told anyone what I was thinking they would have flipped their lids. I knew I was exploring new territory, but I didn't have anyone around me who I trusted to be able to help me explore. What this left me with was a concern that I was going to get led astray somehow, but with an equally strong conviction that there was something out there yet to be obtained. Thus, I pursued this line of reasoning and prayed about it, but did so cautiously and gingerly. I still knew I couldn't discuss it with anyone from my church, which was disappointing, but of the most spiritually advanced of everyone I knew I got an "I can't handle this" sense from them.

Eventually, God brought me an opportunity in the form of a guy around my age, named Ben, whom I had befriended the year prior at a conference. We would chat occasionally on the phone, and we would discuss all sorts of spiritual things, especially about healing and the prophetic—visions, dreams, discernment of spirits, and more.

The first time I ever tried to purposefully ascend into the heavens I was driving alone in my car on a two-hour car trip. I had called Ben to chat on the ride, and we began talking about the idea of freely accessing the heavenly realm. Up until that point in the conversation, I was the only person I knew who believed that was possible. It turned out that the things I had been pondering were things he had recently begun to experience too, and it was a confirmation to me. I don't know what he thought about it at the time but I was relieved to know someone else whom I could share this secret with. It felt validating, and encouraged me that I was on the right path . . .

Thank You For Purchasing This Book

Thank you for reading *Faith to Raise the Dead*. It is my sincere hope that this book has helped equip you to manifest the life of Jesus Christ in your life in a greater way. If you enjoyed it, you will find more free content at www.thekingsofeden.com. Please consider leaving a review on Amazon.com so others can find this book more easily.

Other books by Michael C. King include:

Practical Keys to Raise the Dead
Broken To Whole: Inner Healing for the Fragmented Soul
The Gamer's Guide to the Kingdom of God
The Beginner's Guide to Traveling in the Spirit

The God Signs Series
> **Gemstones From Heaven**
> **Feathers From Heaven**

Appendix I
The Dead Raised in the Bible

Stories of people raising the dead are found in twelve places in scripture, and each one provides its own unique glimpse into the creative and redemptive nature of God. Be encouraged as you read what the Bible says about resurrection life.

1. Elijah raised the son of the widow from Zarephath (1 Kings 17:17-22).
2. Elisha raised the Shunammite woman's son (2 Kings 4:32-35).
3. Ezekiel prophecies and resurrects an entire army in a vision (Ezekiel 37:1-10)
4. A man was raised on contact with Elisha's bones (2 Kings 13:20, 21).
5. Many saints rose from the dead when Jesus died (Matt. 27:50-53).
6. Jesus rose from the dead (Matt. 28:5-8; Mark 16:6; Luke 24:5, 6).
7. Jesus raised the widow from Nain's son (Luke 7:11-15).
8. Jesus raised Jairus's daughter from the dead (Luke 8:41, 42, 49-

55).

9. Jesus raised Lazarus from the dead (John 11:1-44).

10. Peter raised Tabitha/Dorcas from the dead (Acts 9:36-41).

11. Paul was raised by the disciples after a stoning (Acts 14:19-20)

12. Eutychus was raised by Paul after falling out a window (Acts 20:9-10).

Note: Jesus' resurrection (#6 above) has been excluded from the testimonies listed in this chapter as no details of the actual resurrection are given in the text, but His resurrection is the pivotal event around which all other resurrections are made possible.

1 Kings 17:9-24

Then the word of the Lord came to him: "Go at once to Zarephath in the region of Sidon and stay there. I have directed a widow there to supply you with food." So he went to Zarephath. When he came to the town gate, a widow was there gathering sticks. He called to her and asked, "Would you bring me a little water in a jar so I may have a drink?" As she was going to get it, he called, "And bring me, please, a piece of bread."

"As surely as the Lord your God lives," she replied, "I don't have any bread—only a handful of flour in a jar and a little olive oil in a jug. I am gathering a few sticks to take home and make a meal for myself and my son, that we may eat it—and die."

Elijah said to her, "Don't be afraid. Go home and do as you have said. But first make a small loaf of bread for me from what you have and bring it to me, and then make something for yourself and your son. For this is what the Lord, the God of Israel, says: 'The jar of flour will not be used up and the jug of oil will not run dry until the day the Lord sends rain on the land.'"

She went away and did as Elijah had told her. So there was food every day for Elijah and for the woman and her family. For the jar of flour was not used up and the jug of oil did not run dry, in keeping with the word of the Lord spoken by Elijah.

Some time later the son of the woman who owned the house became ill. He grew worse and worse and finally stopped breathing. She said to Elijah, "What do you have against me, man of God? Did you come to remind me of my sin and kill my son?"

"Give me your son," Elijah replied. He took him from her arms, carried him to the upper room where he was staying, and laid him on his bed. Then he cried out to the Lord, "Lord my God, have you brought tragedy even on this widow I am staying with, by causing her son to die?" Then he stretched himself out on the boy three times and cried out to the Lord, "Lord my God, let this boy's life return to him!"

The Lord heard Elijah's cry, and the boy's life returned to him, and he lived. Elijah picked up the child and carried him down from the room into the house. He gave him to his mother and said, "Look, your son is alive!"

Then the woman said to Elijah, "Now I know that you are a man of God and that the word of the Lord from your mouth is the truth."

2 Kings 4:8-37

One day Elisha went to Shunem. And a well-to-do woman was there, who urged him to stay for a meal. So whenever he came by, he stopped there to eat. She said to her husband, "I know that this man who often comes our way is a holy man of God. Let's make a small room on the roof and put in it a bed and a table, a chair and a lamp for him. Then he can stay there whenever he comes to us."

One day when Elisha came, he went up to his room and lay down there. He said to his servant Gehazi, "Call the Shunammite." So he called her, and she stood before him. Elisha said to him, "Tell her, 'You have gone to all this trouble for us. Now what can be done for you? Can we speak on your behalf to the king or the commander of the army?'"

She replied, "I have a home among my own people."

"What can be done for her?" Elisha asked.

Gehazi said, "She has no son, and her husband is old."

Then Elisha said, "Call her." So he called her, and she stood in the doorway. "About this time next year," Elisha said, "you will hold a son in your arms."

"No, my lord!" she objected. "Please, man of God, don't mislead your servant!" But the woman became pregnant, and the next year about that same time she gave birth to a son, just as Elisha had told her.

The child grew, and one day he went out to his father, who was with the reapers. He said to his father, "My head! My head!"

His father told a servant, "Carry him to his mother." After the servant had lifted him up and carried him to his mother, the boy sat on her lap until noon, and then he died. She went up and laid him on the bed of the man of God, then shut the door and went out.

She called her husband and said, "Please send me one of the servants and a donkey so I can go to the man of God quickly and return."

"Why go to him today?" he asked. "It's not the New Moon or the Sabbath."

"That's all right," she said.

She saddled the donkey and said to her servant, "Lead on; don't slow down for me unless I tell you." So she set out and came to the man of God at Mount Carmel.

When he saw her in the distance, the man of God said to his servant Gehazi, "Look! There's the Shunammite! Run to meet her and ask her, 'Are you all right? Is your husband all right? Is your child all right?'"

"Everything is all right," she said.

When she reached the man of God at the mountain, she took hold of his feet. Gehazi came over to push her away, but the man of God said, "Leave her alone! She is in bitter distress, but the Lord has hidden it from me and has not told me why."

"Did I ask you for a son, my lord?" she said. "Didn't I tell you, 'Don't raise my hopes'?"

Elisha said to Gehazi, "Tuck your cloak into your belt, take my staff in your hand and run. Don't greet anyone you meet, and if anyone greets you, do not answer. Lay my staff on the boy's face."

But the child's mother said, "As surely as the Lord lives and as you live, I will not leave you." So he got up and followed her.

Gehazi went on ahead and laid the staff on the boy's face, but there was no sound or response. So Gehazi went back to meet Elisha and told him, "The boy has not awakened."

When Elisha reached the house, there was the boy lying dead on his couch. He went in, shut the door on the two of them and prayed to the Lord. Then he got on the bed and lay on the boy, mouth to mouth, eyes to eyes, hands to hands. As he stretched himself out on him, the boy's body grew warm. Elisha turned away and walked back and forth in the room and then got on the bed and stretched out on him once more. The boy sneezed seven times and opened his eyes.

Elisha summoned Gehazi and said, "Call the Shunammite." And he did. When she came, he said, "Take your son." She came in, fell at his feet and bowed to the ground. Then she took her son and went out.

2 Kings 13:20-21

Elisha died and was buried. Now Moabite raiders used to enter the country every spring. Once while some Israelites were burying a man, suddenly they saw a band of raiders; so they threw the man's body into Elisha's tomb. When the body touched Elisha's bones, the man came to life and stood up on his feet.

Ezekiel 37:1-10

The hand of the Lord was on me, and he brought me out by the Spirit of the Lord and set me in the middle of a valley; it was full of bones. He led me back and forth among them, and I saw a great many bones on the floor of the valley, bones that were very dry. He asked me, "Son of man, can these bones live?"

I said, "Sovereign Lord, you alone know."

Then he said to me, "Prophesy to these bones and say to them, 'Dry bones, hear the word of the Lord! This is what the Sovereign Lord says to these bones: I will make breath enter you, and you will come to life. I will attach tendons to you and make flesh come upon you and cover you with skin; I will put breath in you, and you will come to life. Then you will know that I am the Lord.'"

So I prophesied as I was commanded. And as I was prophesying, there was a noise, a rattling sound, and the bones came together, bone to bone. I looked, and tendons and flesh appeared on them and skin covered them, but there was no breath in them.

Then he said to me, "Prophesy to the breath; prophesy, son of man, and say to it, 'This is what the Sovereign Lord says: Come, breath, from the four winds and breathe into these slain, that they may live.'" So I prophesied as he commanded me, and breath entered them; they came to life and stood up on their feet—a vast army.

Matthew 27:50-54

And when Jesus had cried out again in a loud voice, he gave up his spirit. At that moment the curtain of the temple was torn in two from top to bottom. The earth shook, the rocks split and the tombs broke open. The bodies of many holy people who had died were raised to life. They came out of the tombs after Jesus' resurrection and went into the holy city and appeared to many people.

When the centurion and those with him who were guarding Jesus saw the earthquake and all that had happened, they were terrified, and exclaimed, "Surely he was the Son of God!"

Luke 7:11-15

Soon afterward, Jesus went to a town called Nain, and his disciples and a large crowd went along with him. As he approached the town gate, a dead person was being carried out—the only son of his mother, and she was a widow. And a large crowd from the town was with her. When the Lord saw her, his heart went out to her and he said, "Don't cry."

Then he went up and touched the bier they were carrying him on, and the bearers stood still. He said, "Young man, I say to you, get up!" The dead man sat up and began to talk, and Jesus gave him back to his mother.

Luke 8:41-55

Then a man named Jairus, a synagogue leader, came and fell at Jesus' feet, pleading with him to come to his house because his only daughter, a girl of about twelve, was dying.

As Jesus was on his way, the crowds almost crushed him. And a woman was there who had been subject to bleeding for twelve years, but no one could heal her. She came up behind him and touched the edge of his cloak, and immediately her bleeding stopped.

"Who touched me?" Jesus asked.

When they all denied it, Peter said, "Master, the people are crowding and pressing against you."

But Jesus said, "Someone touched me; I know that power has gone out from me."

Then the woman, seeing that she could not go unnoticed, came trembling and fell at his feet. In the presence of all the people, she told why she had touched him and how she had been instantly healed. Then he said to her, "Daughter, your faith has healed you. Go in peace."

While Jesus was still speaking, someone came from the house of Jairus, the synagogue leader. "Your daughter is dead," he said. "Don't bother the teacher anymore."

Hearing this, Jesus said to Jairus, "Don't be afraid; just believe, and she will be healed."

When he arrived at the house of Jairus, he did not let anyone go in with him except Peter, John and James, and the child's father and mother. Meanwhile, all the people were wailing and mourning for her. "Stop wailing," Jesus said. "She is not dead but asleep."

They laughed at him, knowing that she was dead. But he took her by the hand and said, "My child, get up!" Her spirit returned, and at once she stood up. Then Jesus told them to give her something to eat.

Note: This story is also found in Mark 5:22-43 and Matthew 9:11-26

John 11:1-45

Now a man named Lazarus was sick. He was from Bethany, the village of Mary and her sister Martha (This Mary, whose brother Lazarus now lay sick, was the same one who poured perfume on the Lord and wiped his feet with her hair). So the sisters sent word to Jesus, "Lord, the one you love is sick."

When he heard this, Jesus said, "This sickness will not end in death. No, it is for God's glory so that God's Son may be glorified through it." Now Jesus loved Martha and her sister and Lazarus. So when he heard that Lazarus was sick, he stayed where he was two more days, and then he said to his disciples, "Let us go back to Judea."

"But Rabbi," they said, "a short while ago the Jews there tried to stone you, and yet you are going back?"

Jesus answered, "Are there not twelve hours of daylight? Anyone who walks in the daytime will not stumble, for they see by this world's light. It is when a person walks at night that they stumble, for they have no light."

After he had said this, he went on to tell them, "Our friend Lazarus has fallen asleep; but I am going there to wake him up."

His disciples replied, "Lord, if he sleeps, he will get better." Jesus had been speaking of his death, but his disciples thought he meant natural sleep.

So then he told them plainly, "Lazarus is dead, and for your sake I am glad I was not there, so that you may believe. But let us go to him."

Then Thomas (also known as Didymus) said to the rest of the disciples, "Let us also go, that we may die with him."

On his arrival, Jesus found that Lazarus had already been in the tomb for four days. Now Bethany was less than two miles from Jerusalem, and many Jews had come to Martha and Mary to comfort them in the loss of their brother. When Martha heard that Jesus was coming, she went out to meet him, but Mary stayed at home.

"Lord," Martha said to Jesus, "if you had been here, my brother would not have died. But I know that even now God will give you whatever you ask."

Jesus said to her, "Your brother will rise again."

Martha answered, "I know he will rise again in the resurrection at the last day."

Jesus said to her, "I am the resurrection and the life. The one who believes in me will live, even though they die; and whoever lives by believing in me will never die. Do you believe this?"

"Yes, Lord," she replied, "I believe that you are the Messiah, the Son of God, who is to come into the world."

After she had said this, she went back and called her sister Mary aside. "The Teacher is here," she said, "and is asking for you." When Mary heard this, she got up quickly and went to him. Now Jesus had not yet entered the village, but was still at the place where Martha had met him. When the Jews who had been with Mary in the house, comforting her, noticed how quickly she got up and went out, they followed her, supposing she was going to the tomb to mourn there.

When Mary reached the place where Jesus was and saw him, she fell at his feet and said, "Lord, if you had been here, my brother would not have died."

When Jesus saw her weeping, and the Jews who had come along with her also weeping, he was deeply moved in spirit and troubled. "Where have you laid him?" he asked.

"Come and see, Lord," they replied.

Jesus wept.

Then the Jews said, "See how he loved him!"

But some of them said, "Could not he who opened the eyes of the blind man have kept this man from dying?"

Jesus, once more deeply moved, came to the tomb. It was a cave with a stone laid across the entrance. "Take away the stone," he said.

"But, Lord," said Martha, the sister of the dead man, "by this time there is a bad odor, for he has been there four days."

Then Jesus said, "Did I not tell you that if you believe, you will see the glory of God?"

So they took away the stone. Then Jesus looked up and said, "Father, I thank you that you have heard me. I knew that you always hear me, but I said this for the benefit of the people standing here, that they may believe that you sent me."

When he had said this, Jesus called in a loud voice, "Lazarus, come out!" The dead man came out, his hands and feet wrapped with strips of linen, and a cloth around his face.

Jesus said to them, "Take off the grave clothes and let him go."

Therefore many of the Jews who had come to visit Mary, and had seen what Jesus did, believed in him.

Acts 9:36-41

In Joppa there was a disciple named Tabitha (in Greek her name is Dorcas); she was always doing good and helping the poor. About that time she became sick and died, and her body was washed and placed in an upstairs room. Lydda was near Joppa; so when the disciples heard that Peter was in Lydda, they sent two men to him and urged him, "Please come at once!"

Peter went with them, and when he arrived he was taken upstairs to the room. All the widows stood around him, crying and showing him the robes and other clothing that Dorcas had made while she was still with them.

Peter sent them all out of the room; then he got down on his knees and prayed. Turning toward the dead woman, he said, "Tabitha, get up." She opened her eyes, and seeing Peter she sat up. He took her by the hand and helped her to her feet. Then he called for the believers, especially the widows, and presented her to them alive.

Acts 14:8-20

In Lystra there sat a man who was lame. He had been that way from birth and had never walked. He listened to Paul as he was speaking. Paul looked directly at him, saw that he had faith to be healed and called out, "Stand up on your feet!" At that, the man jumped up and began to walk.

When the crowd saw what Paul had done, they shouted in the Lycaonian language, "The gods have come down to us in human form!" Barnabas they called Zeus, and Paul they called Hermes because he was the chief speaker. The priest of Zeus, whose temple was just outside the city, brought bulls and wreaths to the city gates because he and the crowd wanted to offer sacrifices to them.

But when the apostles Barnabas and Paul heard of this, they tore their clothes and rushed out into the crowd, shouting: "Friends, why are you doing this? We too are only human, like you. We are bringing you good news, telling you to turn from these worthless things to the living God, who made the heavens and the earth and the sea and everything in them. In the past, he let all nations go their own way. Yet he has not left himself without testimony: He has shown kindness by giving you rain from heaven and crops in their seasons; he provides you with plenty of food and fills your hearts with joy." Even with these words, they had difficulty keeping the crowd from sacrificing to them.

Then some Jews came from Antioch and Iconium and won the crowd over. They stoned Paul and dragged him outside the city, thinking he was dead. But after the disciples had gathered around him, he got up and went back into the city. The next day he and Barnabas left for Derbe.

Note: In the above passage while it only states that they thought Paul was dead, it is highly likely he was. Medically speaking, someone who is stoned to death (or a sliver before death) would have such significant total-body injuries including broken bones, brain injury, tissue damage, and internal bleeding that it would be impossible to simply get up and walk back to the city, then leave to travel to another city the next day without a significant divine touch whether dead or alive, and in a short time he would be dead nonetheless. The author presumes that while the text does not explicitly state it, that Paul was dead and the disciples resurrected him before proof of his death could be clearly obtained. Paul makes mention of this in 2 Corinthians 11:24-25, in that same passage alluding to multiple other opportunities for him to have died and resurrected that are not included in the scriptures.

Acts 20:7-10

On the first day of the week we came together to break bread. Paul spoke to the people, and, because he intended to leave the next day, kept on talking until midnight. There were many lamps in the upstairs room where they were meeting. Seated in a window was a young man named Eutychus, who was sinking into a deep sleep as

Paul talked on and on. When he was sound asleep, he fell to the ground from the third story and was picked up dead. Paul went down, threw himself on the young man and put his arms around him. "Don't be alarmed," he said. "He's alive!"

Appendix II

Resurrection-Related Scriptures for Prayer and Encouragement

Numbers 23:19

God is not human, that he should lie, not a human being, that he should change his mind. Does he speak and then not act? Does he promise and not fulfill?

1 Samuel 2:6

The Lord brings death and makes alive; He brings down to the grave and raises up.

Job 33:29-30

Yes, God does these things again and again for people. He rescues them from the grave so they may enjoy the light of life. (New Living Translation)

Psalm 16:8-11a

I keep my eyes always on the Lord. With him at my right hand, I will not be shaken. Therefore my heart is glad and my tongue rejoices; my body also will rest secure, because you will not abandon me to the realm of the dead, nor will you let your faithful one see decay. You make known to me the path of life . . .

Psalm 27:13

I remain confident of this: I will see the goodness of the Lord in the land of the living.

Psalm 77:14

You are the God who performs miracles; you display your power among the peoples.

Psalm 118:17

I will not die but live, and will proclaim what the Lord has done.

Psalm 133

How good and pleasant it is when God's people live together in unity! It is like precious oil poured on the head, running down on the beard, running down on Aaron's beard, down on the collar of his robe. It is as if the dew of Hermon were falling on Mount Zion. For there the Lord bestows his blessing, even life forevermore.

Proverbs 18:21

The tongue has the power of life and death, and those who love it will eat its fruit.

Isaiah 26:19

But your dead will live, Lord; their bodies will rise—let those who dwell in the dust wake up and shout for joy—your dew is like the dew of the morning; the earth will give birth to her dead.

Isaiah 65:20

Never again will there be in it an infant who lives but a few days, or an old man who does not live out his years; the one who dies at a hundred will be thought a mere child; the one who fails to reach a hundred will be considered accursed.

Jeremiah 29:11

For I know the plans I have for you," declares the Lord, "plans to prosper you and not to harm you, plans to give you hope and a future.

Jeremiah 32:27

I am the Lord, the God of all mankind. Is anything too hard for me?

Matthew 7:7-8

"Ask and it will be given to you; seek and you will find; knock and the door will be opened to you. 8 For everyone who asks receives; the one who seeks finds; and to the one who knocks, the door will be opened.

Matthew 10:8

Heal the sick, raise the dead, cleanse those who have leprosy, drive out demons. Freely you have received; freely give.

Matthew 18:19-20

"Again, truly I tell you that if two of you on earth agree about anything they ask for, it will be done for them by my Father in heaven. For where two or three gather in my name, there am I with them."

Matthew 21:21-22

Jesus replied, "Truly I tell you, if you have faith and do not doubt, not only can you do what was done to the fig tree, but also you can say to this mountain, 'Go, throw yourself into the sea,' and it will be done. If you believe, you will receive whatever you ask for in prayer."

Matthew 27:50-53

And when Jesus had cried out again in a loud voice, he gave up his spirit. At that moment the curtain of the temple was torn in two from top to bottom. The earth shook, the rocks split and the tombs broke open. The bodies of many holy people who had died were raised to life. They came out of the tombs after Jesus' resurrection and went into the holy city and appeared to many people.

Mark 11:22-24

"Have faith in God," Jesus answered. "Truly I tell you, if anyone says to this mountain, 'Go, throw yourself into the sea,' and does not doubt in their heart but believes that what they say will happen, it will be done for them. Therefore I tell you, whatever you ask for in prayer, believe that you have received it, and it will be yours.

Luke 1:37

For no word from God will ever fail.

Luke 7:22

So he replied to the messengers, "Go back and report to John what you have seen and heard: The blind receive sight, the lame walk, those who have leprosy are cleansed, the deaf hear, the dead are raised, and the good news is proclaimed to the poor.

John 5:21

For just as the Father raises the dead and gives them life, even so the Son gives life to whom he is pleased to give it.

John 5:25

Very truly I tell you, a time is coming and has now come when the dead will hear the voice of the Son of God and those who hear will live.

John 10:10

The thief comes only to steal and kill and destroy; I have come that they may have life, and have it to the full.

John 11:21-27

"Lord," Martha said to Jesus, "if you had been here, my brother would not have died. But I know that even now God will give you whatever you ask."

Jesus said to her, "Your brother will rise again."

Martha answered, "I know he will rise again in the resurrection at the last day."

Jesus said to her, "I am the resurrection and the life. The one who believes in me will live, even though they die; and whoever lives by believing in me will never die. Do you believe this?"

"Yes, Lord," she replied, "I believe that you are the Messiah, the Son of God, who is to come into the world."

John 14:12-14

Very truly I tell you, whoever believes in me will do the works I have been doing, and they will do even greater things than these, because I am going to the Father. And I will do whatever you ask in my name, so that the Father may be glorified in the Son. You may ask me for anything in my name, and I will do it.

John 15:7-8

If you remain in me and my words remain in you, ask whatever you wish, and it will be done for you. This is to my Father's glory, that you bear much fruit, showing yourselves to be my disciples.

John 16:23-24

In that day you will no longer ask me anything. Very truly I tell you, my Father will give you whatever you ask in my name. Until now you have not asked for anything in my name. Ask and you will receive, and your joy will be complete.

Acts 26:8

Why should any of you consider it incredible that God raises the dead?

Romans 4:17

As it is written: "I have made you a father of many nations." He is our father in the sight of God, in whom he believed—the God who gives life to the dead and calls into being things that were not.

Romans 8:10-11

But if Christ is in you, then even though your body is subject to death because of sin, the Spirit gives life because of righteousness. And if the Spirit of him who raised Jesus from the dead is living in you, he who raised Christ from the dead will also give life to your mortal bodies because of his Spirit who lives in you.

1 Corinthians 15:12-22

But if it is preached that Christ has been raised from the dead, how can some of you say that there is no resurrection of the dead? If there is no resurrection of the dead, then not even Christ has been raised. And if Christ has not been raised, our preaching is useless and so is your faith. More than that, we are then found to be false witnesses about God, for we have testified about God that he raised Christ from the dead. But he did not raise him if in fact the dead are not raised. For if the dead are not raised, then Christ has not been raised either. And if Christ has not been raised, your faith is futile; you are still in your sins. Then those also who have fallen asleep in Christ are lost. If only for this life we have hope in Christ, we are of all people most to be pitied.

But Christ has indeed been raised from the dead, the firstfruits of those who have fallen asleep. For since death came through a man, the resurrection of the dead comes also through a man. For as in Adam all die, so in Christ all will be made alive.

1 Corinthians 15:53-58

For the perishable must clothe itself with the imperishable, and the mortal with immortality. When the perishable has been clothed with the imperishable, and the mortal with immortality, then the saying that is written will come true: "Death has been swallowed up in victory."

"Where, O death, is your victory?

Where, O death, is your sting?"

The sting of death is sin, and the power of sin is the law. But thanks be to God! He gives us the victory through our Lord Jesus Christ. Therefore, my dear brothers and sisters, stand firm. Let nothing move you. Always give yourselves fully to the work of the Lord, because you know that your labor in the Lord is not in vain.

2 Corinthians 1:9-10

Indeed, we felt we had received the sentence of death. But this happened that we might not rely on ourselves but on God, who raises the dead. He has delivered us from such a deadly peril, and he will deliver us again. On him we have set our hope that he will continue to deliver us . . .

2 Corinthians 1:20

For no matter how many promises God has made, they are "Yes" in Christ. And so through him the "Amen" is spoken by us to the glory of God.

Ephesians 5:14

This is why it is said: "Wake up, sleeper, rise from the dead, and Christ will shine on you."

2 Timothy 1:10

. . . But it has now been revealed through the appearing of our Savior, Christ Jesus, who has destroyed death and has brought life and immortality to light through the gospel.

Hebrews 6:1-3

Therefore let us move beyond the elementary teachings about Christ and be taken forward to maturity, not laying again the foundation of repentance from acts that lead to death, and of faith in God, instruction about cleansing rites, the laying on of hands, the resurrection of the dead, and eternal judgment. And God permitting, we will do so.

Hebrews 11:19

Abraham reasoned that God could even raise the dead, and so in a manner of speaking he did receive Isaac back from death.

Hebrews 11:35

Women received back their dead, raised to life again. There were others who were tortured, refusing to be released so that they might gain an even better resurrection.

James 1:17

Every good and perfect gift is from above, coming down from the Father of the heavenly lights, who does not change like shifting shadows.

1 John 3:21-22

Dear friends, if our hearts do not condemn us, we have confidence before God and receive from him anything we ask, because we keep his commands and do what pleases him.

1 John 5:11-15

And this is the testimony: God has given us eternal life, and this life is in his Son. Whoever has the Son has life; whoever does not have the Son of God does not have life. I write these things to you who believe in the name of the Son of God so that you may know that you have eternal life. This is the confidence we have in approaching God: that if we ask anything according to his will, he hears us. And if we know that he hears us—whatever we ask—we know that we have what we asked of him.

Revelation 11:11

But after the three and a half days the breath of life from God entered them, and they stood on their feet, and terror struck those who saw them.

References

Anonymous Source, Personal Interview, 14 Jan, 2017

"Authority." *Dictionary.com*, www.dictionary.com/browse/authority?s
=t. Accessed 11 Mar. 2017.

"Incipient." *Dictionary.com*, www.dictionary.com/browse/incipient?s
=t. Accessed 5 Oct. 2016.

Gregory, Philip Woodward, Edmund G. Gardner, and George F.
Hill. *The Dialogues of Saint Gregory: Surnamed the Great; Pope of
Rome & the First of That Name. Divided into Four Books, Wherein
He Entreateth of the Lives and Miracles of the Saints in Italy and of
the Eternity of Men's Souls.* London: P.L. Warner, 1911. Print.

Fortuna, Jeannie. Telephone interview. 06 Oct. 2016.

Gladney, Wanda. Telephone interview. 17 Oct. 2016.

Hebert, Albert J., S.M. *Saints Who Raised The Dead: True Stories of 400
Resurrection Miracles.* 2nd ed. Charlotte: Tan, 2004. Print.

Johnson, Tyler. *How to Raise the Dead.* Charleston: n.p., 2010. Print.

Johnson, Tyler. Personal Interview, 22 March, 2016

King, Michael C. *Practical Keys to Raise the Dead.* Charleston: n.p., 2016.
Print.

King, Michael C. *The Gamer's Guide to the Kingdom of God.* Charleston:

n.p., 2016. Print.

LeClaire, Jennifer. "Prophet Bob Jones Passes Away." Charisma
News. N.p., 11 Oct. 2016. Web. 28 Feb. 2017. <http://www.
charismanews.com/us/42794-prophet-bob-jones-passes-
away.

Martin, Ernest L. "Simon Magus Begins Universal Church." Good
News May 1964: 9 . Print.

Mayes, Keith. "What is Quantum Mechanics?" *Theories with Problems*.
N.p., n.d. Web. 9 Mar. 2017. <http://www.
thekeyboard.org.uk/Quantum%20mechanics.htm>.

McCraty, Rollin. "The Energetic Heart Is Unfolding." *HeartMath
Institute*. N.p., 22 July 2010. Web. 09 Mar. 2017.
<https://www.heartmath.org/articles-of-the-heart/science-
of-the-heart/the-energetic-heart-is-unfolding/>.

Medic, Praying. *Divine Healing Made Simple*. Charleston: Inkity Press,
2013. Print.

Murray, Richard K. The Question of Hell. Georgia: n.p., 2007. Print.

"S.C.J. FAQ: Section 12.35. Jewish Thought: What does Judaism
believe about Satan?" Ed. Daniel Faigin. N.p., 12 Mar. 2014.
Web. 11 Nov. 2016. <http://www.scjfaq.org/faq/12-
35.html>.

Strong, James. Strong's Exhaustive Concordance. Peabody, MA:
Hendrickson, 2007. Blueletterbible.com. Web. 5 Oct. 2016.

About the Author

Michael King is a prolific writer by day and a Registered Nurse by night. He hungrily explores all things spiritual and his love for God has given him a passion for signs, wonders, and miracles. Michael is married to a beautiful wife who doubles as his professional editor. He is known by family and friends for his proficiency in the prophetic and in healing prayer and energy work. His blog, thekingsofeden.com, focuses on spirituality with a hint of health-related topics and a dash of his fiction and fantasy writing. He is available for speaking engagements on request.